D0397050

WHAT HAPPENS
TO ROVER
WHEN THE MARRIAGE
IS OVER?

Also by Patti Lawson

*The Dog Diet: What My Dog Taught Me About Shedding
Pounds, Licking Stress, and Getting a New Leash on Life*

WHAT HAPPENS TO ROVER WHEN THE MARRIAGE IS OVER?

And Other Doggone Legal Dilemmas

PATTI LAWSON

Illustrations by David Voisard

Skyhorse Publishing

Skyhorse Publishing books may be purchased in bulk at special discounts for sales promotion, corporate gifts, fund-raising, or educational purposes. Special editions can also be created to specifications. For details, contact the Special Sales Department, Skyhorse Publishing, 307 West 36th Street, 11th Floor, New York, NY 10018 or info@skyhorsepublishing.com.

Skyhorse® and Skyhorse Publishing® are registered trademarks of Skyhorse Publishing, Inc.®, a Delaware corporation.

Visit our website at www.skyhorsepublishing.com.

10 9 8 7 6 5 4 3 2 1

Library of Congress Cataloging-in-Publication Data is available on file.

Cover design by Jane Sheppard
Cover photo credit: Jerry Waters

Print ISBN: 978-1-5107-1153-2
Ebook ISBN: 978-1-5107-1154-9

Printed in the United States of America

This book is dedicated to Rodney Morrison, a great Dog Dad and my wonderful husband and partner in life. Thanks for supporting and loving me in all things.

CONTENTS

INTRODUCTION

I've heard fellow lawyers refer to certain cases they regretted accepting as a "dog of a case," but it wasn't until I actually represented a St. Bernard against an unscrupulous pet store that the phrase had any real meaning to me. Canines are in the courtroom today as defendants, plaintiffs, victims, and way too often as pawns or bargaining chips as their human companions part ways. Despite having four legs, canines actually have no real "standing" in court . . . that's the legal term meaning that you have a right to be there. That's where you come in. As your dog's human guardian it's your responsibility to make sure your pet doesn't get lost in the legal labyrinth, or, worse, be denied the legal remedies she deserves.

Animals have always been designated as property in court going back to the old laws of replevin. Cattle and other livestock were possessions, a major source of food, as well as income, and most legal disputes centered on these issues. The domestication of pets, and dogs in particular, necessitates a change in the property classification of pets that are now members of the family. Animal rights groups are more plentiful than ever, and due to their huge presence legislation concerning the rights of animals and their owners is changing rapidly. Keeping up with the changes as well as how they apply to your pet is crucial. *What Happens to Rover When the Marriage Is Over?* is not a legal reference book, and will not prepare you to become the go-to legal eagle for dogs. It will give you practical advice and share personal stories to give you a better understanding of the legal system and your pet. It's crucial that you know how to keep custody of your pet should you divorce; that you don't risk confiscation of your pet by a humane officer if you violate a city ordinance; that you know your housing rights and those of your dog, plus a myriad of other issues. *What Happens to Rover When the Marriage Is Over?* is about all the issues dogs might face as living beings in our world. Only we can make sure that our dogs "pawsitively" enjoy every legal right and protection available. For all they give to us, it is very little to give to them.

Most of all, this book is about loving and protecting the dog(s) in your life. I adopted my dog Sadie during a time of great stress and discord in my life. I had no idea how she would change my world and open my eyes to the wonder of all animals. I feel it's the least I can do to try to change the legal world for Sadie and all of her species who have not received fair treatment in American courts. My hope is this book will make pet parents more aware of the greater consequences our pets face from a legal system that is antiquated in the majority of rulings and laws for companion pets. But also to let them know about the great resources and kindred spirits ready to work for a better world. If this book is even one small step in that direction, then Sadie has done a great job at allowing me to put into words what she has taught me with her actions.

Chapter 1

IN THE BEGINNING THERE WAS DOG
(Who Let the Dogs In?)

I have two toothbrushes in my bathroom. I don't have a husband, a live-in boyfriend, or a roommate. I have a dog. I brush her teeth every night. She sleeps on my bed; she rides in my car. She has total freedom to go wherever she wants to go in our home. She's allowed on the furniture. She has almost as many toys as I have shoes. I take her everywhere with me, and if she isn't welcome, I often don't go. She goes out the door with me in the morning when I go to work, and I drop her off at day care, just like the parent of any two-legged child. I have photos of her on my desk and bulletin board. I talk about her in conversations that she probably has no business in, but I don't care. I cook for her, make sure she gets proper nutrition and medical care, and in all ways I share my life with her. The day I let a little eight-week-old puppy into my house, she ran into my heart and has occupied it for ten years now.

Shortly after I adopted Sadie, I found out she'd been exposed to the parvovirus and might die. That day my life changed forever. I fell in love for the first time in my life. Truly in love. That amazing, "I can't live without you" all-consuming forever-commitment love I'd been unable to feel for anyone or anything in my life until I ran home in my high heels to take her to the vet. I scooped her out of her crate and buried my face into her soft little body. Nope, through two husbands and other relationships that were supposed to last forever, I knew this love was different and would never end. My love for my dog Sadie filled a missing part inside of me that no one had ever even come close to touching.

Sadie is like the air I breathe; I feel suffocated when she's not near me. I feel incomplete when she's not with me. I have no apologies for my great love of this precious dog. The day I went to see about getting a dog I had two criteria:

1. I didn't want a dog that would lick my face.
2. I didn't want a dog that would shed all over my house.

I kiss her right on the mouth with no reticence, and I let her lick my face without reserve. I've gone through more vacuum sweepers than you should need in a lifetime because Sadie is a long-haired dog. I have more black clothes than a ninja, because Sadie has black hair and I choose to believe you can't see it on black clothing. If you don't want to leave my house with dog hair on your clothes, don't sit on my furniture.

I tease her and I chase her. I grab the long hair "feathers" on her leg when she walks by, and I roll on the floor with her. I pull her ears out like wings and tell her she looks like a bat. I trace the black lines on her face and am jealous of the "permanent eyeliner" that emphasizes her beautiful eyes. I take her lips and pull them into a comical smile. She lays her head on my chest and looks into my eyes. In her eyes I see wisdom that only dogs have. I put her toys on my head and any number of silly things to amuse her, and in doing so I make myself happy. If she's out of my sight for too long, I call out, "Where's my dog?" She comes running. I talk to her. She knows about all my challenges, fears, failures, victories, and hopes that I have for our future. In all things she is my confidant and I am hers.

I know everything about her . . . each inch of her hairy little body. I check for bumps and patches on her skin that feel unusual. I check her eyes and wipe away the "eye boogers." I breathe deeply of her dogness and it reassures me that all is not only right in my world—our world—it's wonderful. I hold her paws. I kiss that sweet space right between her nose and her eyes. I pat her cool smooth stomach. I scratch her chest, and when she paws me in the car I give in and scratch her head. I hold her close and rejoice when she joyously greets me each day when I pick her up from day care. I relish it when she jumps on me like I've been gone for months when it's only been a little over eight hours. I wake at night to listen to her steady, even breathing and her little yips as she chases a squirrel in her dreams. I've woken up panicked in hotels because I didn't feel the weight of her body on the bed, and then remembered that I had to leave her at home.

It's the most awesome responsibility and privilege to be responsible for her life and her well-being. I ask her, "Am I doing okay? Am I all that you imagined your 'mom' would be? Is your life turning out the way you wanted it to?" In her eyes I see the answers to my questions.

According to the 2015–2016 American Pet Products Association (APPA) National Pet Owners Survey Statistics, more than ninety-four million Americans let dogs into their lives and families in 2015. I believe at least half of them feel very close to how I feel about my dog. We've integrated our dogs into our lives and in all aspects; they are family members. We buy clothes for them. We take them on vacation. We purchase health insurance for them and make sure they're included on our automobile policies. For some of us, the relationships we have with our dogs are most often the longest ones in our lives. Although dogs have had connections with humans for centuries, I believe the shift in our deep emotional attachment to our dogs is relatively new. In my opinion, we longed for an attachment for something that loved and accepted us for ourselves. Ultimately, this longing became a necessity brought about by the changes in our country, the rampant rise of materialism, and a lack of deep meaning in our lives.

It all seems to have happened so suddenly, and maybe the rise of social media and cable television has made it seem that way. Could it have been Oprah and Martha Stewart who unabashedly brought their dogs out of their own living rooms and into ours that made people rush to have a dog in their home and family? What transpired to make someone like me, who never had a dog of my own, and millions of other pet parents become so crazy in love with our dogs? Did we all get swept into a massive popular trend? Was it suddenly cool to have a dog? Or was it more that society became restless and people were searching for consistency and lasting love in an ever-changing and often confusing world?

I believe most people live the life Thoreau eloquently described as "quiet desperation." The majority of Americans don't find passion and fulfillment in their jobs and work environment. More often we work to provide for our needs than because it is something that inspires and completes us. We have "Take Your Dog to Work Day," which makes that one day of the year satisfying to many employees. Some entrepreneurs have even created their own businesses in part so they could have their dog with them at work. At Replacements, Inc. in North Carolina, where you can find just about any china pattern in the world, founder and CEO Bob Page created the business so he could bring his dog to work, and he allows his employees to do the same. Employees at Replacements consider this perk to be one of their most important benefits. I was happy to shop there with Sadie, even though she made me nervous when she got close to the displays. Interestingly, Replacements reports that customers have broken china in the showroom, but none of the customers' or employees' dogs have broken anything.

Our devotion to our dogs grows deeper as they grow older. We can't bear the thought that their lives are flying by seven times faster than ours. We grieve deeply when they are gone. There are pet crematories, pet funeral homes, and pet cemeteries. Contemplating the unexpected event that we would die before our dog, we include them in our wills, naming guardians and leaving money for their care. Every aspect of pets today is big business, but at the heart of it all is that profound bond we have with our canine soul mate. Because of that bond millions of Americans let dogs into their homes and lives. That bond propels us to seek out the best food for them and every other conceivable comfort to make their life the best it can possibly be.

Dogs not only dominate the American home scene, they're everywhere. Dogs have roles on television shows and in movies; they're used in advertising; and countless new businesses are created around them and their owners. The number-four top commercial in the 2016 Super Bowl was Doritos Dogs, in which dogs plot to enter a supermarket to get Doritos and devise an ingenious way to accomplish it. Advertising uses dogs to sell everything from Ikea kitchens to allergy medicine and just about anything else you can imagine. Car manufacturers have introduced dog-friendly features; and Subaru touts that their cars are "dog approved." Subaru's Share the Love Program promotes their dog-friendly car and raises money for animal rescue and other worthy causes. Commercial vacuum sweeper manufacturers have special models for pet hair, and along with thousands of dog boutiques and specialty stores in the United States, pets have their own box store chains to fulfill their every need, real or imagined.

Corporations have let dogs into their corporate culture as brand ambassadors, because if people love dogs and their product/service is associated with a dog, then people will love it. Dogs can be the perfect "spokesperson" for brand recognition. Ever hear of a dog getting a DUI and ruining the image of the company it represents? Dogs don't give statements to the press that are offensive, aren't seen using a different product than the one they're getting paid to bark about, and they never bite the hand that feeds them.

Dogs used in commercials and movies are protected by standards as to how long they can work, breaks, and other important regulations to ensure their health and safety. Dogs have been part of the advertising scene for a long time. One of the most iconic dogs in advertising history had passed away before he ever became famous. Nipper, who got his name from nipping visitors at his home in England, lived a normal dog's life from 1884–1895. Following Nipper's death, his owner, the English painter Francis

Barraud, painted a picture of Nipper looking into a phonograph machine. He eventually sold it to the Gramophone Company, and Nipper's image was patented in 1900. In 1990, RCA "hired" a two-month-old puppy named Chipper who was used with Nipper's image in campaigns. Everyone remembers the Taco Bell Chihuahua and Spuds McKenzie. Today, dogs are present in many commercials, if not as a "spokesdog," then as part of the family portrayed in the commercial. The Greyhound Bus Line has used a greyhound dog as its logo since 1930. However, it wasn't until 1957, when they introduced Lady Greyhound on *The Steve Allen Show*, that the company raced to the head of the public transportation pack.

In the 1950s and 1960s, most dogs were still treated like animals and kept outside. According to PetMD, today almost half of our family dogs share our beds. Lassie and Timmy had a deep bond and loyal partnership on the popular television show in the 1950s, and while the show may have popularized the collie breed, it was also the beginning of recognizing the dog as much more than an animal that lived in the backyard. John Provost, who played Timmy (1957–1964), actually had to go and live with the dog who played Lassie for three days to see if they were compatible before he got the part.

Dogs were featured more prominently as inside-dog family members in later television series, such as *Married with Children* and *Frasier*, and in the Bush's Best Bean commercials. Buck, Eddie, and Duke all portrayed the present-day American family dog who has free rein of the house and shares in the privileges and perks of its two-legged family members. Somewhere along the line, the term "dog owner" was substituted with "pet parent," signifying the role of dogs more as "fur children" than less important members of the family hierarchy. Many states and cities have used the term "guardian" in their legislation and ordinances, indicating that we are more protectors than masters of our dogs.

Then there are the beloved cartoon dogs that are part of American culture and loved by millions. Marmaduke, Scooby-Doo, Snoopy, Astro, and Brian Griffin all contributed to the humanization of the American dog. Snoopy best exemplifies the relationship between a person and their dog as a confidant, friend, and family member. Charlie Brown, with all his insecurities, social ineptness, and failures, always has the loyalty and companionship of Snoopy.

The medical field allows dogs trained as special therapy dogs into hospitals, nursing homes, and rehabilitation facilities. Hershey Medical Center in Pennsylvania began its pet therapy program in 2005. Certified therapy dogs provide patients comfort and stress relief; provide mental stimulation; reduce depression and anxiety; lower blood pressure and respiratory and heart rates; and encourage better communication between family members, patients, and medical providers. Visits are provided in almost all adult units seven days a week. The special dogs in this program also sit with family members of acutely ill patients in critical care units, providing much-needed consolation. Hundreds of hospitals in the United States have some type of dog therapy program for patients.

I once represented an elderly man in a nursing home when I received a call from the facility inviting me to attend his birthday party. As I listened to the details of when and where, the caller told me that it was really my dog Sadie that the gentleman had requested at his party. She asked me to come early and bring Sadie to visit other residents who would not be able to attend. As a fairly new dog mom, I'd never heard of dogs visiting nursing homes and was happy to oblige. Since then, Sadie has made numerous trips to nursing homes even though she is not a trained therapy dog. Most hospitals require that dogs are certified therapy dogs, but nursing homes often do not. When one of my sisters went to a nursing home for rehabilitation, this facility also welcomed dogs, so Sadie went to visit her and many of the other residents. All across the country, nursing homes and hospitals, including renowned children's hospitals, such as Texas Children's Hospital and Children's Hospital of Pittsburgh, have let dogs in because they are good medicine.

As much as the legal system has been slow to recognize pets as essential family members, they have brought dogs into the courtroom and the prison system where they perform vital services. Dogs provide comfort and support to witnesses, in particular children and victims of crime. The Children's Advocacy Center in Mississippi began using a German shepherd named Vachss in the 1990s. In 1994, Vachss received the Hero of the Year award for comforting children. Since then, hundreds of jurisdictions across the country have partnered with various organizations to provide canine comfort in the courtroom.

Dogs were brought into the prison system as early as 1981, when a Catholic nun in the state of Washington began the Prison Pet Partnership to help rehabilitate female inmates. The women were part of a program to train dogs to assist disabled persons, and it was successful for both human and canine participants. Since then, programs to bring canines and cellmates together for a mutual purpose have evolved across the country. In Kansas, as well as in other states, racing greyhounds who are retired escape euthanasia by going to prisons where they are taught dog decorum, learn to walk on a leash, become housebroken, and are trained in other qualities that make them ready for adoption.

Schools have welcomed dogs in for activities that benefit students emotionally and academically. Members of Tails of Joy in Hartford, Connecticut, participate in Reading Education Assistance Dogs (READ) with their trained therapy dogs. Dogs are assigned to a child who needs help with reading for a period of several weeks. The dogs are trained to sit quietly and do what dogs do spectacularly: listen. The student reads to the dog, then at the end of the time period the student reads aloud to the class with his paw partner at his side. The student then receives his choice of a new book paw-printed by his tutor with a tail. Dogs are involved in a myriad of programs in schools, helping to lick bullying, improve communication with autistic children, and reduce stress.

Dogs have also been brought in—maybe reluctantly on the dog's part—to pop culture. Paris Hilton helped popularize the accessory dog. Suddenly countless numbers of young girls were getting miniature dogs and carrying them around in designer bags.

If dogs were only let into the lives of great pet parents, it would be a better world for them. However, dogs are so loving, so compliant, and now so big business, that they've also been dragged into the lives of people who may not have their best interests at heart.

One such group, a direct result of the Paris Hilton dog accessory fad, is the pet trendologists. These are the people you see on the morning television shows talking about everything that remotely relates to dogs. They stage massive productions, such

as dog fashion shows, Yappy Hours, Matchmaking with Mutts, and dozens of other events. They create magazines that promote celebrities with dogs, celebrity status for dogs, and all sorts of ridiculous things that dogs have no interest in, such as dog beer. Unlike the informative magazines that promote dog health and good nutrition, and provide necessary and useful information to make dogs' lives better, the trendologists' publications are often just one more way to promote themselves. They strive for recognition and often succeed at becoming celebrities in their own right. They can be seen all over the Internet in photos with movie stars and socialites and dogs. These "Doglebrities" start businesses with clever names that provide services most dogs would rather skip. Ever hear of a gym where you can bring your dog? They exist, but the last place I can think of my dog or any dog picking for exercise is a sweaty gym. They use dogs to pave the way to fame and fortune and are often successful doing it. They can tell you what your personality is by the dog you have, this season's hottest nail polish color for your dog, and help you find a mate by using your dog to attract one.

Pet trendologists don't represent the millions of pet parents today who are devoted to the best welfare for their dogs and in all matters consider what is best for them. They are a strange breed unto themselves who seek profit from pets. They see their dogs much like the society mothers see their teenage daughters—as a way to do the things they didn't get to do and turn their dogs into commodities and "dogutantes." Rare is the photo of a dog at a "trendy" event where it looks happy or relaxed. However, pet trendologists are part of the dog culture in our country today, and these events are most often not regulated or held to any legal standard for the comfort and best interest of the dogs. I'd like to see how a pet trendologist would feel if placed in an uncomfortable costume and paraded before a loud and often inebriated crowd. I've never seen a mutt that actually drank martinis, but "Martinis and Mutts" is one such popular event this crowd is fond of. Unlike the use of dogs in movies or television, these events are not governed by rules for the safety and best interest of the dogs. Many of these events claim to raise money for various dog charities. In my experience, the cost of producing these elaborate, over-the-top festivities often far surpasses what could be raised in a less ostentatious manner that doesn't involve uncomfortable situations for dogs.

The integration of millions of dogs into our family and society has created countless opportunities for new businesses, professions, and products. This growth necessitated the creation of regulations and oversight for the services and products provided to dogs and by dogs, as well as laws governing dogs' behavior in public and in all aspects of life that regulate the actions of their human counterparts.

The world that I share with Sadie is, for the most part, insular and idyllic. Those of us who love our dogs and have made them members of our family and share our lives with them know there is a bigger world outside that governs many of our actions and what we can and cannot do with them outside our doors.

We let the dogs into our homes and into our hearts, but when we take them out into the larger world things change. We must be aware of their standing in society and the laws that regulate their behavior and our treatment of them. Most everything we do is governed by legislation that was passed with initial good intentions, and dog law is no different. When people hear the term "dog law," the first thing they usually envision is the dog catcher. Dog catchers have evolved into animal control/humane officers that do much more than catch stray dogs. That might not seem important to you as a dog parent, but it's *imperative* that you have a good general understanding of what it means to bring a dog into your life and into the public, as well as your subsequent responsibilities and rights under the law. Unfortunately, animal law has been slow to change from the view of dogs as property to that of family member. Your dog is your fur child inside your home, but that changes the minute her paws hit the sidewalk. When we bring dogs into our lives we must also bring an understanding of the laws that will affect our life together.

Study after study has been done about the reasons people love dogs as much as they do, but there is still no certain conclusion, no definitive answer. Maybe it's because there are as many reasons why we love our dogs as there are people or dogs. Maybe it's just because they simply love us back. No matter the reason, that love propels us to take care of them in all aspects, including legal issues.

In the beginning there was dog, and dog parents know that was a very good thing. I let my dog into my life, and it was the best thing I've ever done. I didn't get my dog to become a celebrity, meet celebrities, or make money. I didn't get her because I wanted to be part of a popular craze, to meet friends or a mate. I got my dog at a time in my life when I was hurting emotionally and seeking comfort. I remembered my horse from my youth and how much she meant to me and the special moments I shared with her. When I got Sadie I lived in the city with a very small backyard and getting a horse was out of the question, so I thought a dog would be a good substitute. Although I didn't know it at the time, I got her because I needed her.

I did realize a lifelong dream of writing through the inspiration of Sadie, and she's earned a little money for her bank from book royalties. My love for Sadie has led me to a concern for all animals, which is prevalent among most dog parents. Some dog owners even become vegetarians due to the love of their dog, which is transferred to all living creatures. How can I ignore the dog my neighbor has tied in the backyard during all kinds of weather and is never free to run? As a lawyer and a dog mom, how can I be silent concerning the lack of vigorous prosecution of animal abusers? Love of our dog leads to love of all animals, and we become acutely aware of all the cruelty and injustice they suffer. By bringing a dog into our life, we get an awareness of the role all animals play in our lives and in society.

This love of other animals caused me to perform an illegal U-turn the day a person threw a bird out of the car in front of me. I caught her, named her AbiGal, and she was part of my family for almost four years. She was a cheerful and beautiful cockatiel with a sweet, yet feisty, personality that was always amusing. Sadie found her intriguing, and although she wasn't exactly in love with her, she accepted her into our little family and the two of them had some nose-to-beak contemplative moments. When Abi died unexpectedly, Sadie grieved right along with me, and for months afterward would sleep in the spot where Abi's cage had been.

If you're reading this book, you are no doubt a dog parent. You are someone like me who has let one or more dogs or other pets into your life. As part of your life, they are part of your greater

world. You shop for them, you take them on walks, you love them. You relate to the dogs you see in commercials and most likely enjoy movies about dogs. Protecting your dog, keeping her safe, making sure she has a good life is part of your life plan, which makes your dog integral to every aspect of your life.

That's how it was with Bill Robertson and his wife and the multiple adopted dogs they shared in a large home on several fenced acres in an upscale Philadelphia suburb. Canine and connubial bliss reigned from the wine cellar to the large outdoor pool. Then they got divorced. If you don't think the law can intrude in your private life and that of your dogs, you will have a big shock if you ever end up in family court. The Robertsons let these dogs into their lives, but keeping them in proved to be quite a different story.

Chapter 2

THE CUSTODY OF CANINES
(Dividing the Dog)

People have always fought like cats and dogs in divorce court. However, the number of cases where people are actually fighting *over* the dog or cat has increased substantially in the past several years. Many of these cases get a great deal of media coverage, particularly where large amounts of money are spent on legal fees such as the case of "Gigi" mentioned in the Introduction. However, for every sensational case you see on CNN or in the headlines of a newspaper, thousands of couples parting ways wrestle with this problem daily in family courts. Dogs, while considered "persons" in their owners' minds, are not given the same status in court as human children, although it's easy to apply the same principles for canine custody as used in child custody. A Pennsylvania couple tackled this problem, albeit not cheaply, and finally arrived at a reasonable solution for the people and the dogs.

Mr. Robertson is a successful financial planner in Philadelphia. He was married for thirty-three years to the mother of his four daughters. During the marriage his wife was a stay-at-home mom to their four children and filled the role of corporate wife. Family was important to the Robertsons. Their lovely home had been built to foster togetherness and contained all the elements that made it the place where the kids and their friends loved to hang out. The large, sprawling home was set on three acres and had a disco in the basement, a soda fountain bar, a gym, a pool, and as many dogs and cats as possible. The warm kitchen opened into a comfortable family room where animals and people spent many happy hours in front of the fireplace and watching television.

The Robertson kids grew up and went off to college and careers, then the Robertson marriage came to an end. At the time of the divorce, the family had three rescued golden retrievers, several cats, expensive furniture, numerous cars, and lots of investments. As the divorce made its way through the procedure of dividing assets, few problems arose. It was easy for the separating spouses to choose cars, agree on an equitable distribution of financial assets, and agree that the husband would keep the house and the wife would pick out a new one. In one twenty-minute walk through the seven-thousand-square-foot house armed with Post-it notes, they agreed, without rancor, who would take what furniture. The only problem was they could not agree on who should keep the dogs.

Mrs. Robertson thought she should get the dogs because she was the one who stayed at home with them every day and walked them and fed them the majority of the time. Mr. Robertson was certain the dogs should stay in the only home they had ever known so they could continue swimming in the pool and run freely on the property.

Mrs. Robertson said the dogs would be lonely at home all day because they were used to her being with them. Mr. Robertson said the dogs would miss the weekend trips to the mountains and beach he took them on. This went on for two years. The property settlement was signed, the deeds were transferred, titles to cars signed off on, investments disbursed, but the dogs remained in limbo.

Finally, after lawyers drained the separate property of both spouses and caused a huge decline in their financial resources, they decided to use a family law mediator. It took only one session for the custody of the dogs to be decided. The mediator had both parties submit evidence of the two main standards used in child custody cases. Who was the primary caretaker of the dogs and what was in their best interest? The mediator was able to help the couple see that both of their arguments for custody for keeping the dogs fit in these standards. Mrs. Robertson's argument for keeping the dogs had been the "primary care" standard, and her husband's was "in the best interest of the dogs."

In the Robertsons' case, both spouses played important roles in the lives of the dogs. It was true that Mrs. Robertson was the primary caretaker—she took them to the vet, fed them, and took them for walks—but it was equally true that it would be unfair for the dogs to be taken from their home with their favorite lounging areas, the yard they loved to run in, and to deny them of their swimming pool privileges. The Robertsons were finally able to put an end to the dogfight and agree on the following canine custody arrangement.

1. The Robertsons would share joint custody of the canines.
2. They would be solely responsible for all of the dogs' expenses while in their individual custody, including food, new leashes and collars, treats, toys, and other items.

3. They would bear equally the cost of veterinary care for the dogs, and no medical decisions would be made for the dogs without the consent of the other party, except in an emergency situation. Each party would execute a Medical Power of Attorney in favor of the other person in case of a life-threatening emergency, and if one person could not be located that authorized the person who was with the dog to make any necessary decisions.

4. The dogs would reside with Mrs. Robertson from Monday morning when Mr. Robertson would drop them off on his way to work, until Friday evening when he'd pick them up on his way home.

5. Both Mr. and Mrs. Robertson would have the right to take the dogs on a two-week vacation annually, and other trips as agreed to.

6. Holidays would be split every other year:
   - During odd-numbered years, Mr. Robertson would get the dogs on Thanksgiving, Easter, and Memorial Day. Mrs. Robertson would get them on Christmas, New Year's Eve, and Labor Day.
   - During even-numbered years, Mr. Robertson would get the dogs on Christmas, New Year's Eve, and Labor Day and Mrs. Robertson would get them on Thanksgiving, Easter, and Memorial Day.

7. The dogs would always spend the Fourth of July with Mr. Robertson because they were afraid of fireworks and were used to taking shelter in the wine cellar during that celebration.

8. Changes in the schedule had to be requested two weeks in advance.

This worked amazingly well for the Robertsons and their grown children. In fact, when Mr. Robertson adopted a new dog, this dog was also included in the custody agreement. As for the cats, since the house provided more than enough room for Mr. Robertson and the dogs, the cats were granted sole possession of the third floor of the former marital home.

During the two years when custody of their dogs was pending, the Robertsons were cordial and accommodating; however, that's not always the case. In the movie *When Harry Met Sally*, Billy Crystal tells his newlywed friends that sooner or later they'll be fighting over an eight-dollar dish that will one day cost them a fortune at the legal firm of That's Mine, This Is Yours. While humorous, it's not so funny when you find yourself in front of a judge who views your dog no better than a coffee table with a pulse, and that's exactly the situation you'll encounter in the majority of courts today. Keep in mind that even though dogs are regarded as property by the court, they are not automatically factored into any agreements as your house would be. Dogs and other pets only become an issue when both parties want custody of them.

A lot of divorces and other relationships that end don't involve pets, but when they do, its unknown territory for most couples. I've personally talked to dozens of couples with sad stories of the dog they lost in the divorce. Years later, they're still angry, sad, or both. With a little preparation, a lot of common sense, and a big serving of kindness, you can get through this and keep your beloved canine companion with you. Dismissing unrealistic expectations that a court hearing will solve your problems is paramount. The court will be of little or no help to you.

The first thing you have to accept is that courts today still hold the view that animals are property. Despite the high-profile cases in the media involving celebrities and other unique issues, the law has no provisions for pets as anything more than property and often will not even address the pet custody issue. If you're facing a pet custody issue, and you understand this, you can prepare adequately and not waste time and money attempting an avenue of recovery that in all probability will never happen.

It *is* possible to avoid an acrimonious custody fight over Rover even if it's not entirely amicable. If you're not married or cohabitating with someone right now and you have a pet, then before you share a residence or last name with someone it's essential for you to have a "petnuptial" agreement. This needs to be separate from any standard prenuptial you enter into for financial or property issues, because prenuptials often cover a number of issues, and when one or more of these is challenged when the couple divorces the agreement comes under scrutiny. In many jurisdictions if one part of a contract or agreement is flawed, the entire document is thrown out. Don't take this chance with your dog. It's one thing to lose out on money or cars, but a living creature that you love is quite another situation.

I've created a "petnuptial," which is a simple one-page legal document that declares whom your dog belongs to and who will get her if you split up. At the back of the book is a sample petnuptial, which you can use to create your own. Then, should you ever

part ways, it will clearly establish whom the pet belongs to. Of course, you must continue to provide care, love, and every other need your dog has and to constantly look out for her best interest. That's because in relationships and marriage, sometimes property is deemed commingled. That means ownership transfers to the other person through any number of acts (these are discussed later). Since your dog is property, this could happen. Just make sure you take care of your dog so when the two-legged companion goes in another direction your four-legged companion will be at your side.

In any relationship that is ending, be it a marriage, civil union, or other partnership, you must first try to get an agreement with your spouse or partner that your dog will remain with you. It might be impossible for many reasons, but you at least have to try. If you can have a rational conversation with the departing spouse that you should keep the dog, make sure it ends in a written agreement that confirms custody of the dog to you and get it notarized. It doesn't have to be prepared by an attorney or have a lot of unnecessary legalese. A simple one-page document will work just fine as long as it's clear that Rover remains with you. Keep this document and enter it into your court file as part of your property settlement. A judge's indifference to the custody of the pet also works in your favor; they really don't care who gets the dog, so you can agree to anything with your partner.

As civil as the Robertsons were, they couldn't reach an agreement with each other about the dogs. Unfortunately, before they discovered mediation, they'd spent thousands of dollars on attorney's fees with no result. They were getting nowhere in the court system and had nothing to lose by trying the services of a mediator. Once it's clear that you are at an impasse with your spouse over the custody of Rover, ask them to participate in mediation. If you live in a jurisdiction where mediation is used, this is an excellent option and should be attempted before you involve your lawyers to try to get a judge to listen to your dispute.

Mediators charge by the hour. That's it. Not by the hour for each of you, just for the time you use them and for the time they review your case before the actual mediation. They are extremely economical when you consider what you're paying your attorneys. For example, if the wife has an attorney who bills her at two hundred and fifty dollars an hour and she calls to find out something about her husband, she will be put on hold while the lawyer calls the other attorney to see if he can get the question answered. All the while the wife is on hold, the "meter" is running. As soon as the husband's attorney picks up the phone, another meter starts running at that lawyer's hourly fee. So, if the husband is paying his lawyer an hourly fee of three hundred dollars an hour, while the two lawyers are talking—maybe about the case or maybe about golf or a new Mercedes—combined the couple is getting billed a whopping five hundred and fifty dollars an hour! A mediator is much more cost effective and more efficient than a court with a crowded docket so it may be months before a hearing is scheduled.

Mediators are trained problem solvers. A mediator is a neutral third party who has no interest in the outcome and is trained to help people reach resolutions in many different types of disputes. As a certified family law divorce mediator, I've seen many seemingly insurmountable problems go away after a few mediation sessions. Mediators listen to both sides of the story and suggest, not order, a solution.

Mediation is much less formal than a court hearing and is always held in a neutral location. I often use the conference room of a legal organization I belong to or my own dining room. The only criteria for the location of the mediation is that it has no personal meaning for either party. Your lawyers should not be present at the mediation; it would be counterproductive to have them present. This is your attempt to solve the custody issue between the two of you and the mediator. During parenting plan mediations, children are never present, and your contested pet shouldn't be either. It's not a contest where the dog is placed in the middle and you both call her name to see whom she responds to. Mediators are excellent listeners and can often hear things neither party realizes they are saying and bring great insight to the dispute.

You can bring the same type of evidence to a mediation that you would present in court. Since it's less formal, you'll be able to speak freely. The mediation usually starts with both parties sitting with the mediator at a table. Unlike depositions that might be held as part of your divorce case, the mediation is not recorded and a court reporter is not present. The mediator will make a brief introduction and explain how the mediation will proceed. I find it helpful to have a flip chart of a short list of rules that I explain at the beginning. The rules are simple and basically require the parties to be respectful, not to interrupt, to ask for a break if they need it, and to remain calm and open to the process.

The mediator might ask each party to write down what they expect out of the mediation and not just the end result. Then each party is given a chance to make an opening statement. This is your chance to tell the mediator your side of the story. Each party must respect the other and not interrupt them when they are speaking.

After the introductory session, the mediator will meet with each party separately. This is the time to present any documentary evidence you have. The mediator will make notes and ask you questions. This might continue for several meetings. You'll be able to give the mediator questions to take to your spouse and vice versa. The mediator will only share information with the parties that they have authorized her to disclose.

Once the mediator feels sufficient information has been exchanged and shared, she will bring both parties together and make a recommendation for resolution of the matter. The mediator's recommendation is not binding, and both parties can disagree and walk away. However, if the mediation is successful and both parties agree, this matter won't be part of your court case. It can be put in the final order without the court's approval.

The decisions reached in mediation should be put in writing and include:

- Who gets physical custody of the pet?
- Are you going to have shared custody?
- How financial obligations for the pet will be handled if custody is shared.
- What veterinarian will you use?
- Will the noncustodial ex have visitation?
- What restrictions will apply to visitation?
- Any other aspect of the dog's future if you are sharing custody.

This is the time to get every issue you've agreed to in writing. Remember, you can agree to anything at this point, but if you take the matter to court, the decision is out of your control.

If the mediation fails, then you can move forward and hope to get the court's assistance in the matter. If the court decides the placement of your "pet property," it will be put in your final divorce order. Keep in mind that final orders from a judge are just that: final. If you choose to appeal, it's a long, complicated process, and in the meantime the well-being as well as the placement of your beloved pet must comply with the order. You'll have to rely on your lawyers and hope they draw a judge who will be sympathetic to your issue of pet custody *and* willing to deal with it. It's important that during your mediation you keep working until you reach an agreement or it becomes clear that you won't be able to reach an agreement.

When you find yourself in court, remember that the court still views animals as property. Knowing this, the easiest, fastest, and least expensive route to gain custody of your dog is to prove that she is your "separate property." No matter what jurisdiction you reside in, separate property is an accepted standard when reaching a property settlement in a divorce case. Separate property is anything owned solely by one spouse, and there are myriads of evidence to prove this. Of course, your dog has to actually *be* your separate property, not a dog you acquired jointly.

While there may be slight differences depending on your jurisdiction, usually anything left to you as an inheritance; something you can show ownership of prior to marriage; something you purchased with your own money, not marital funds, and was used solely by you, all of these can denote separate property. It's probably rare that a dog is bequeathed to someone in a will, although it's possible and will be discussed later in this book. If you received a dog through a bequest in a will, she is your separate property unless you "commingled" her into the marriage. Commingling most often occurs with money, not living creatures. For example, if you inherited fifty thousand dollars and placed the money in a joint bank account where you both had access to it, it would no longer be separate property. If you had nothing to do with your dog, never took care of her, didn't like her, gave her to your spouse, or some other action that clearly indicated you didn't accept ownership of the dog or want her, your case could be decided swiftly. The dog could be awarded to your spouse in the property settlement as she is no longer your separate property due to your actions that basically commingled her into the marital joint assets.

Gifts are also separate property, and if the dog was a gift from your spouse or someone else and you have the papers to prove it, for example, adoption papers in your name, breed registration papers showing you as the owner, a card stating that the dog is a gift to you, or any other document proving the dog was a gift solely to you, she is your separate property and should be awarded to you.

If you purchased or adopted the dog prior to marriage, you need the sales receipt from the breeder or the adoption papers. After reading this book, you'll know you need to have a petnuptial separate from any other prenuptial agreement to ensure your dog stays if your mate strays, but these documents can go a long way in proving the dog is separate property obtained prior to the marriage. Additional records will bolster your case: dog tax, dog license fee, vet bill, and boarding kennel receipts, as well as any other papers showing that you were the one who bore the expense in providing for your four-legged separate property. Note the use of generic terms: something, it, and property. This keeps the argument in the perspective of the court by using terms recognized in property settlements. If you're at this stage, you failed to convince your spouse that your dog-daughter belonged solely to you, and the mediator wasn't able to persuade your soon-to-be ex that your dog needed to stay with you. For court, keep it simple and present the pet as a piece of property that you hold the ownership deeds for.

If you acquired the dog during the marriage and essentially it was a "joint ownership dog," not your separate property, and she becomes the "bone of contention" in the divorce, you must try to convince the court that you should have custody of your dog. Hopefully you'll get a judge who's a dog lover and will be willing to apply the standards used to determine custody of children to the custody of your dog, but don't count on it. Despite what you hear in the media, whether or not a judge will consider the custody of your dog is uncertain at best. If you haven't agreed with your spouse or partner who gets the dog and you decide to split, you better know what these standards are, because they will be your best shot of walking out of court with Rover.

The day I showed up for my divorce hearing with no clue about what was going to happen was the last time I ever entered a courtroom without being thoroughly prepared. Since we had no children I hadn't bothered to research any issues of custody and just assumed that Tiffany, *my dog*, would be going home with me. I couldn't have been more wrong. Had I known the two standards that are used in almost every jurisdiction in determining custody of children, I would have harbored no such hopes, because I came up woefully inadequate in each standard. In pet custody cases, if you can get the court to consider the custody issue of your pet beyond the property classification and the answers to these two questions are in your favor, then you'll have a pretty good chance of getting custody:

1. Who is the primary caretaker?
2. What is in the best interest of the pet?

Sounds simple enough, but in many relationships it's not that easy to determine. In mine, it was pretty much a slam dunk for my husband. After all, I'd taken off for law school and left Tiffany with him.

Although I failed miserably at proving I was Tiffany's primary caretaker, it wasn't because I hadn't paid attention in law school and didn't know any tactical legal maneuvers. It's because I simply wasn't the person who cared for her most of the time, and that's the criteria for determining the primary caretaker. It's the person who cared for the pet most of the time. After all, when you don't know what the dog eats, or how often to send her outside, or the best way to remove dog slobber from inside car windows, and don't have any clothes covered in dog hair, then you probably weren't the person taking care of your so-called companion animal. Hindsight is 20/20, but when you're looking at the back end of your pet walking away from you, maybe for the last time, it's little comfort thinking about what you could have done to be designated as the primary caretaker.

You must understand the concept of *primary* caretaker if you are facing a canine custody dispute. This standard is often successfully argued in property and animal cases. If you find yourself before a judge who's not going to hear any touchy-feely entreaties, it won't do you any good to tell him that you and Rover are soul mates and that the two of you most likely will starve to death if separated. Plus, if you were going to do that, you might want to have a more convincing argument than starvation. Dogs don't lose their appetite very often, and if you're like me, you'd probably just console yourself with food anyway. You get the picture here—you must use the language of the law. Remember, mediation is informal, court is not.

Your chance for success is greatly increased by presenting simple and convincing evidence that clearly proves you were the person the animal depended on. There are no complicated formulas or hidden nuances that will dazzle the judge. The simple question will be: Did you or did you not take care of the dog? Were you the person who had the vet on speed dial? Tearful dramas are the stuff court TV shows are made of, and yes, oceans of tears roll through divorce court, they just aren't very effective at turning the tide in your favor for winning custody of your pet.

While lawyers (excluding me, of course) are accused of making outrageous arguments that border on being absolutely ridiculous, there are some things that just won't fly in court and will not help you get custody of your dog. However, here are ten basic responsibilities that a pet primary caretaker performs. If you have proof that you performed the majority of these, you are well on your way toward proving that you were the primary caretaker of your pet.

1. Did you feed your dog daily? Did you manage your dog's diet knowing what she could and could not eat?
2. Were you the one who purchased the dog's food and favorite treats, taking her along to the pet store for a new leash or toy?
3. Were you the one who took the dog to the vet? Are you familiar with any medical issues your dog has? Do you have a file of her medical records?
4. Did you dispense medicine to the dog when needed? Did you sit with her when she was sick: comfort her, notice when she was not feeling well?
5. Did you take your dog with you when you traveled or boarded her at a safe and comfortable kennel when you couldn't take her with you? (Photos and Facebook are good evidence.)
6. Were you the one who gave the dog her bath and brushed her teeth? Did you take her to the groomer when needed?
7. Did you exercise the dog regularly—take her for walks more than once a day?
8. Did you have playtime with your dog? Do you know her favorite activities? Did you throw balls in the yard, play tug-of-war, or teach her tricks and new activities, such as agility exercises?
9. Did you train your dog or were you the one who took her to obedience classes? Are you the person whose voice she responds to?
10. Are you the one your dog looks to as her "person"? Does she want to be with you? Does she sleep with you? Does she count on you for her needs?

Of all the judges in West Virginia at a time when custody of pets was almost unheard of, we got a judge who took a great interest in the future of our mutually acquired dog, Tiffany. She was one issue I never thought would be part of the divorce. I was prepared to give up my share of almost everything we had acquired together and take nothing from what my husband had before I met him, but when *my* dog was listed in my husband's petition, I was blindsided.

The main reason I lost custody of Tiffany all those years ago was because the judge didn't believe that I was the primary caretaker, and back then I had no idea what that even meant. Sure I had just finished law school and felt ready to take on the best legal eagles out there, but when selecting my classes during law school, I failed to include a family law class. The only divorce I planned on handling was my own, which I was positive would be very simple. That is until I was confronted with this quandary of a term: primary caretaker. Did dogs have different levels of caregivers supplying different services to them? In the few seconds I was given to ponder this question, I realized I was more like the absentee caregiver, and I knew that was not going to be good for my case.

The judge's patience was nearing an end. Had I or had I not provided the majority of Tiffany's necessary care during the marriage, and if not, why? In a *Legally Blonde* moment I blurted out, "Your Honor, the reason I didn't care for her during the past three years is that I didn't live with her."

This proved to be a most unacceptable answer, as the judge stared at me sternly and lobbed another question,

which also seemed to call for a simple enough answer that had nothing to do with whether Tiffany's leash would be in my hand after the proceeding.

He wanted to know what I'd done on vacations during my three years of law school. What this had to do with my seeming lack of care for my dog, I had no idea. I thought maybe he wanted to see who would be providing Tiffany with the most fun in the future, and if there was one thing I knew how to do, it was have fun, so I launched into a lengthy, but honest, answer I was sure would score me points.

"Well, the usual things. I rested, went to visit my family in Pennsylvania, took a few trips to the beach, went skiing, learned to sail, went shopping in Miami once, and took a cruise to recover from trial advocacy."

"Did you take your dog with you on any of these trips?" he asked.

"Well no, the cruise ship of course didn't allow dogs, and you know how it is in law school. I doubt I would have been very good company for her . . . I slept a lot the first few days of vacations and I just wanted to get away. You know what I mean."

Turned out that whether this had been his law school experience or not just didn't matter, and fun in the future for Tiffany was the last thing he was looking for. My lack of caring for and involvement with Tiffany over those three years did not meet the standard he kept referring to, and I was unable to provide a shred of acceptable evidence to prove otherwise.

As the final divorce hearing went on, I realized that primary caretaker was a simple enough standard that every divorce court litigant should know. As in child custody cases, John and I could have agreed to almost any type of arrangement for the physical custody of Tiffany. Neither of us had a clear separate property claim to Tiffany. We hadn't actually purchased her. Our five-year-old nephew found her wandering the streets and he gave her to *me.* He didn't give me any type of note or card I could use as proof. Additionally, shortly after I was attached to Tiffany, a neighbor kid claimed it was his dog. When I cried and didn't want to give her back, my husband gave him one hundred dollars and the family let me keep her. John didn't get a receipt or he could have proved that Tiffany was his separate property and the decision would have been in his favor. Or, if he'd written a note or card to me saying Tiffany was a gift to me, she could have been my separate property and custody would be mine.

Our judge made it clear that it was of paramount importance that Tiffany go with the person who had taken care of her, provided a stable environment for her, and had been responsible for her safety and health. He wasn't interested in the future, he wanted to know about the past, and that's the time period that is examined in custody cases. Judges aren't interested in what you tell them is *going* to happen, but what has *been* your pattern and practice as a parent, whether of a child or a dog.

Perhaps it was because John and I had a prenuptial agreement that was not challenged and just about every issue in dissolving our marriage was already decided before the day of the final hearing, but for whatever reason, our judge was more than willing to deal with the custody of our dog. He began his decision process with the primary care standard, a foundation to build on. Even in cases where an item clearly is property, such as a house or boat, the primary caretaker standard can be applied to a certain extent when dividing marital assets. For example, let's say you owned a house before you got married and retained the deed in your name during the marriage. If your spouse took care of all the maintenance on the house, made substantial improvements, and added significantly to its value, it's possible the court would award him (or her) a portion of the increased value and their separate funds used for this purpose. If you're not in a financial position to pay your spouse his share, the court can order that the property be sold and the proceeds split in order for the equitable distribution or the community property standard be met for the division of the property. This can also happen with other property, such as a boat. If you had a boat and all you ever did was ride in it once in a while, never cleaned it, paid for licenses or fees, or any other expenses, such as maintenance, docking, or storage, you could possibly be left on the shore watching while your ex sails off with the vessel, just like I watched Tiffany and her fluffy tail walking away from me after the hearing.

There are two types of property settlements in divorces: equitable distribution, where things are divided "equitably" based on a number of factors, often giving the judge wide discretion with a result that may not always be fair; or community property, where anything acquired during the marriage with very few exceptions is split down the middle. Depending on the state you live in, one of these standards is used to separate your marital assets, and if one of them is your dog, you better hope you live in the state that applies equitable distribution if you're depending on the court to make the decision. Think about it, in a community property state the ruling might be that you get the crystal and your spouse gets the dog. No difference, just dividing things evenly is the goal. You have a better chance for a fair, rational decision in an equitable distribution state. In the case of companion animals, the custody issue is all or nothing and doesn't include a portion of the value of the dog awarded to the noncustodial spouse. Tangible real or personal property's value can be apportioned; that's not the case with a living companion animal.

Courts recognize a set of responsibilities that are necessary and make common sense when it comes to raising children. Children are psychologically bonded to their caregivers, and courts realize this emotional bond is important for the child's developmental journey. Psychologists have successfully advocated that it's necessary for children's stability to remain with their primary caregiver. Likewise, veterinarians, animal behaviorists, and ethologists (specialists in the study of animal behavior) validate the bond between animals and their caregivers. Animals have grieved themselves to death at the loss of their companion caregiver. In Vilmos Csányi's book, *If Dogs Could Talk: Exploring the Canine Mind,* the Hungarian ethologist recounts the story of a stray dog that came to the university laboratory where he worked. The night janitor took charge of the dog, providing all his care, and the two became inseparable companions during the nights they spent in the lab. At the end of his shift, the janitor often took the dog home with him, and when he didn't the dog waited anxiously for the custodian to arrive for work each evening. One night the janitor didn't return to work; he had died. The other workers in the lab soon noticed the dog was missing and began searching for him. He was found sitting outside the apartment building of his deceased master. Every dog owner is convinced of the innate mutual understanding between them and their canine companion. Your animal is bonded with you if you've been the person who provided for her care, the one she depended on; you owe it to her to make sure this bond remains intact.

You can successfully argue the primary care standard even though the court won't grant "child" status to your pet. The key for success is to be organized and present simple evidence. Someone who has no knowledge of the habits, needs, or routines of the animal will not be able to convince the court they were the caregiver for the animal they now want. In fact, such a person would have as much of a chance of getting custody of the pet as a man in a most absurd Texas case.

In this case, three dogs had been purchased jointly by a couple when they lived together before marriage. In time, the couple married and moved from New England to Texas, where a series of unfortunate events occurred. The husband was convicted of several crimes and sentenced to thirty years in jail. After spending more than two hundred thousand dollars on her husband's legal defense, the wife gave up and filed for divorce, asking for most of their property, including the dogs.

Obviously, having nothing much to do in prison but watch the calendar slowly move toward the thirty-year emancipation date, the husband filed papers asking the family court to award him custody of the dogs. He claimed he was their primary caretaker even though he'd been incarcerated for five years at the time the divorce was filed. Now, I do know many jails have work release programs, but release programs to care for your own dogs is not a prison rehabilitative service. Despite having been unavailable for the slightest need of the dogs for more than five years, the husband wanted them. Ignoring the fact that they couldn't live in his cell with him, he still wanted them. It was impossible for this guy to think that he'd have someone else care for the dogs until he was released, because by that time the dogs would be more than two hundred and ten years old in human years. He didn't state in his petition what he was going to do with them or how he'd care for them behind bars, but in our justice system, everyone is entitled to their day in court. You can pretty much file anything you want to if you pay the filing fee in your jurisdiction, but it doesn't always mean you'll be heard, let alone prevail.

For whatever reason, disbelief perhaps, the Texas judge was intrigued and decided to rule on the man's petition in the divorce case. His ruling determined that this man had abandoned the dogs and the wife got custody of the three dogs. The court didn't even entertain the ridiculous pleading of the man that he was the primary caretaker of the dogs, but awarded custody based on a legal premise used in child custody cases when someone asserts that they are the primary caretaker. If you're not there, you aren't taking care of the children or the dogs, and if you abandon your family, you don't have much of a chance later to ask for custody of your children. In other words, whether you leave for law school or jail (and there are those who think most lawyers should end up at the latter destination anyway) there's no difference in the eyes of the court. There are, of course, exceptions to every legal principle, and couples often make arrangements that one spouse will go away to school in preparation to better provide for the family, but that clearly was not the case here.

Because there are no statutes that specifically define "pet parents," there are no mandates of what pet primary caretakers should be responsible for and, as in my divorce case, courts often rely on extensive experience in child custody cases. Our judge's job was to divide our property in an equitable manner, and this piece of property, albeit on four legs with a heartbeat and a name, was going to go to the person who had taken care of it.

That day in court, my husband had a firm grasp of what a primary caretaker was and not just because his secretary had researched the information for him. He knew because he'd lived it—this was his reality.

The 1979 movie *Kramer vs. Kramer*, in which Dustin Hoffman and Meryl Streep portray divorcing couple Ted and Joanna Kramer, brilliantly depicts the role of a primary caretaker. Hoffman's character had no choice but to pick up the slack and learn almost instantly how to care for his son when his wife walked out. In a short time he became an expert parent. His conversations changed, his priorities changed. He learned to cook, wash clothes, do the grocery shopping, pay the bills, and everything else about his son he'd missed while he pursued a career in advertising.

Necessity truly is the mother of invention, and without me in the house, the same thing happened to my ex-husband. He had integrated Tiffany into every aspect of his daily routine. Tiffany was his companion, and he knew what being her primary caretaker was all about.

If you get a judge who will listen to your claim as primary caretaker of your dog, you'll need evidence to prove it. If you truly have been the primary caretaker, this evidence was created long before the divorce papers were drawn up. If it's *your* dog and you were the one caring for it the majority of the time, you'll have the necessary proof to convince the judge. Keep in mind, most judges who will even briefly entertain such an argument will most likely have as much interest in who gets Rover as which one of you will be eating from the good china. The key is to keep it short, have the proper evidence, and, as hard as it is, keep emotion out of your argument; in other words, "Just the facts, ma'am."

There was no way I could convince the judge that I'd been Tiffany's caregiver. Although we'd been married for eight years, we only had Tiffany for half of that time, and for three out of those four years I had been at law school. My claim was just as pathetic as that of the Texas inmate. You can't feed a dog over the phone or in a prison cell, and you can't take her to the vet from eight hundred miles away.

As if my absence wasn't enough, there was my soon-to-be ex-husband with pristinely accurate records of what seemed to be Tiffany's every meal, veterinary appointment, walk, and bowel movement for the last three years. Yep, he looked just like Dr. Doolittle with his records and his understanding of what was involved in the care and feeding of this particular dog. My ex had learned all he could about divorce law, but most importantly, he had fallen totally in love with Tiffany in my absence, and this was one girl he wasn't going to let go of. No one in that courtroom could doubt his sincerity about parenting Tiffany.

Were you the one who wouldn't get off the couch to take the dog for a walk? Were your recently polished nails wet every time the yard needed to be cleaned? Loved the dog from afar, but begged off the bath? Enjoyed riding in your fancy car, but never took your dog along? Have no idea whom the dog goes to when she is sick? Have no idea what "your" dog eats or if she takes any medication? If so, you haven't been the primary caretaker of the "marital dog."

All of these activities are major primary caretaking duties, and if you want a pet that your soon-to-be ex is also claiming, it's essential that you have proof that you were the person this animal depended on for everything from fresh water to adequate dental care. However, if you didn't perform these duties, you need to ask yourself why you want this dog. On the other hand, if you have a spouse challenging you for custody of your dog and you are the primary caretaker, it won't be difficult to prove. Again, I caution all couples that are parting ways . . . rare is the court that will deal with pet custody, so try to work it out between yourselves first.

Common sense will guide you, and you can refer to the same standards delineated in your state's child custody statutes. In short, what it takes for the day-to-day care as well as the yearly necessities to provide for a child is almost identical to the needs of your pet.

So how do you prove to the court that you were/are the primary caretaker of the pet? You'd think that if you were the one who fed the dog you'd get to keep the dog. Not so fast, though. There are a great deal of caretaking duties necessary for the proper treatment of a dog. Granted feeding is right up there, but many things go along with it. Before we got Tiffany, my husband and I had a dog named Carlyle. I spotted Carlyle one Sunday with his cute little head poking up out of a cardboard box along the roadside with a FREE PUPPIES sign as we drove home from New Hope, Pennsylvania. I begged John to turn around and stop, and before he could protest too much, I had Carlyle on the seat between us headed to his new home.

Carlyle would never come to John when he called him; instead he ran around and around our house each time he got loose, often making John miss his train to the city for work. After futile attempts to lasso him, lure him with food, and chase him into the open garage failed, John discovered one foolproof way to capture Carlyle.

He'd back the car out of the garage, open the back door, and since Carlyle loved a car ride even more than chasing the ducks at the park down the street, he'd gallop down the hill and leap into the backseat. John would close the door quickly, drive the car back into the garage, shut the garage door, and let Carlyle out of the car and into the house.

I took Carlyle swimming at the duck pond and slept in front of the fireplace with him. When he was a puppy I carried him up and down the stairs because he was afraid of them. I took Carlyle for walks, allowing him to carry a big stick that extended out several feet from both sides of his mouth, but he balanced it perfectly, making everyone we encountered move out of his way. I gave him baths on the back patio, I put bows on him for photographs, I jumped in the pool and swam with him.

After our neighbor witnessed one particularly embarrassing Carlyle chase, which resulted in John falling and ripping his pants, he said, "John, why don't you be the one who feeds Carlyle and maybe then he won't run away from you."

Clearly frustrated, John replied, "Feed him? Feed him? If it wasn't for me, this dog would starve, and he still won't come to me."

Sadly, this was true, because in those days I never even prepared food for myself. We operated a restaurant in Center City, Philadelphia, and Carlyle and I just waited for John to bring us food from the restaurant. We'd sit on the back patio together every night waiting for John to trudge down the hill from the train stop with our dinner. I don't even remember what the kitchen in that house looked like! Yet, even though John performed the most essential and necessary chores of a primary caretaker for Carlyle, feeding, I did everything else for Carlyle and was the one he considered his "person." I have no doubt Carlyle would have remained with me had our marriage ended then.

Primary caretaker duties include companionship, playing, and anything essential for the well-being and survival of your animal. The following activities are all primary caretaker duties, and you should know as much about these things as you know about your own needs. However, for court, evidence must be documented. Records are gold, so keep track of everything you possibly can if you see a rift in the romantic landscape that could be permanent.

Perhaps you're thinking: *Are you crazy? Who can remember all of this, and how could it ever be presented briefly and in concise form?* It can be hard to recall all the details when standing in front of a judge, let alone recite the inventory of your terrier's toy box. That's why you must know without doubt that you'll need *proof* that you are the person who knows this animal best. You do numerous things for your animal without a second thought. Using this list as a guide, you can create a great record of the life you share with your dog and the services you provide. You'll need a file with all important papers and documents about your pet's life with you. This file should include:

1. Dog tax records that clearly show your name as the responsible owner and that you paid the fee. It's a good idea to attach your personal check or credit card receipt to the invoice.
2. Adoption papers or purchase papers from a breeder showing that you were the person who acquired the dog and paid.

3. All medical records that clearly note you were the person bringing the animal to the vet. Again, attach the receipt for payment.

4. Photographs of important events with you and your pet, including holiday photos, Christmas cards, and vacations. Your dog should also be featured prominently on your Facebook page—she's an integral part of your timeline!

5. Hotel receipts for stays where you took your pet that show the "pet fee" paid by you.

6. Receipts for any major purchases for your pet, training classes, or other expenses you bore the sole responsibility for.

7. Membership cards to any organization you and your pet belong to. For example, a Tails of Joy club, READ (Reading Education Assistance Dogs), any therapy organizations, or social groups such as an agility club or dog hiking group.

8. Receipts for boarding or pet sitters who have cared for your pet.

9. Your daily calendar noting all important appointments including those for your pet.

10. Pet catalogs addressed to you and correspondence addressed to you and your pet. (Don't laugh, my dog Sadie often gets more mail than I do!)

I regret that it took a divorce for me to understand that a *primary caretaker* is nothing more than the person who loved the dog and loved spending time with her, as well as caring for her and meeting and providing for her needs. One of the greatest gifts my dog Sadie gives me every day is that she needs me. Providing for her needs and sharing my life with her is a joy not a chore.

In my absence, my ex and Tiffany had bonded; they became part of each other's lives. As much as she waited for him to come home at the end of the day, it was clear from his detailed records and recitations that he anticipated this daily reunion as much as she did. If you want the pet only as a grab for power, were not bonded to the pet, and did not provide her care, successfully proving your role in her life as a primary caretaker will be difficult and is a challenge you shouldn't attempt, because you also have to consider the second standard: in the best interest of the pet. How can it be in the best interest of your dog to be with a person who knows nothing about caring for her or providing for her needs?

Best interest is a broad term that can be interpreted quite narrowly. What is in the best interest of the dog? The answer isn't hard to determine when considered logically and honestly in light of what truly is best for your dog. Is one partner moving into a high-rise building where the dog will have little chance for outside exercise? Do you have children the dog is comfortable with? Perhaps the children and the dog should stay together. When parents split up, the dog is often a great source of comfort to children. Consider the age of the dog, since change can be stressful for older dogs. Dogs are routine oriented and are often confused by big changes, particularly as they age.

Is one of the partners going to travel a great deal for their job, thus placing the care of the dog in the hands of a stranger? Does one of the spouses work long hours so the dog will be alone the majority of the time? Who can go home at noon to let the dog out? Is one partner moving into a neighborhood near a busy highway? There are so many things to consider, but the primary rule should be: What is best for my dog and will cause the least disruption in her life? This takes a selfless spirit that, unfortunately, is rarely present when couples split up. If you are bonded with your dog, you know her needs and what she enjoys. When you know these things, you know what is best for her. Perhaps a good example of lack of concern for the best interest of pets is exhibited in a Connecticut case in which three horses were caught up in a debacle of a marriage.

Meet the Kellys, whose court case reads like a *Saturday Night Live* skit. The Kellys, like many divorcing couples, had a lot more going on between them than divvying up their marital assets, which included the three horses. The Kellys seemed quite ill matched and probably should not have wed in the first place. Before meeting Mrs. Kelly, Mr. Kelly had planned to become a priest. Instead he found himself married to an ambitious lawyer, while he labored for the homeless, earning very low wages. If you think someone who had planned a life governed by a vow of poverty would be fair and reasonable in splitting marital property, you'd be wrong. Mr. Kelly's dreams of a peaceful and reverent life, perhaps in a church rectory, were a distant memory in the marital domicile. This union was far from happy, and it seems once the priesthood goal was abandoned, so was all reason. Mr. Kelly escaped the turmoil of his marriage by viewing porn on his computer. Mrs. Kelly endured by "working" late, not alone, and often not at the office.

There were three or four separations during the marriage, and the predictable marital disputes such as money and affairs, as well as other issues. One such instance concerned a website the couple had created together about their horses. When the marriage started to fail, the husband linked the horse website to another website that expressed his disillusionment with the marriage and his opinion of his wife. Anyone who logged on to the jointly created horse website was immediately routed to www.mywifeisabitch. com. Again, not the best move to ensure celebrating a silver anniversary. After a hearing on marital alimony that evidently didn't go in the husband's favor, he broke every telephone in the house and sent emails to all his wife's relatives calling her derogatory names. (These happenings would *never* have occurred had Mr. Kelly kept his original career plan.) During the telephone destruction, the Kelly cat and dog as well as Mrs. Kelly had been terrified. The court issued a restraining order that banned Mr. Kelly from the marital home, his wife, the cat, and the dog. Even after these insane actions, Mr. Kelly asked the court for custody of the horses, thinking he had a chance to get them because they didn't witness the telephone terror rant.

At the time of the final separation, the couple was living in a jointly purchased home that had a horse stable. When the couple separated for the final time, Mrs. Kelly was awarded the marital home, the horses, the dog, and the cat. However, Mr. Kelly appealed, remaining adamant in his pleadings that he wanted custody of the horses.

Unlike the typical family dog, the couple's horses were expensive show horses and considerable marital assets had been used to purchase them as well as the property with the barn. At the divorce hearing, the wife produced credible testimony that during the marriage the defendant had little or nothing to do with the three horses: Shadowfax, Quinn, and Maestro. The only remote involvement he had with them was creating a complicated financial scheme for purchase of the marital home, which included the horses' stable. His tenuous claim to the horses was that without his efforts to arrange the financing, they could not have purchased the marital property; thus there would have been no barn and no horses. The wife claimed that he never shoveled one pile of manure, let alone fed, brushed, or exercised the horses. Allegedly he had ridden Shadowfax once, and the details of said ride in the court notes indicate that he was "not an accomplished rider." One can assume from this note that the husband had not established any type of bond with Shadowfax or the other horses, and most definitely not with the cat or dog.

Similar to the Texas inmate husband, this man had nowhere for the horses to live because he was living at his parents' house while the divorce was pending. Because he'd been served with a restraining order after the phone incident, it was impossible for

him to keep the horses in the marital stable, as he was prohibited from going there.

While this case may seem somewhat humorous, as you read between the lines, it's a sad example of a power grab for living creatures with no regard to their well-being or a person's actual relationship with them. Where was he planning to keep the horses? He couldn't even afford independent living for himself, let alone was he able to pay for board and care for the horses at a commercial stable. Why he wanted them was never spelled out, and he obviously had neither the interest nor the ability to ride them.

When it's time for you to make your case that the dog belongs to you and depends on you, remember you must be ready with records that reflect the true arrangement you had with the pet. Mr. Kelly had nothing to offer the court as evidence that he was the primary caretaker of the horses; neither was it in their best interest to go with him. Mrs. Kelly seemed quick to point out her husband's shortcomings in every area, including with the horses, but this isn't necessary.

Custody issues over your pet can be avoided entirely with a few simple options in the event you and your partner go separate ways. If you have a dog before you enter into a marriage, domestic partnership, or other arrangement with a two-legged being, you must create a document that clearly outlines that the dog is yours and you have no intention of her ever becoming joint property. I suggest you create a petnuptial by following the example at the end of this book.

Don't risk the future of your dog by failing to protect her in the event you end up in divorce court. Of course, anything can be challenged in court, but by having a petnuptial you will have proof that you owned your dog before the marriage and that your partner entered into it without duress and with full knowledge of the facts.

There are situations where someone should *never* have custody of a living creature, and if one of these circumstances was prevalent in your relationship, don't be silent about it. You must speak up if your spouse has ever caused harm to your pet or intentionally placed them in a dangerous situation. If you were a victim of domestic abuse, be very outspoken about the abuse, providing court records if possible, but make certain your spouse does not get the dog under any circumstances. There is a strong connection between animal abuse and domestic violence, which is covered in chapter 4, but the rule here is never, ever leave a pet with someone who has abused you.

If your partner has a severe alcohol or drug abuse addiction, speak up. What happens to the pet when your spouse is drunk or under the influence of drugs? A pet is in danger when in the care of people who can't take care of themselves.

If your partner has mistreated the pet in the past, even if it didn't result in physical harm, make it known. Abuse is never a one-time incident, and retaliatory abuse over a human partner directed at a pet is common and a risk you should never allow your pet to bear.

Don't make a condemnation of your ex's lack of involvement, but moreover portray the real life you've shared and enjoyed with your dog. Under all the anger and accusations when the human relationship ends, there's another relationship that's not ending— the one you share with your dog—and you have the ability to show the court that you deserve to continue that relationship. It's a good idea to develop the no-grudge policy that all dogs possess in dealing with your ex. Think about it, has your dog ever reminded you that you stepped on her paw or forgot to refill her water bowl?

As for the Kellys, the court apparently made the right decision for the horses and awarded them to the wife, who was indeed their primary caretaker. It was also in the best interest of the horses for them to remain living in the barn. However, this was not the basis of the court's decision. The caretaking and well-being of the animals were obviously considered by the court, because the official opinion made note of the wife's personal involvement with the animals and the husband's lack thereof. The horses, the cat, and the dog were distributed in the property order along with the division of finances and other personal items and real estate. Among other things, the former Mrs. Kelly got to retain her interest in her law firm, had her maiden name reinstated, and paid Mr. Kelly for his share in the marital home. Mr. Kelly received no alimony, but he did receive enough money to move out of his parents' home and was ordered to transfer ownership of the joint website to his wife with the removal of the link to www.mywifeisabitch.com.

Things turned out okay for me and my ex-dog and ex-husband. He took Tiffany back to Hilton Head, South Carolina, where she loved to run after birds on the beach and walk in the evenings with him. I had visitation every year, and sometimes more, and she never forgot me. As time went on and I was busy establishing a legal career, traveling, and working long hours, I knew the right decision had been made. I'd think of her safe and content with a person I once loved very much and knew he loved her and would never let her down.

Of course, the time came when I got *the call* I will never forget. It was July 16, 1999, the day John Kennedy Jr., his wife, and her sister perished in a plane crash off the coast of Martha's Vineyard. While John and I had remained mostly cordial after our divorce, we were not close, but when he said hello I knew something was wrong. With a halting voice and obvious crying, he told me that Tiffany was gone. He relayed how in past months he'd had to carry her up and down the stairs. He told me how she had no energy, slept most of the time, and described a most desolate situation. He told me that the day before she'd quit eating and had gotten very sick.

He'd taken her to the vet and was given a very grim prognosis, so he took her home and prepared to say good-bye. He told me he'd spent several hours talking to her, stroking her fur, and showing her pictures of the three of us. He'd let her lick ice cubes, and then he carried her down the steps for the last time. He put her in the passenger seat of his convertible and took her for one last drive to the beach she loved. Through his tears he assured me she had not been in pain as he carried her to the beach and sat down to hold her as the seabirds gathered. John said Tiffany sniffed the sea air, looked at the birds, and put her head on his chest as if to say she was ready to leave—no use looking at birds you can't run after anymore. And then . . . she was gone.

I cried for everything lost with her passing. I cried for the end of my marriage that I'd never grieved for. I cried for the little puppy that my nephew had brought to me in Columbia, South Carolina, saying in his small kindergarten voice, "Aunt Pat, I found you a dog."

I cried remembering the time she threw up in my car and seemed frightened I would be angry. I wasn't. I cried thinking about the night after she was spayed when I stayed up all night giving her ice chips. I cried as I recalled watching her burying treats in the yard when she first came to live with us like she was saving them in case there was no food one day. I remembered her riding in the basket on my bike, her soft fur blowing in the wind. I cried for all the memories I didn't get to make with her because of decisions I'd made. But I didn't cry for the life she'd had with John—it was the best one she could have lived.

If you can walk away from a divorce or the end of a relationship knowing that the right decision was made for your dog, then you will have no regrets over her. We all have regrets, but we don't need to have them about our dog if we keep her best interest foremost and provide for her needs. Tiffany brought us together in the end; we were able to let go of a lot of bitterness and remorse. Grieving over our dog enabled us to mourn for what we also lost as a couple, but it enabled us to move on. We no longer needed to catch birds that we were just too tired to chase.

ESSENTIAL ELEMENTS WHEN DIVORCING WITH A DOG

1. Begin before the relationship starts, making sure you have all the proper documentation to show this was your pet before the relationship began.
2. If you haven't done that, try to work things out with your spouse/partner and get a notarized agreement that your pet is your separate property.
3. If that doesn't work, find a mediator, preferably one who has experience in animal custody issues, and if not in child custody issues. Your State Bar Association or Supreme Court will have a list of mediators and what they specialize in.
4. Work hard during the mediation to present the best evidence for retaining custody of your pet.
5. If you reach an agreement, have the mediator put it in writing, get it notarized, and make it part of any property agreement you reach in your divorce.
6. If you are unsuccessful at mediation, be prepared to make the separate property argument in court. Unless you know

your judge is sympathetic to animal issues and will consider a pet custody issue, this is your best tactic.

7. If your pet clearly is not your separate property, remember the two standards used in child custody: primary caretaker and in the best interest of your dog. Be ready with clear and convincing evidence to show you fulfilled these standards.

8. Remember the end of a marriage doesn't have to mean the end of your relationship with your dog.

9. If you share custody of your dog with your ex, make sure your dog has continuity in her life and make visitations as easy as possible. Don't hold on to grudges.

10. *Before* you think of getting into another relationship, make sure you've done *everything* you can to make sure your dog is separate property.

After a divorce almost everything in your life changes, often including where you live. If you are not retaining ownership of the marital home and not purchasing a new house, you most likely will be renting. Don't get discouraged if all of the rentals available in your area state they don't allow pets. Understanding both sides of the pet rental dilemma is essential in order for you to obtain new housing with a lease that includes your dog.

Chapter 3

THE PROPERTY PET PREDICAMENT
(Renting with Rover)

It's so discouraging for pet parents seeking a place to live. They get to the end of a perfectly great rental advertisement to see the words: No Pets. I brought my dog Sadie home to a house I owned, so I never imagined myself being in that situation. I was wrong.

Life has a way of bringing unexpected changes, and Sadie and I weren't exempt. April 28, 2008, we walked out our front door for the last time. The weeks leading up to this day had been hectic. Yard sales morphed into moving sales. Packing boxes were everywhere, and a poster I'd kept for years was prominently and temporarily taped to the mirror in my bathroom. The photo was of a night moon over the ocean with the caption: "There is a time to leave even when there is no certain place to go." This was our reality.

Finally, the movers had taken what we wanted to keep to a storage unit, the house had been cleaned for the last time, the refrigerator we'd stood in front of a million times was empty, and the house echoed with each step we took. I threw a few old comforters on the floor of our bedroom, placed the pillows and blankets into a makeshift bed, and lay down to spend the last night in the first house I'd ever bought on my own, the one I'd brought my little puppy home to. A confused Sadie stood stiffly looking at me for a few minutes, but when I patted the place beside me she gingerly stepped on the blankets, lay down, and sighed. We fell asleep in the light of the one small television we'd kept for this last night. Call me crazy, but I felt it important to spend this last night in our home together. I had no idea what tomorrow would bring.

The next morning we put the blankets and television into the trunk of the car. I took hold of Sadie's leash, and we walked the block and a half to the state capitol for our closing. The cavernous building was quiet at this early hour, and I could hear Sadie's paws clicking on the marble floor. We went straight to the department of administration's reception area, and I told the receptionist we were there for a property closing. She removed her glasses and looked from me to Sadie—I guess sleeping on the wooden floor of an eighty-five-year-old house hadn't done much for our looks— but she said to take a seat.

The lawyer I had been working with on the sale appeared and tousled Sadie's ears, offering us coffee and water, which I accepted, as we followed him into an elegant conference room. I took a seat and Sadie stood looking around. Our beverages arrived and, as usual, Sadie loudly lapped up her water while the other govern- ment officials necessary for the closing began taking their seats. No one said a word about a dog being there.

Finally, everyone was in place. One man couldn't be quiet any longer and finally said, "I see you've brought your dog." To which I replied, "Well, it's her house too, and you might need her paw print on the sales contract," which broke the ice.

Sadie lay down under my chair, papers were passed around, terms gone over, signatures put in place, and I was handed a check. I showed it to Sadie for her approval, which brought on a great deal of laughter. I shook hands with the new owners, and Sadie was greeted by many of the officials. In less than thirty minutes our house now belonged to the state of West Virginia, and we were officially homeless.

I'd made temporary arrangements to stay with my boyfriend, who was most generous to share his small condo with me, Sadie, and her crate, which took up much of his living room. I'd accepted a new job and needed to find a new place to live while I wrestled with the many decisions at this intersection in my life. No problem. However, it was a *big* problem. Almost every advertisement listed in our local paper prohibited pets. Many allowed cats, but not dogs. (Dogscrimination!) One complex about fifteen miles out of town advertised itself as pet friendly so we went to see it. It was run-down at best, and the dog area was a muddy mess.

The houses for rent that allowed dogs demanded deposits that were more than the monthly rent. We traipsed through houses that cost more per month than my mortgage had been, apartments that were about the size of one of the bedrooms in my former house, and some that were in downright dangerous locations for dogs and people. What's a pet parent to do in this situation?

Meanwhile, Sadie was miserable. She hated staying in the condo when I went to work. The balcony doors that opened over the pool sounded like thunder and she was frightened. She barked and barked. Rodney got notices from his condo board. She barked some more. The neighbor downstairs began complaining. I'd go there at lunchtime and slink through the lobby, avoiding any other residents or the management. Then I'd be greeted by a frantic Sadie barking and whining in her crate. It was stressful for everyone, and the pressure to find a pet-friendly rental was intense.

I finally found a perfect house and bought it, but not everyone wants to own a house or can afford to do so. Many people are in a city temporarily and just want a decent place to call home for a few months with their best friend. Do pet parents have a legal right to rent property with a dog? The short answer is no. The one exception, and often on a case-by-case basis, is service dogs. We live in an unreasonable world, yet "reasonable accommodation" is the standard used in the Federal Fair Housing Act that determines what is reasonable for disabled persons to request and for their accompanying service dogs.

What many people tend to overlook is that the Americans with Disabilities Act (ADA) prohibits discrimination against disabled individuals in *public* places. So there are requirements for accommodation of service animals and even pets in some *public* housing, but the protection in privately owned rental property is sometimes minimal at best. Federal mandates address the matter directly. For instance, under federal law 42 U.S.C. § 3604(f)(3)(B) it is illegal to refuse to make "reasonable accommodation" for impaired tenants if the landlord will not suffer "financial or administrative burdens" because of those accommodations. The Department of Housing and Urban Development declared that a landlord's waiver of its no-pet policy to impaired tenants with companion dogs does, in fact, constitute such a reasonable accommodation. Further, Section 504 of the Rehabilitation Act of 1973 and the Federal Fair Housing Amendments Act of 1988 require that disabled individuals be given equal rights to housing that is also offered to those without disabilities. Section 504 of the Rehabilitation Act of 1973 prohibits discrimination on the basis of disability in all programs and activities that receive federal funding or are operated by the federal government. The nebulous concept of "reasonable accommodation" was originated in this act and became the model for the Fair Housing Act.

The federal Housing and Urban Development department (HUD) has a regulation titled "Pets in Elderly Housing," which is referred to as the "Pet Rule."

This rule has been through many incantations: 1986, 1996, and again in 1999. This is a narrow regulation that applies only to federally assisted rental housing designed for individuals sixty-two years of age or older or disabled individuals regardless of age. What's great about this regulation is that it not only protects the rights of disabled individuals who need a service animal, it also allows for "most" federally funded housing to allow residents to have pets. Landlords are allowed to place "reasonable" restrictions on the pets, such as size and number, but not on service dogs. This doesn't cover what most people know of federally funded housing, the Fair Housing Act Section 8 housing, which has no provision to allow pets, but must make "reasonable accommodation" for service animals.

One thing to keep in mind, while disabled tenants are protected, as previously pointed out, landlords are not required to suffer financial or other burdens by waiving the no-pet policy. Courts have ruled that disabled tenants can only qualify for the no-pet waiver if no other reasonable alternatives are available for a companion dog. Landlords' rights to deny a no-pet waiver have been upheld for various reasons, including if the disabled tenant doesn't abide by the general rules of occupancy or the companion dog is a safety threat to other tenants. This restriction is particularly problematic in jurisdictions with breed-specific legislation, which is discussed later. However, the basis for most breed-specific legislation is determined by labeling certain breeds "dangerous," often without a valid factual basis, thus eliminating certain certified service dogs merely because of their breed. HUD reviews complaints and concerns regarding landlords who refuse tenants with assistance animals.

So for pet parents, there's *some* good news for us here. When we're old and if we have no money and can qualify for federal elderly designated housing, we can have a pet! Seriously, this is a great law, as the love and companionship of a dog, particularly in later years, is priceless. I constantly see photos of pets that need homes because their elderly pet parent has moved into private assisted living or a nursing home and they aren't allowed to take their canine companion along. More private housing alternatives for elderly people need to become aware of how important an animal companion is to the health and well-being of their elderly residents and follow the example of the federal law.

Rental policies in private housing are covered by city or county ordinances. The ordinances cover everything from eviction to deposits, and in many cities pets are covered with special regulations. Most often the regulations regarding pets cover the following:

- Number of pets
- Type of pet

- Breed-specific exemptions
- Licensing requirements

Most rental housing restrictions on the number of pets set the limit at two. Not two cats and two dogs and two birds. Just two pets in one apartment allowed and no more. Private landlords who are particularly pet friendly might allow someone to have more than two dogs or two cats if the prospective tenant has a compelling enough reason. Many cities have restrictions on the number of pets in residential properties, rental or owned, and without a special license you must abide by the limit.

Landlords can legally permit certain pets and ban others. I called a rental complex that advertised, "Call about pet accommodations," only to learn that they only allowed cats. I told the rental agent that my dog really liked cats, but she hung up the phone. Any animal banned by state or local laws will also be banned by a rental company or private landlord. Usually this includes any type of exotic animal, such as large snakes or farm animals in an urban situation.

However, breed-specific legislation has certainly made it possible, and in some areas mandatory, to prohibit certain breeds of dogs

© DAVID VOISARD

in rental units or privately owned homes. Most often pit bulls or pit bull–type dogs, including bull terriers, American Staffordshire terriers, or any other dog exhibiting pit bull physical characteristics, are banned as well as rottweilers, cane corsos, Doberman pinschers, huskies, German shepherds, and others, depending on the location. If you want to rent a residence and have one of these breeds, providing that there is not a breed-specific law in your location, it is essential that you are prepared to convince your landlord that you and your dog will be excellent tenants.

You can expect a potential landlord to require that your dog have a current license. Dog licenses are required by city and county governments. Dogs must be licensed, but cats do not. (Dogscrimination!) Licenses are usually a nominal fee for which you receive a metal tag for your dog's collar. Where I live, dog licensing is set forth in the state code at WV Code §19-20-2. In my county, the fee is three dollars per dog per year. In New York City it's eight dollars and fifty cents per year for spayed/neutered dogs and thirty-four dollars per year for unspayed/unneutered dogs. Dog licenses have a number that identifies your dog and will be helpful if she's ever lost. It is a requirement that the dog tag be displayed on your dog's collar. Additionally, most states require rabies vaccines, and tags are issued to show compliance with this law. This is covered in detail in chapter 9. All of this must be up to date if you want to convince anyone to rent you a place to live with your dog. Few cities go beyond breed restrictions on the above list to regulate private property rentals. Most landlords do require damage deposits and have rules for dogs, such as barking, common areas, and picking up poop. There may be other hurdles to get over, one being pet rent.

Pet rent is relatively new and becoming more and more prevalent in rentals that allow pets. Like hotels, which will be addressed in chapter 8, there's a great difference between allowing pets and being pet friendly. Tolerating is not the same as welcoming. Burdensome restrictions, exorbitant fees and deposits, and a lack of accommodations for dogs outdoors are all warning signs that the landlord might grudgingly allow pets for the money, but is not keen on the idea.

Pet rent is a monthly fee you pay for the entire length of time you reside in the rental property. The amounts vary from landlord to landlord within the same city as well as among the different types of rentals. Pet parents desperate for a home to share with their dog may not think much of a fifty-dollar-per-month fee—after all, our canine soul mates are priceless, right? Not really. If you sign a two-year lease it will cost you one thousand two hundred dollars for your dog to live with you. Pet rent is not returned like a deposit. Pet damage deposits are paid up front and should be a reasonable fee to cover any potential damage. It usually amounts to something like this fee structure a pet parent recently paid in a midsize California city to move into a downtown condo with two medium-size dogs.

First month's and last month's rent at $1,500 per month.	$3,000
Pet damage deposit at $250 per pet.	$500
Security deposit: $1,500	$1,500
Pet rent at $25 per dog	$50
TOTAL	$5,050

This particular pet parent had to pay five thousand and fifty dollars just to get all ten of their legs in the front door! Pricey, but it could be more if it was New York, Los Angeles, or another large metropolitan city.

A fair pet security deposit is anyone's guess, but should not be more than half a month's rent or less. You do have the possibility of getting at least part of it back and it is a one-time fee. However, pet rent seems to know no boundaries and no end.

Landlords are within their legal rights to charge pet rent as long as it's applied on a nondiscriminatory basis. This doesn't stop landlords from charging more for large dogs than for small dogs, even though there is no factual evidence that big dogs cause more damage than little ones. Actually, puppies cause more damage, so, technically, small dogs are more likely to cost you your damage deposit.

Like me, many pet parents believe their darling fur angel will never damage anything, and pet rent makes us uneasy. Pet rent is separate from a damage deposit. It's basically just a fee for your pet to live with you. It's to ensure your dog isn't going to hold any wild parties or invite the entire complex over to watch Animal Planet, but chewing the woodwork or staining the carpet is a possibility and would be covered by your deposit, which will be in addition to the monthly pet rent.

True pet-friendly properties often use portions of the pet rent to provide accoutrements for the dogs, such as walking trails, a fenced area, and waste disposal bars located around the property. Smart landlords know the more amenities that their properties provide, the more attractive to tenants they are, and that makes the property more valuable on the rental market. Pet parents want their home to be equally comfortable for them and for their dog. The extras are important. Some landlords use the pet rent for additional maintenance on their properties. Hallways and common areas get more wear and tear when many dogs traverse them three or four times a day. Landscaping can also suffer from dogs being dogs, as all pet parents know, and pet rent fees often cover extra lawn care and cleanup. Don't hesitate to ask a prospective landlord what, if anything, the pet rent provides for your dog.

The city of West Hollywood, California, went several steps further when they created specific ordinances to allow tenants to have pets in private housing. The ordinance basically says that certain individuals, despite a pet prohibition clause in their lease, may have up to two dogs. The tenant has to meet specific criteria as follows[1]:

1. The tenant owning the pet(s) is more than sixty-two years of age, or is disabled, or is living with HIV/AIDS;
2. The tenant does not reside in a condominium;
3. The pet or pets are domesticated dogs, cats, or birds weighing not more than thirty-five pounds;
4. The pet does not interfere with other persons' quiet enjoyment of the premises or otherwise constitute a nuisance, a threat to health, safety, or welfare of other persons on the premises;
5. If a licensed physician has prescribed a companion pet as necessary for the patient's welfare or treatment, the landlord may not charge any security deposit. Otherwise, the landlord may require an increase in the security deposit of not more than 25 percent of the existing deposit, but in no event an amount that brings the total deposit to more than allowed by the California Civil Code.

Another interesting and great part of this ordinance is that it allows for the replacement of pets that pass away. Tenants have to replace the pet with a pet of the same kind; for example, a dog for a dog or a cat for a cat, and they can't be any larger than the previous pet. I once lived in a condominium complex that passed new association rules that prohibited pets, but grandfathered in (lawyer talk for allowed them to stay) any pets residing in the building before the rules were changed. The new rule clearly stated that if your dog or cat died they could not be replaced.

1. West Hollywood, CA, City Code Section 17.52.010.

There was a feisty older lady living on my floor who had two Yorkies, both of which were quite old. She was livid about the new rule, expressing her dissatisfaction to anyone who would listen. She'd always had dogs and had no intention, as she said, of "leaving this earth alone without the comfort of my dogs." In her heavy Irish brogue she told me, "You watch, Pat, if anything happens to one of my babies, I'll have me another one so fast their heads will spin." I thought she was just upset and would adjust in time, but I was wrong.

About six months after the rules were implemented I shared the elevator with this lady and, as usual, she was holding both dogs. I greeted her and the dogs, but immediately realized something was different. One dog seemed to have shrunk considerably. Same name, different dog. Seems one of this lady's dogs had died, but she didn't tell anyone and replaced it immediately with the new dog and no one, except for me, was the wiser. The West Hollywood ordinance makes it much easier and certainly less stressful than what my neighbor was willing to do to keep a dog.

Many cities have various regulations concerning renting with pets and are largely limited to the items listed previously with slightly different aspects. In New York City tenants may keep pets unless the lease specifically prohibits it. So, if the lease doesn't mention pets, you're free to share your apartment with Rover. If the lease does prohibit pets and you disregard it, you still have a chance if you don't hide or conceal the pet. The law says the clause is not enforceable if a tenant "openly and notoriously" had a pet for at least three months and the landlord knew it and took no action.[2] You would have to be open about the dog, making it visible and making sure the landlord knew about the dog's presence. He'd probably take you to court anyway, which would be an ordeal and probably expensive.

2. NYC Admin. Code § 27-2009.1(b).

Westchester County, just outside of New York City, adopted a pet law in recognition of the increasingly important role that pets play in our lives. The county stated: "Because household pets are harbored for reasons of safety and companionship, as well as the physical and emotional well-being of their owners and there is currently a housing emergency, it is necessary to protect pet owners from retaliatory and other evictions and to safeguard the health, safety, and welfare of tenants who harbor pets."[3]

The majority of municipalities don't even address the issue of pet-friendly or pet-free rentals. It is up to the property owner/landlord to decide what the pet policy will be. In these cities you won't have any laws or regulations to use for support of having your pet. This decision will be completely between you and your landlord.

So what's a pet parent to do when seeking housing for you and your four-legged roommate? My first piece of advice is to not give up. There are different types of rental properties and your chances of getting your dog on the lease varies from type to type. Rental properties are usually in the following categories:

- Privately owned rental property with an individual owner/landlord. This can be a house, apartment, condo, or co-op.
- Planned unit development: condos that are governed by numerous rules and restrictions even though you might be renting from the owner of your unit.
- Co-ops, which have different rules from condos, since it's not deeded individual ownership but a complicated structure that means the other owners on the co-op board have to approve you and your dog.
- Apartment complexes owned by a corporation and managed by a management company.

3. Westchester County Code, section 695.01.

All of these properties, as different as they are, have one thing in common. You will have a landlord, whether it's an individual, a corporation, all the other occupants/owners in the building, or a management company. Mr. Landlord calls the shots when it comes to who does and who doesn't get to lease their property. Landlords, no matter what their status, have rental property to make money. A rental house or condo is an investment. The number-one reason landlords are reluctant to rent to pet parents and their fur children is actually not damages. It's relatively easy to replace carpet or woodwork, but getting sued for something your dog does is a large financial threat. It's simple—liability for your dog's actions is the number-one reason for prohibiting dogs in rentals. Landlords don't want to get sued. Even if they're found not guilty, it's expensive to defend a lawsuit. Many landlords have heard horror stories of lawsuits, and without checking the law or the facts of the case, they think it's easier to say, "No pets," than to carefully screen for responsible pet parents and well-trained dog tenants. They don't want to deal with the chance of being held responsible for the actions of a dog, such as a bite or worse. Many landlords aren't aware of the actual laws, often causing unnecessary concerns.

We live in a litigious society. Lawyers are quick to sue anyone, and clients are not scarce. Landlords have a legitimate fear of being sued, unless they know the realty of lawsuits involving pets. Landlords are not strictly liable for harm caused by a dog that is legitimately on their property and not liable at all for a dog that has no business on their property. Strict liability is the legal standard that holds a person responsible no matter the actual facts of the action. The single most fearful potential lawsuit landlords face is if a tenant's dog bites someone on their property. Fear not, the legal standard allowing each dog basically one free bite is discussed in chapter 7, but the landlord has to be *aware* of the dog's characteristics in order to be held responsible. Additionally, if the landlord had no actual knowledge that the dog was even on the property, they are not liable for its actions, the owner is.

So what about these "no-pets" landlords? Some of the more common reasons landlords do not want to allow pets are listed below; knowing these will give you an advantage in negotiating with a prospective landlord to get your pet in the door.

- Complaints from other tenants about barking
- Pets unattended outside in common areas
- Dog waste not being picked up and disposed of
- Dogs jumping on other tenants
- The odor in a rental unit from a dog or cat
- Fleas and/or ticks
- Tracking in mud and dirt in hallways
- Growling or aggressive behavior toward other tenants

No matter which type of property you're considering renting, when seeking housing with a dog there are some things you need to do first. These are important even if you're looking at a pet-friendly property. Your chances of getting her in the door are greatly improved if you show a potential landlord all her good qualities. This can be done in a number of ways.

Don't count on a future landlord to be interested in looking at pages and pages of your photo album, seeing her first little collar or scarf, or anything else you consider endearing and precious. Instead, prepare a package of factual information about your dog, much like you would make for yourself if you were applying for acceptance as a buyer from a co-op board. Meet any misgivings or potential problems head-on. For example, if you work, explain that you will come home at noon to take your dog out or provide the name and phone number of a responsible dog walker you've hired. Address any of the reasons on the list above before the landlord brings them up.

Prepare what I call a "Rover Résumé" for your dog. You can present this to a landlord or co-op board. You should put the Rover résumé and important documents in a folder to give to the landlord. The actual résumé should be one page and include the following information:

1. Age and breed of your dog
2. Brief history of your dog's life with you
3. Any training your dog has received
4. What their living experiences have been: for example, hours left alone, etc.
5. References from former landlords if applicable.
6. Name and telephone number of veterinarian.
7. References for your dog. Yes, references! Former neighbors, boarding kennels, veterinarian, trainer, neighbors.
8. Emergency contact for dog if you're not home.

Include the following documents:
- recent vaccination record;
- certificates of training received, such as the AKC Canine Good Citizen program;
- one or two photos of you and your dog;
- adoption or AKC registration papers; and
- a copy of the current dog license receipt.

The folder should also include a pet responsibility contract, which details how you will be responsible for your pet and what you can promise as a good tenant. Basically, the document is to show that you are a responsible pet parent willing to take on the liability involved for your dog. The résumé for my dog Sadie is located in the back of the book; use it as a guide to create one for your dog.

In addition to your dog's résumé and the accompanying documents, no matter which type of property you seek to lease these additional steps go a long way toward getting you the keys to a new dog-friendly home.

1. Even if they don't advertise that the property is pet friendly, ask anyway. A well-prepared pet parent often takes a reluctant landlord by surprise and they will give you a chance.
2. Offer to pay an extra deposit. Even in pet-friendly properties an extra deposit is standard for pets. This might sway a landlord who's on the fence in your favor.
3. Promise to get renter's insurance that will include a damage clause for your dog.

Before you start your search talk to other pet parents; they're the best source possible for information about housing with pets. Talk to pet parents at the dog park, at the vet, walking on the street, in pet stores, in parking lots. Wherever you see a person and a dog, ask them if they know of any pet-friendly rentals. Eavesdrop on any conversations you hear about dogs and weasel into them with your questions. Dog parents are usually eager to help other dogs and their person in any manner possible. I learned that when I adopted Sadie and received endless good information, often from complete strangers with dogs. "Go to the dog runs and ask people how they got their apartments," suggested Diane West, the publisher of *New York Tails*, a magazine for city pet owners. "That's the best advice I've heard, and it actually works." The website (www.newyorktails.com) is a great resource for pet parents looking for pet-friendly housing in New York City. The site contains a list of real estate agents in the city who specialize in finding pet-friendly rentals, and you can register for the type of housing you're looking for and receive email notifications when one becomes available.

As with everything else, the Internet is a great resource when searching for a pet-friendly property. Renters beware, though, the pictures on websites often don't accurately represent the property, so prepare to be disappointed. The People with Pets website (www. peoplewithpets.com) lists pet-friendly property for several major cities in the Unites States. Many of them are large complexes with high fees and lots of restrictions, but you can find smaller properties if you're persistent. Rent.com, a national website, also lists pet rental properties (www.rent.com/pet-friendly-apartments). Dealing with a landlord in a privately owned property is often better than a large, corporate-owned property where property managers don't have the authority to make exceptions or agree to modified terms for fees and other restrictions.

Craigslist is another good source, but again, as with anything on the Internet, be overly cautious and don't take anyone at their word. Craigslist has a section in the rental advertisements that signifies if dogs or cats are allowed. But remember, even if it doesn't say pets are allowed, you might be able to convince a landlord that your dog is rental worthy if you use the tools described previously.

I did an experiment and called random rental advertisements in my area that clearly stated, "No pets." You may be surprised to hear that these were nice people and many of them were pet parents. So, why didn't they want pets for tenants?

Overwhelmingly it was because of irresponsible pet parents in the past. Almost every one of the reasons listed for prohibiting pets in this chapter has been the fault of an irresponsible pet parent and not the dog. A landlord in my town had many stories of tenants who left dogs alone for days, including one time he had to use his pass key to feed and water the dog. He had no idea where the tenant was and had to call animal control. All appearances said the dog was abandoned, and it turned out it was. The tenant was soon sent packing as well.

Landlords have had tenants who let the dogs use the apartment as if it was a grassy area for bathroom trips or chew doors and woodwork. They told of renters who just opened their door and let the dogs run free outside, resulting in numerous problems with other tenants. One renter couldn't sleep because their dog was barking, so they tied it in the complex courtyard and then no one could sleep. Inconsiderate, uninformed, lazy, irresponsible people should not have a dog, let alone have it in a rental property so it can reflect all its owner's bad qualities.

Landlords told me about making a concession and being taken advantage of. One tenant brought a medium-size dog to meet the landlord, but he soon noticed she moved in with a Great Dane that had puppies not long after. Many landlords found it easier to just say no up front, but were not completely against making decisions on an individual basis. Every landlord I talked to said a Rover résumé and the accompanying documents would lead them to believe the pet parent was responsible and consider making an exception. Several of the landlords said a pet responsibility contract would be the ultimate assurance that the pet parent was serious and viewed their dog as a family member and would make a good tenant.

Here are a few helpful tools for landlords to assist in the pet rental dilemma. A useful tool is a pet checklist, where you can get all kinds of essential information about the potential tenants, both human and canine. Using a pet screening checklist, offering refundable pet deposits, or having a separate lease for the dog that makes the tenant liable for anything the pet may do would help offset costs and possibly exempt renters of monthly fees and reward pet owners for keeping their animals under control.

A sliding scale for pet rent could be created. The possibility of a decrease in pet rent after a certain number of months without any problems from the dog and a favorable inspection of the premises would provide an incentive for pet parents to try harder to make their dog a positive part of the rental community.

Before signing a lease, make sure both you and your dog can live with the terms. I know the desperate feeling to get a rental property with your dog and to get it as soon as possible. I tried to convince myself I could live with conditions I know neither Sadie nor I could manage. One landlord said I'd get my fee back at the end of the lease if there was no evidence of the dog in the house. Really? How was I supposed to manage that? I wondered if she made the same promise to parents with kids.

One very nice condo owner was willing to rent us the perfect place. It was the right size, the right price, and close to everything. It had lots of room for walking and was in a safe area. However, until he received a dirty look from a lady in the lobby as we were leaving, he neglected to tell me that the condo rules said you had to carry your dog in and out of the building and hold them in the elevator. Since I usually arrive home with files, groceries, a purse, and mail, I can't see how I'd also carry a thirty-five-pound, silky-haired, wriggling Sadie and make it to my apartment on two feet. I really wanted to rent that perfect apartment, so I thought of a few creative solutions.

Perhaps I could train Sadie to carry my purse in her mouth, while sitting on my back as I crawled across the lobby dragging any packages along with me. I also thought of getting one of those large soft-sided carry-on suitcases and fitting it out with a screen to let air in. I'd simply pop Sadie into it and pull her in and out of the building. The trial run of the first option ended with Sadie and me both tangled in her leash with a bag of oranges rolling all over the floor. And any attempt to get her in a suitcase was futile, so, unfortunately, I had to pass on the otherwise great offer.

Other pet parents have similar stories of unreasonable restrictions. One landlord said they would prefer the dog be muzzled at night to ensure there was no barking. Another landlord insisted the dog wear some type of "socks" so the hardwood floors wouldn't get scratched. That too proved an impossible condition for the dog dad.

It's definitely getting easier to rent with Rover, but it still takes persistence and charm to find the right place for you and your dog to call home. Pick and choose your battles in the landlord-tenant skirmishes. Some restrictions you can adapt to, and you'll know immediately if you can even attempt to give others a try. Don't count on the enforcement of any law to force a landlord to rent to you, except for the rare ones like those mentioned in this chapter or provisions for service dogs.

After you settle into your new home with your sweet dog and all is well in your world take a look around. Not all dogs are as lucky as yours. There has been a shocking rise in animal cruelty cases in recent years. Neighbors in a Miami suburb complained about numerous dogs and people at a house in their subdivision, yet they never went to see what was going on there. They were "shocked" when police discovered one of the biggest dogfighting rings in South Florida on their street. Barking dog keeping you awake? There might be a very good reason for it. What's a pet parent to do if the neighbor next door is making life miserable for their dog? Should you mind your own business, or is the welfare of all dogs your business? How do you get the laws against animal cruelty enforced? My dog Sadie and I found ourselves facing these questions in our former home one night when a sweet puppy needed our help.

Chapter 4

ABUSE OF ANIMALS
(Does Your State Law Have Teeth?)

S adie and I used to live in a not-so-elegant and sometimes downright dangerous section of town. Although the beautiful West Virginia state capitol was only two blocks behind our house, and in between, the street was lined with stately older homes that were well kept by their owners or had become branches of state offices and posed no safety threat whatsoever, it was quite a different scene in front of our house. Immediately across the street, and for several blocks in that direction, the houses had fallen into disrepair, had been purchased by disreputable landlords, and were inhabited by not-so-nice, if not criminal, tenants. These people never had jobs, therefore they didn't have to get up for work, which meant they had no concept that the rest of us might need to sleep at night. I had experienced numerous skirmishes with different tenants from across the street over the years, beginning with a shooting my neighbor and I witnessed in the middle of the street.

On one very frigid December night at a rat-trap apartment hidden by the house directly across the street, Sadie and I found a very cold, hungry, skinny, and sweet pit bull puppy.

This was one of my first holiday seasons with Sadie, but already I'd found her company better than that of most of the people I knew I'd encounter if I went out to ring in the new year. We'd enjoyed a leisurely dinner and were watching television in the living room, which was on the side of the house that faced the slumlord apartments, when we heard what sounded like the sad, urgent cries of a dog. I cautiously opened the front door and listened. Yes, it was definitely the yipping of a very little or very young dog, but who knew what could be going on over there.

This particular apartment had been the scene of numerous early morning visits by the city police and county sheriff. And I had called Mr. Slumlord in the middle of the night about these tenants more times than I could remember. The infractions that I knew about included everything from setting off post-midnight firecrackers in the street months after the Fourth of July to stealing the newspaper from my front porch and throwing beer bottles in the yard. As for more serious infractions, let's just say that more people left the apartment in law enforcement vehicles than taxis.

Knowing all of this I couldn't ignore the puppy's cries and neither could Sadie. She'd begun to whine and paw at the front door, nudging me with her nose, which moved my conscience to grab my coat, a flashlight, some pepper spray, Sadie on a short leash, and go out the front door. Lucky for me, Sadie does not bark a lot, and she was silent right along with me as we crept down the alley in the direction of the puppy's cries.

We slipped silently behind the house where the apartment was located. I shined my light on the front porch, where the yowling had turned to whimpering, and there, shuddering in the beam of my flashlight, was a pit bull puppy. Sadie was not tall enough to reach the porch, but she stood up on her hind legs and tried to get closer to the puppy. The puppy got down on its stomach and inched its way over to the porch railing. The closer it got, the worse it looked. This dog was so skinny that even in the dark I could see its ribs. The porch was covered in dog waste, and there was no blanket or shelter of any kind for this poor puppy. Her eyes were matted, and she had no water or food.

It was a foolish move to disregard our own safety, but with my hand on the pepper spray in my pocket we went up on the porch and pounded on the door. The puppy clung to the side of my leg and began licking my shoe, but it felt like she was licking my heart in an effort to keep it from breaking for her. I pounded louder and pressed my face to the dirty glass to see if any lights were on in the interior of the apartment, but it was dark.

I wanted to take the puppy with me, but instead went back across the street for water, a blanket, and food. I returned without Sadie to tend to the puppy and, thankfully, no one had returned to the apartment. The frail puppy exhibited as much enthusiasm as she could physically muster at the sight of me and loudly lapped up the water and began gobbling the food.

"Hang in there, little girl," I told the neglected puppy, then I returned home to call the police. She was so hungry that she didn't even lift her little head out of the bowl as I left.

The police in any city are always busy with "serious" crimes, and many cities, including mine, have few animal control officers. At best they were available only during regular daytime hours and this being New Year's Eve meant drunks took priority over dogs. Wrestling with my conscience about the welfare of the puppy, and the potential problems I could bring on myself for taking the puppy, took only a few seconds to resolve. Before she knew it, she was safe and sound in my basement with a blanket, water, and a treat. I had no idea what I would do with her in the morning.

When Sadie and I went downstairs the next morning, the little puppy was whining at the basement door. As I opened the door she scrambled out and followed me to the back door, then she ran out into the yard with Sadie. I redialed animal control, and explained the situation. An officer promised to come to the house. He arrived as Sadie and the puppy were finishing their breakfast and I told him the story and offered to show him where the puppy had been.

As we walked down the alley he told me that pit bulls in particular are often treated badly from puppyhood in order to make them "mean" and teach them to fight or be fierce protectors for drug dealers. This was before Michael Vick and the Bad Newz Kennels were common knowledge, and I couldn't believe this adorable dog was most likely headed for a miserable future. I thought of how soft this little puppy was and how terrified and sad she looked and knew whatever the officer said, this was one dog whose future would not be in the fighting ring, protecting drug dealers, or any other nefarious duty, no matter what I had to do.

The officer looked at the porch, which appeared more horrible in the daylight. He shook his head. He took out a citation booklet and began writing a ticket to the occupants for violation of several city dog ordinances. The ticket indicated that the dog had been seized and the owners would have to attend a hearing and petition to get the dog back. If they didn't do so in a certain amount of time, the dog would be forfeited and become the property of the county.

He placed the ticket on the door and we walked back to my house. I asked the officer what would happen to the dog if the people never appeared. He said the dog would most likely be adopted, but anyone who wanted to adopt her would have to pass a screening test in order to prevent her from going to a similar home. It was scant assurance, but it was better than nothing, and the officer was kind and I was well acquainted with many of the workers and the director of our local shelter, so I knew the dog would be in good hands.

I nervously waited for the occupants of the apartment to return. I had scary visions of potential scenarios should they come pounding on my door demanding to know where their dog was. I happened to be walking out my front door to work a few days later when they jumped out of a cab. I lingered on the front porch, pretending to search for something in my purse as they stumbled down the sidewalk and onto their porch. When they saw the citation on their door they just turned around and ran. They never read it, and they never looked back. I can only imagine what they were running from. I was just relieved that they were gone. In a few weeks a pile of junk was removed from the apartment and placed out for trash—the usual indication that tenants were gone. That was the easiest eviction I'd ever witnessed from those apartments.

I called the shelter daily to check on the dog and a few weeks later was thrilled to learn she'd been adopted and would, by all indications, have a much different life than she had been headed for.

This is just one dog in a medium-size city that was lucky enough to have a crazy neighbor who ventured out in the night to help. Even though we have amazing dog rescue organizations in the United States with thousands of dedicated volunteers, there are untold numbers of dogs that are not so fortunate.

In Charleston, West Virginia, Debra Linz's neighbor kept their dog tethered to a tree with a heavy chain in all kinds of weather, with no shelter, twenty-four hours a day year-round. When Ms. Linz researched her local laws to see what could be done, she was surprised to see there was no law prohibiting such treatment. She befriended the neighbor and the dog and made anti-tethering legislation an issue in her community. Along the way she produced an award-winning news story about this cruel practice, got important legislation passed on the city and county levels, and no doubt saved hundreds of dogs from such treatment. Known as the Linz Law, it now extends to the entire county.

A doctor let his dog run free with no collar, no identification of any kind, and carelessly entrusted the dog's care to neighbors. The sweet black-and-white dog lived down the street from a popular boarding kennel and would camp outside the door, hungry for food and affection. She became friends with one of the kennel worker's dogs and found a family in the clients and staff of the kennel.

Not all stories of neighbors and pets have such happy endings, though. Sometimes it's the neighbor who's a danger to your pets. Two family pets in a fenced yard excitedly scarfed down mysterious hamburgers laced with razor blades. They survived after extensive surgery and rehabilitation, but eating was never a joyful experience for them again. The dog's neighbor, who had long complained of their barking, was arrested and convicted of animal cruelty. There are countless stories of dogs being poisoned where the neighbor who didn't like dogs for any number of reasons was responsible.

All of these are examples of animal abuse and/or neglect. Pet Abuse.com lists almost twenty thousand *recent* cases of animal abuse in the United States alone. These are only the *reported cases*. What about the thousands of dogs that suffer in silence because no one ever reported their abuse? What about the countless dogs with owners who neglect them on a regular basis? What does this have to do with you or me, responsible pet parents who have taken dogs into our families and our hearts?

As mentioned in chapter 1, loving our dogs leads to caring about how they are treated. Pet parents can play an important role in the prevention of abuse and neglect just by being a good neighbor to both the people and animals next door. We know our dogs must have rabies tags and licenses, but it's also important to have a general understanding of the animal abuse and neglect laws in your city and state. Pet parents can change cruel practices and help eliminate neglect by supporting new legislation to enrich the lives of our four-legged citizens.

Dogs love so freely and bring such joy to our lives that becoming educated about the abuse and neglect of animals is one way you can help other animals have a life as good as the one you provide for your dog. As a pet parent you need to be informed about animal abuse and neglect for the following reasons:

- To better protect your own dog and your other pets.
- To help animals get out of abusive and dangerous situations.
- To help keep your community safe from animal abusers.
- To keep animal abusers from committing future crimes that harm people.

Our first duty in the fight against animal abuse and neglect is to protect our own dogs, which will serve as a good example to others. I am an overprotective dog mom and make no apologies for it. I know many pet parents who have lost their dog through a simple lapse in judgment and were devastated. Listed below are some of the ways I protect Sadie from potential harm. You can make these simple actions part of your routine to keep your dog safe.

1. I never leave her out in the yard for long periods of time without checking on her.

2. I watch if she has a particular interest in an area of the yard and make sure nothing harmful has caught her attention.

3. I walk my yard weekly, checking the fence, seeing if any objects I don't recognize are there or if it needs repair.

4. I never leave her in the care of strangers. People have offered to watch her when I'm outside a store waiting to have something brought out, but I always thank them and decline. I just ask someone if they could bring out what I need, not an entire order of groceries or a cumbersome item, and people are always glad to help. I like shopping at outdoor markets, like farmers' markets, when possible, and dog-friendly stores.

5. I never allow anyone to give her a treat, except my bank. I take the treat, thank the person, and say she'll eat it later. She never does.

6. I never leave her in the care of anyone I don't know very well, and even then it's rare.

7. I don't leave her in the car so I can just run in somewhere. Drive-through restaurants or those that offer curbside pickup are ideal when you have your dog in the car.

8. I'm watchful of people who are overly friendly when we are on walks in the city; those who want to pet her and who ask a lot of questions. People Sadie doesn't seem to like get very little of our time. Dogs know when someone is a threat to them or their person.

9. I never let anyone pick her up from day care unless it's my boyfriend. The day care has signed permission forms and will not release your dog to anyone unless they have your written permission.

10. I'm particularly careful with her on vacations. Dogs get lost way too often and it's totally preventable. Leashes are invaluable, and Sadie always has her leash on even when we are on the beach. She does get unleashed for a run after

a pack of seagulls when we are on a remote beach without threat of an adjacent road. I'd rather get out of breath running with her to chase birds than take any risk. She is *never* without a collar with an identification tag.

Although animal law as a practice for lawyers and a course of study in law schools has developed mostly in the past ten years, the Animal Legal Defense Fund has been fighting for more than thirty years to protect the lives of and advance the interests of animals through the legal system. Founded in 1979 by attorneys active in shaping the mostly unheard-of field of animal cruelty laws, the Animal Legal Defense Fund (ALDF) has tirelessly campaigned for stronger enforcement of anti-cruelty laws and more humane treatment of animals in every corner of American life. These people are dedicated to defending dogs. As pet parents, we have this incredible support team to turn to when confronted with animal abuse or neglect.

Strong and well-crafted legislation makes it possible for injured and mistreated dogs to be rescued, but a law can only work when animal abuse and neglect are reported. It's rare for any person who breaks the law to turn himself or herself in and for animal abusers it's perhaps even rarer.

As a special prosecutor, I sought justice for victims of fraud. Most of these people suffered emotional and financial harm. It was rewarding to see victims get restitution and criminals made responsible for the harm they had caused. Most of the people in my cases put the experience behind them and were made as whole as possible, which is the best result justice can deliver. But what about the victims in animal abuse cases? What about the dogs that are murdered or maimed so badly they have to be euthanized? Dogs that survive a severe beating or poisoning suffer long after the horrible act is over and bear physical and emotional scars for the rest of their lives. Often the culprit is the dog's owner who never shows remorse.

When a dog is killed or harmed, its human companions share its sorrow and pain. These pet parents often feel burdened by guilt as well, searching for some way they could have prevented this. For the rest of their lives, they will worry about the safety of their pets, their children, and relatives, and their world is forever viewed with mistrust. Their feelings are similar to those who have had a human loved one murdered, but pet parents often receive little sympathy or understanding, and there are no support groups for them to turn to. The "it was only a dog" attitude is sadly prevalent. Animal abuse is a repulsive crime that the toughest laws will never punish in a manner equal to the crime or make the victims, humans and animals, whole again.

As pet parents, we need to know the difference between abuse and neglect. The law delineates between abuse and neglect using varying criteria in different jurisdictions. Abuse is intentional cruelty. Neglect, while just as cruel, is held to a different standard. The harm to the animal is often as painful and destructive despite how it's labeled in the law. What difference does it make if someone starves a dog to death through neglect or kills it by shooting it with an arrow? Abuse and neglect are both crimes.

They both cause injury to a living creature. There's no excuse for either one. The phone number of the humane officers, the sheriff, or police department in your area should be on the refrigerator right next to your vet's information, it's that important.

I cringed along with the rest of the country and was outraged at the crimes of Michael Vick and his cohorts at the Bad Newz Kennel, where dozens of pit bulls were subjected to shocking treatment and killed. While we have nothing to thank them for, the case informed America that such horrendous crimes prevail and of the widespread intentional cruelty to animals. Why would a professional football player with fame and money possibly commit such horrendous crimes? Testimony from the proceedings made it clear: Vick was a willing, active participant; he didn't just bankroll the operation. The only good news to come out of the Bad Newz Kennel was that Vick and his fellow criminals were punished under both state and federal laws. The immense global publicity brought an awareness to the horrific practice of dogfighting, as well as animal abuse in general.

Dogfighting is a felony crime in all fifty states, and eight states have taken it a step further by prosecuting this crime under the RICO (Racketeer Influenced and Corrupt Organizations) Act. This is the law that is most often used against organized crime and allows for penalties of three times the actual damages, enhanced jail time, and the prosecution of more individuals than those actually engaged in the crime. Anyone who was involved in planning, providing money or services, or participating, such as betting or even attending, can be prosecuted for dogfighting under the RICO Act.

Animal abusers can be the person next door or a high-profile person, such as Michael Vick. The excuses for animal abuse are as diverse as the abusers. In 1985, Dr. Stephen R. Kellert and Dr. Alan R. Felthous studied one hundred and fifty-two criminal men. They identified nine reasons for animal cruelty. Ever since this groundbreaking study other organizations continue to report that they see these nine typologies over and over again. They are:

1. To control an animal.
2. To retaliate against an animal.
3. To retaliate against another person.
4. To satisfy a prejudice against a species or breed.
5. To express anger through an animal.
6. To enhance one's own aggressiveness.
7. To shock people for amusement.
8. To displace hostility from a person to an animal.
9. To perform nonspecific sadism.[4]

A few years ago, there were still four states without anti-cruelty laws for the protection of animals. At that time a reporter in Columbus, Mississippi, wrote: "Forty-six states have laws making at least some type of animal cruelty a felony. Four states don't. Mississippi counts itself among the four. With our poverty and health issues, it's hard enough being a human here. If you're a dog or cat, forget it."

A sad statement, but despite legislation and enhanced penalties, this is still reality for animals in our country, and dogs in particular. Thankfully, Mississippi passed felony animal cruelty legislation in 2011. Idaho was the last state to pass felony animal cruelty legislation; however, it was extremely liberal—it lacked "teeth" for sufficient punishment and penalties. The statute permitted three misdemeanor crimes during a fifteen-year period before a person could be prosecuted for a felony. It was good news in 2012 when Idaho

---

4. Kellert, S. R. and Felthous, A. R. 1985. Childhood Cruelty Toward Animals Among Criminals and Noncriminals. *Human Relations* 38:1113–29.

passed felony provisions for cockfighting, cruelty, neglect, and abandonment. This is an impressive and significant accomplishment by citizens and the legislature and fantastic news for the animals that live in Idaho. According to the Animal Legal Defense Fund legislative rankings in 2015, the five states with the strongest animal legislation are the same ones that have topped the list for the last eight years.

1. Illinois
2. Oregon
3. Maine
4. California
5. Michigan

The states at the bottom of the list were:

46. North Dakota
47. Utah
48. Wyoming
49. Iowa
50. Kentucky[5]

The ranking is determined by the overall strength and comprehensiveness of the state law. Fifteen criteria are applied to give each state a score, thus determining its place in the ranking. Does your state have real teeth in your animal protection laws? States improved their rankings in one or more of the following ways:

- Expanding the range of protections for animals
- Providing stiffer penalties for offenders
- Strengthening standards of care for animals

---

5. *Animal Legal Defense Fund 2015 U.S. Animal Protection Laws Rankings.*

- Reporting of animal cruelty cases by veterinarians and other professionals
- Mitigating and recovering costs associated with the care of mistreated animals
- Requiring mental health evaluations and counseling for offenders
- Banning ownership of animals following convictions
- Including animals in domestic violence protective orders
- Prohibiting convicted abusers from gaining employment involving animal contact
- Strengthening provisions on the sale and possession of exotic animals
- Expanding humane officers' powers to be the same as other peace officers[6]

This list is a great tool for pet parents wanting to make a change in their community. It's an excellent guide of what your laws *should* include and can be used to draft legislation.

Laws defining animal cruelty vary from state to state. The laws are differentiated by severity of the crime, whether it's defined as abuse or neglect, and by penalty. Abuse, generally the intentional harm to an animal through any number of means, is punished more severely and is a felony in every state. Neglect, on the other hand, is considered less severe and is often a crime of omission rather than commission. Neglect, of course, can result in the death of an animal, and many states determine punishment for neglect by the severity of the actual act.

Almost all state laws contain prohibitions and punishments for abuse, including the following:

- Fighting
- Bestiality (sexual abuse)

---

6. Used with permission from the Animal Legal Defense Fund.

- Physical harm or killing: beating, burning, choking, hitting, mutilating, poisoning, shooting, stabbing, torturing
- Retaliatory abuse: harming a pet by any of the above or other means to punish a person
- Any means of physical harm to a pet to force a person to be quiet or compliant of their own physical abuse

Notice how several of these prohibitions relate directly to the reasons cited in the Kellert and Felthous study.

Even though dogs are used in product research by companies in the United States, and many scientific experiments where they are subject to *intentional harm*, most laws exempt this practice from criminal prosecution. Dogs end up in testing labs and other research facilities by various routes, including being gathered from shelters, picked up from "free to a good home" ads, kidnapped, taken by other deceptive means, or when they are no longer useful to puppy mills or are sold by their owners for research. Dogs are also bred specifically for testing purposes, most commonly beagles. Almost all large pet food companies have dogs that live on their premises and test food. A major pet food company I went to visit as part of a media event has more than eight hundred beagles living there in lovely conditions, but what about human interaction and bonding? Greyhounds that are no longer fit for racing are also prey for research labs. Many pet parents take a stand against using dogs for research by lobbying Congress to ban it and boycott the products of companies using animals for research.

Animal neglect is regulated differently by individual states but usually includes:

- abandonment without proper food, water, and shelter;
- failing to provide medical care;
- neglecting to provide proper food, water, and shelter;
- hoarding;

- puppy mills;
- starvation; and
- tethering a dog outside without proper care: i.e., shade, shelter, use of a heavy chain or collar, water, in extreme temperatures (both hot and cold), and for extended periods of time

Unlike abuse cases that are rarely witnessed when a dog is killed or tortured, animal neglect cases are reported more often by neighbors or other concerned people who witness it. Neglect happens over a period of time, but the cases can be challenging because they're sometimes difficult to identify. A lack of humane officers makes investigating them difficult, and prosecutors with far too many cases often fail to prosecute them. It's a sad fact that understaffed prosecution offices often have to make hard choices about which case to take to trial. The most heinous cases that get a lot of publicity and public outcry usually go to trial. Prosecutors receive a great deal of criticism when they offer a plea bargain, but some punishment is better than none at all, and as pet parents we can help others understand that. The good news is that through lobbying and public attention brought to the issues of animal cruelty and neglect, many county prosecutor offices now have a specific attorney or two assigned only to animal cases. Pet parents should become acquainted with local prosecutors, as they can be a valuable resource for animal abuse and neglect cases.

It becomes even more difficult when there are cases of mass neglect, such as in hoarding or puppy mills. Limited resources coupled with a lack of personnel restrict the prosecution and discovery of these appalling cases. When organizations such as the Humane Society of the United States or the American Society for the Prevention of Cruelty to Animals (ASPCA) get involved, national publicity follows, bringing much-needed awareness and funding to these cases. These organizations have been criticized for only getting involved in cases that garner national attention and provide opportunities for fundraising, but such criticism is often unfair. Moreover, they're the only organizations large enough with the equipment, contacts, money, and manpower to effectively conduct such rescues. Don't hesitate to report animal abuse and neglect to them.

One fact that's true of many crimes, and maybe even more so in animal crimes, goes back to the ancient laws of replevin that animals are property. People are outspoken in defending their actions over their property, and this is even more so for dogs. I've had neighbors who vehemently use foolish defenses to justify unsafe and neglectful actions with their dogs. It's even more prevalent when dogs are used for a specific purpose that borders on neglect. In many situations they have big organizations to support them: hunting clubs, national dog racing organizations, breeders, pharmaceutical and cosmetic companies, farm organizations, and others. These organizations have well-paid lobbyists who have historically opposed animal legislation that would infringe on their individual uses for dogs. If these groups aren't large corporations with endless funds to promote their agenda, they are supported by big business, and money is no object.

The motto of the ASPCA is: "We are their voice." These animals cannot speak for themselves and rarely defend themselves against people who abuse or neglect them because it's often people who have cared for the animal. Pet parents appreciate the remarkable qualities of dogs and the unconditional love they bestow on us. Unfortunately, they sometimes love their human masters even when those masters hurt them. Rarely do you hear of a dog that bites the hand that feeds her—quite the opposite. I have read countless accounts of rescued dogs that were timid, scared, malnourished, and injured, yet they remained loyal to their "person." Rescue groups I've been involved with have recalled heartbreaking stories where a dog simply did not want to leave its abusive master.

Reporting abuse or neglect is your first step in helping put a stop to such treatment of dogs. If you see a neighbor's dog being treated badly, you must act. First, determine if it would be safe to approach the neighbor and offer help. Is the dog being chained out for long periods of time without shelter, water, or food? Is the dog left home alone all day with no way to get outside? Does the neighbor have too many animals that they simply can't care for? Does the dog cower when approached by its owner and seem frightened? That could mean that the dog is also being abused and you should do everything you can without endangering your own safety to determine the situation.

Know the laws concerning animals in your state, city, county, condo building, or subdivision. These laws and regulations will be discussed further in chapter 9. Laws can easily be found online at the websites of your state legislature, city, or county websites, or the Animal Legal Defense Fund website (www.aldf.com). You should have copies of the regulations if you live in a condo or subdivision.

The standards for determining neglect in many states are terribly inadequate. Overall, the majority of states only require that the dog have shelter, water, and food. At best, most of these laws provide minimal standards, if any at all, and the term "adequate shelter" is used in the majority of laws with no definition of "adequate."

In New York, the law requires that outdoor dogs must have shelter that is suitable to the breed of the dog, its physical condition, and the climate of the area. For cold weather they require a structure that is sturdy and in good condition that has insulation, has a waterproof room, and is large enough for the dog to stand and turn around in, and lie down with its legs outstretched.[7] New York ranks fortieth on the ALDF rankings for 2015.

---

7. N.Y. AGM. LAW § 353-B: Appropriate shelter for dogs left outdoors.

Conversely, Ohio, which ranks twenty-seventh, has a very poor law for animals left outside, which fails to require any specific humane requirements for shelter for dogs and allows tethering:

"All dogs, regardless of age, must be kept confined on the premises of the owner, keeper, or harborer at all times. Acceptable methods of confinement include a fence, a tethering device, a dog pen, inside a house or garage, or under adequate supervision.[8]

Palm Beach County, Florida, has a near-perfect law for the care of animals and how they must be housed. This law can serve as a model for legislation in other jurisdictions. The state of Florida overall is in the top tier of state rankings by the ALDF, coming in at number fourteen, but if all counties adopted the Palm Beach standards it would surely be even further up the list. However, Manatee County, Florida, is known for unfair treatment of dogs, poor animal shelter management, and has had several national high-profile dog bite cases. In one case, which will be discussed in chapter 7, two dogs were unjustly killed in a dog bite case. Subsequently, the Manatee County law used to murder two beloved Australian shepherds was declared unconstitutional. This is one of thousands of examples of how laws can vary greatly within one state. If the Palm Beach statute (seen below) was adopted nationally, it would be a major step in reducing the number of abuse, neglect, and animal cruelty cases in the United States.

Sec. 4-24. Animal care; manner of keeping. (Palm Beach County, Florida)

(a) It shall be unlawful for any person keeping an animal to fail to provide for that animal:

---

8. Ohio Revised Code Section 955.22C.

(1) clean, sanitary, safe, and humane conditions;

(2) sufficient quantities of appropriate food daily;

(3) proper air ventilation and circulation;

(4) adequate quantities of visibly clean and fresh water available at all times; and

(5) medical attention and/or necessary veterinary care when an animal is sick, diseased, or injured. Upon request by the division, written proof of veterinary care must be provided.

(b) It shall be unlawful for any person keeping an animal to fail to provide shelter for that animal.

(1) Shelter for dogs, cats, and small domestic animals must:

a. provide adequate protection from the cold and heat. When the outdoor temperature falls below forty (40) degrees Fahrenheit, all cats, small domestic animals, and those dogs that cannot tolerate such temperatures without stress or discomfort (i.e., short-haired breeds, sick, aged, young, or infirm) must be moved indoors or provided adequate heating to maintain a temperature above the forty (40) degrees Fahrenheit range. When the outdoor temperature rises above eighty-five (85) degrees Fahrenheit all dogs, cats, and small domestic animals must be provided air-conditioning, a fan, or another cooling source to maintain the temperature in the shelter at or below eight-five (85) degrees Fahrenheit;

b. provide protection from the direct rays of the sun and the direct effect of wind and rain;

c. provide a windbreak and rain break;

d. contain clean, dry bedding material;

e. provide protection from the elements at all times;

f. provide sufficient space for each animal to comfortably stand up, sit down, lie down, and turn around in the shelter. If the shelter is used for more than one (1) animal at the same time, it must provide enough space for each animal to comfortably stand up, sit down, lie down, and turn around simultaneously; and

g. provide a solid roof.

(2) Shelter for equine, bovine, ovine, and porcine normally maintained in outdoor areas must:

a. provide protection from the direct rays of the sun and the direct effect of wind and rain;

b. provide a windbreak and rain break;

c. provide a solid roof;

d. provide protection from the elements at all times; and

e. provide space for each animal to comfortably stand up, sit down, lie down, and turn around in the shelter. If the shelter is used for more than one (1) animal at the same time, it must provide enough space for each animal to comfortably stand up, sit down, lie down, and turn around simultaneously.

(c) It shall be unlawful for any person maintaining equine or ovine to fail to keep hooves trimmed so as to prevent lameness and extreme overgrowth causing deformities.

(d) No person shall tether an animal to a stationary or inanimate object as a means of confinement or restraint unless such person is with the animal and the animal is at all times visible to such person. Choke or prong-type collars shall not be used on an animal while such animal is tethered. As used in this chapter, tether means to restrain an animal by tying the animal to any object or structure, including, without limitation, a house, tree, fence, post, garage, or shed, by any means, including, without limitation, a chain, rope, cord, leash, or running line. Tethering shall not include using a leash or lead to walk an animal. Notwithstanding the foregoing, an animal may be tethered while actively participating in or attending an organized show, field trial, agility event, herding contest, or other similar exposition or event of a limited duration that involves the judging or evaluation of animals.

(e) Any dog maintained outdoors for all or part of the day in a fenced yard or other type of enclosure shall be provided a minimum of eighty (80) square feet of open space. An additional forty (40) square feet shall be required for each additional dog kept in the same enclosed area. Each dog shall be provided sufficient shelter within the enclosed area. Any enclosed area where a dog is confined shall be kept free of objects that may injure the dog and shall be cleaned regularly to remove feces. Dogs shall not be maintained outdoors during periods of extreme weather, including, but not limited to, hurricanes, tropical storms, and tornados.

(f) Animals must be given appropriate daily exercise.

(g) No humane slaughter of animals as defined in Florida Statutes §§ 828.22 and/or 828.23 shall be done within earshot or view of the public.

(h) It shall be unlawful for any person to tease or molest any animal.

(i) It shall be unlawful for any person to:
    (1) leave an animal in any unattended motor vehicle;
    (2) transport an animal in any motor vehicle without adequate ventilation or in unsanitary conditions; or
    (3) subject or cause an animal to be subjected to extreme temperatures that adversely affect the animal's health or safety.

(j) It shall be unlawful to transport any animal on a public road in any vehicle unless the animal is safely and humanely restrained (at a minimum by a harness with double tethering for dogs) so that the animal is unable to jump or fall out of the vehicle. When animals are transported in a pickup truck with a metal bed, the animals shall be provided protection from the metal bed.

(k) Animals shall not be allowed on any median or in any roadway, highway, or street intersection for any purpose other than crossing the same.

(l) Any person trapping an animal must:

    (1) use a humane trap;

    (2) provide protection from the direct rays of the sun and direct effect of wind, rain, and irrigation/sprinkler system;

    (3) provide fresh water in the trap;

    (4) remove the trapped animal within twenty-four (24) hours of capture. All trapped dogs and cats must be returned to their rightful owner, or to a governmentally operated animal shelter or humane society in the county; and

    (5) make every attempt to locate the offspring of any lactating/nursing mother. No trapped animal shall be killed in any manner other than a method approved in the American Veterinary Medical Association Guidelines on Euthanasia, as may be amended from time to time.[9]

If you discover the laws in your state or town are lenient and don't provide strict penalties, seek out other concerned pet parents and begin contacting legislators, city councils, county

---

9. Code of Laws and Ordinances Relating to Palm Beach County Government § 4-24.

commissions, mayors, board presidents, police departments, or anyone you can think of to start change. Find out which officials have dogs and approach them first. You can easily become active in the animal community. Go to city council and county commission meetings. Attend special days at your state legislature that are set aside for animal welfare. Use social media to get the word out about laws that are not strong enough or a lack of enforcement of good laws.

You can start at your local shelter. Shelters are the safe havens for abused, neglected, or abandoned animals. You will only know if your shelter is adequately serving this purpose if you get involved. Volunteer at the shelter and be observant. Is the shelter clean? Are the dogs there being treated humanely? Does the shelter have a sufficient vetting process for prospective adopters so that dogs aren't going from a bad situation to one just slightly better or even worse? Are the employees dedicated to the well-being of the animals or just collecting a paycheck? Volunteering at the shelter is a great opportunity to meet and become familiar with the animal control officers, which will be of great assistance should you need to report abuse or neglect.

Shelters should never send a dog out of their protected environment to a home where abuse or neglect has occurred. Shelters must investigate potential adopters thoroughly. Following are some suggestions you can bring to your shelter if it isn't already implementing them.

1. Require a thorough application, valid ID, and have a reliable person verify all the information before considering the person as an adopter.
2. Criminal background checks will reveal if the person has been convicted of animal cruelty. Local police departments can do these with no charge and they shouldn't be a problem

if your humane officers are part of the police department. Anyone with a conviction for animal cruelty should be banned from the shelter at all times and *never* be allowed to adopt an animal.

3. A home visit is important to see where the dog will live and also how any other pets in the home are being treated. Most shelters ask that you have a fenced yard, but without checking they can't verify that. Properly trained volunteers are invaluable in this step, as the shelter employees are often overworked and simply can't do home visits.

4. Are the screeners at the shelter trained in adoption procedures? Gut instinct goes a long way if the screener is trained and has experience, but even then there's no way to be 100 percent sure the person will be a good pet parent.

5. Listen to any children who are with the adopter. Kids generally tell the truth. If they say their last dog got killed, ran away, or is just "gone," find out what happened.

Become aware of everyday situations of neglect or abuse you can see just about anywhere. The following situations can't be ignored. They require attention and at least cause suspicion for the welfare of the dog when it's not in public.

1. Watch for dogs left in cars. The temperature in a parked car can rise thirty degrees per minute even with the windows cracked and cause heatstroke, permanent brain damage, or death to a dog in a matter of minutes. Call the police, but if the dog is clearly in distress, rescue them by any means possible. Only nineteen states—Arizona, California, Delaware, Florida, Illinois, Maine, Maryland, Minnesota, Nevada, New Hampshire, New Jersey, New York, North Carolina, North Dakota, Rhode Island, South Dakota, Tennessee, Vermont,

Virginia, Washington, West Virginia, and Wisconsin—have statutes that specifically prohibit leaving an animal confined in a vehicle.

2. Pay attention to dogs that are treated badly by being yelled or sworn at, jerked on their leash, called bad names, and/or appear scared of their owner.

3. Watch for signs of dogfighting. Pit bulls in particular that have a lot of scars or are wearing a heavy studded collar and chain are often used in fighting or by drug dealers to protect their stash. In this case you can get an animal officer to check for the dog's license, and in doing so he may discover enough evidence of fighting to seize the dog.

4. Does a dog look malnourished? Do you see certain dogs running loose and scavenging for food behind restaurants or dumpsters?

5. Does a dog look defeated—sad, listless, no tail wagging? If so, something is probably wrong with their home situation, and through a little detective work you could help this dog. I have seen dogs like this used in begging schemes and, in fact, I helped rescue one.

I was heading to my local farmers' market and saw a man with a large backpack literally hurl a very small dog to the grass. I quickly turned around and drove back, but they were gone. I did call and report the location, description of the man and dog, and what I had witnessed to the police.

The next day at lunch I saw this same man with other men and the same dog. They were taking turns walking through the farmers' market begging with the dog as their prop. To the surprise and embarrassment of my boyfriend, when I saw them in the parking lot I jumped up and ran after the man with the dog.

I asked him what he was doing with the dog and he said he needed food for it. I asked where he lived and he pointed to the area under the interstate bridge. I offered to take the dog. He said no. The dog was apparently very young and was in bad condition. He was extremely dirty with tangled hair and eyes almost matted shut. I said I'd get food if he would wait, but he said he couldn't. I called the police. He was long gone when they arrived.

So I called a friend of mine who helps dogs in an "underground" sort of way. He was ecstatic when he heard my story, as he'd been trying to buy this dog for about four weeks from these men. He'd seen the dog in many different panhandling scenarios with them. Each time he offered to buy the dog the price went up. I told him where the guy told me they were "living." Around 5 a.m. the next day I got a call from my friend, who told me the dog was safe. The dog now lives with a very nice woman and will never be part of a begging scheme again.

This wasn't a case where any of these men cared for this dog, nor had they bonded with it. They would never tell my friend where they got it and most likely have moved on to another town and have another dog that I can only hope gets rescued.

As responsible pet parents, unless an unforeseen or extraordinary event occurs, abuse and neglect will never be part of our dogs' world. We must be aware of the "other" world that millions of dogs live in, make sure our dogs never fall into the hands of anyone who would harm them, and most of all speak up at every opportunity and do everything possible to stop animal abuse, rescue the dogs that have been victimized by an abuser, and keep our elected officials informed of the problem so stringent legislation "with teeth" is in place in our state.

I don't know what happened to my dog Sadie before I adopted her. I've been told bits and pieces of what is known of the first eight weeks of her life, but one strange thing has never been explained. Sadie is afraid of people with crutches, wheelchairs, or walkers and people who limp. I have no idea why she is frightened of these things, it's just *very* evident that she is.

I first noticed this when we walked on the river path by our house. She was no more than three months old when a man who limped quite noticeably and walked somewhat sideways encountered Sadie and me on the path. She began a low growl as he approached, which escalated into her standing on her tiny hind legs and barking shrilly, and as he passed she hid behind my legs. I looked at her as if seeing her for the first time because I had never witnessed any type of blatant dislike bordering on fear from Sadie.

I began seeing this same reaction every time we were near a person in a wheelchair, and more so if it was a man. Sadie was with me for book signings of our first book at Book Expo America, and she loved all the people coming to our publisher's booth. She posed for photographs and was having a great time until someone with crutches, a wheelchair, braces, or a limp came to our booth to get a book signed. First the growling, then the high-pitched bark, then she'd retreat under the table and growl and bark intermittently. I apologized to people, saying I'd adopted her and she obviously had a bad encounter with someone in the past. On our book tour, in store after store there was at least one of these incidents. Sadie turned into a different dog when confronted with anyone who had a physical impediment.

Then her worst nightmare came true. I had an accident and broke my ankle. I came home from the hospital with a walker until they could set it. Sadie came running to the front door to greet me and went crazy—barking, backing away from me, growling—and hid behind a chair. I tried to coax her to me, but she wouldn't come until the walker was out of sight.

The next morning was a struggle as I tried to make my way with the clumsy walker to my car while Sadie growled, snarled, and tugged on her leash. She appeared relieved to reach the Jeep and hop into the back compartment, until she saw that was where the walker was going and leaped to the front seat.

I picked her up from day care that evening with a fresh new cast and a pair of crutches. Her behavior was even worse. She had to be coaxed out from behind the door and carried to the Jeep.

I placed the crutches in the passenger seat, and Sadie retreated to the backseat. I could hear growling and an occasional bark over the radio. When we got home, I carefully placed the crutches under my arms and opened the back of the Jeep to retrieve Sadie, and she leaped into the front. It took a long time, but I finally hobbled myself into exhaustion and got her in the house. I placed the crutches in the spare bedroom, but that didn't solve the problem. She would go to the door and bark and growl at them.

She hated me crawling up the steps and would bark and whine. This went on for two miserable weeks until I begged for a walking cast earlier than the doctor felt was best, but he relented when he witnessed Sadie's behavior.

What caused this? I'd rather not know, but I do know it was something profound, and most likely very painful for her. Let's do our best as pet parents to prevent abuse and neglect and bad memories for our four-legged companions. Let's do our part so that when a person strikes out and harms an animal, our laws will have the necessary strength to bite right back and provide swift justice and punishment.

An important change in policy at the FBI went into effect in January 2016. The FBI has routinely tracked reported crimes and kept a database that has proved extremely valuable in prosecution of crime. Now the agency's Uniform Crime Reporting System will add cruelty to animals as a category. This reporting system will create a better picture of animal abuse and help implement new strategies for intervention in animal abuse and enforcement of laws across the country. Presently, only a third of communities in the United States are participating, but that will greatly enhance the abatement of and punishment for animal cruelty.

The reporting and tracking system will cover four categories:

- Simple and gross neglect
- Intentional abuse and torture
- Organized abuse, such as dogfighting and cockfighting
- Animal sexual abuse

It's a great and noble goal to work to eliminate animal cruelty, but the reality is that despite our best intentions and efforts, like other crimes, it will continue. Every pet parent can make a difference by helping only one dog and protecting their own, paying attention to the status of laws in your state and in particular your local community, volunteering at the shelter or other dog rescue organizations, and being a watchful friend to your four-legged neighbors. Even if we guard our own dogs relentlessly, the unforeseen might happen and they will go missing. Just the thought of this puts most pet parents into a near panic attack, but knowing what to do in this worst-case scenario is crucial. West Virginia Supreme Court Justice Robin Davis and her husband had every available resource for the best care and protection of their beloved golden retrievers, yet one went missing. Their story has important lessons for all of us. Thousands of dog missing posters, television advertisements, billboards, and monetary awards later, one question remains unanswered: How did this dog disappear?

Chapter 5

DOG . . . GONE
(Send Rover Right Over)

The billboards appeared suddenly, and they could be seen everywhere in Charleston, West Virginia. A beautiful golden retriever had gone missing. Not just any dog, this beauty was one of two goldens the family cherished. The dog's parents were a West Virginia Supreme Court Justice and one of the most prominent trial attorneys in the eastern United States. Bronze sculptured images of Tad, the missing dog, and his brother made up a gigantic fountain in the middle of the circular driveway in front of the family's West Virginia mansion. Live-in staff helped tend to the dogs, but the family members were the main caretakers and loved the dogs immensely.

I had been a guest at the house for a friend's wedding reception in my pre-dog days. I was astounded by the splendor of the house, but I was blown away by the dogs' quarters. The dogs had a separate entrance to their luxury spa/kennel/playroom. They entered their suite by walking over a series of grates. First their feet were sprayed with warm water, then they were blown dry before entering the house. Inside the spa were raised bathtubs with massage sprayers, every toy and agility contraption imaginable, and what appeared to be their own private kitchen. Why any dog would run away from such an amazing home was unimaginable.

In spite of all this, Tad seemed to just vanish into thin air. Tad had not been feeling well the night of his disappearance and had vomited in the house. His mom let him out the back door to get some air. She returned in ten minutes, but Tad was gone. An immediate search for Tad began, but there was no response. His dad neglected his law practice and trekked miles over the hilly, wooded subdivision where the family home was located. He biked and hiked for days, getting little sleep as he tried to find his beloved dog. If Tad had wandered away and fallen down because he was sick, he would have been found, but there wasn't the slightest sign that he had passed through the brush or foliage. None of the neighbors had seen him.

A large reward was immediately offered. There was no response. The billboards went up within the first week, and local media were obsessed with the story. Reporters climbed the hillsides following Tad sightings. Entire talk radio shows were devoted to the missing dog, and search parties were organized and combed Kanawha County for weeks. Missing Tad posters were everywhere: on vehicles, on poles, on bulletin boards. If ever a dog should have been located, it would have been this missing golden.

At first they thought someone might have stolen the dog and was quite possibly holding him for ransom. The family is perhaps one of the most well-known families in the state. The construction of their house had been news throughout the state, and the big cases the law firm won were always front-page news. Success like this more than likely had ruffled some feathers. Yet there was never a demand for a ransom or any viable leads. There was no end to the speculation of where Tad was and what had happened to him. Not even the elaborate security cameras at the property provided the slightest clue.

Dogs go missing in only two ways: either they are stolen or they get lost. It depends on the source as to how many dogs get lost in the United States each year, and surprisingly there have been no valid surveys to document any of these numbers. They vary wildly, ranging from the American Humane Association's number of ten million pets gone missing each year, to a standard often used in advertising pet finder services that one in three dogs will go missing, to a microchip company's estimate of two thousand five hundred dogs a week, or one hundred and thirty thousand a year. These numbers become quite insignificant when your dog is the one missing.

The numbers are a little more solid for stolen dogs, because stolen dogs are usually reported to the police. Petfinder.com reports that two million dogs are stolen a year. Tad's parents were both lawyers, yet there was nothing the law could do to assist in finding him or any other dog that somehow gets lost, because getting lost is not a crime, just as there's no crime committed if you lose your wallet.

In the case of stolen dogs, the good news is that in most jurisdictions in the Unites States they are still considered property. It becomes a crime when a person decides to keep the dog when the owner is known, the same as if someone finds your wallet and helps himself or herself to the cash. Theft of personal property is a crime. Stealing a dog is a crime in all fifty states.

As pet parents we have two responsibilities when it comes to lost or stolen dogs:

1. Make sure we take every precaution so our own dog doesn't get lost or end up in a situation where it could be stolen.
2. Pay attention and assist in the return of any dog that appears lost and alert authorities if we witness the theft of a dog.

If your dog has ever been missing, even for as little as five minutes, you know the heart-pounding, shortness of breath, absolute panic the thought of her not returning brings on. I'm accused of being an overprotective dog mom, and I readily admit it. However, I'd rather micromanage my dog and her safety than end up a statistic. I'm neurotic about keeping Sadie safe on a leash. My job as Sadie's protector is knowing where she is at all times, and that means never allowing her out of my sight off the leash unless she is in our fenced yard. I don't even allow her off the leash in other people's fenced yards, because I have no idea how solid the fence is or what type of lapses there might be in the fence. I check our fence weekly, making a game of it by rolling a tennis ball along the fence for Sadie to go after. It's the only way I have peace of mind letting Sadie out into the yard alone for any length of time. Even with all this, I've experienced two severe episodes of panic when I thought Sadie had disappeared.

These are the basic tools that will help ensure your dog never gets lost or stolen.

1. Make sure your dog has a collar with an ID tag, and that she is on a leash at all times when outside of your home.
2. Have a good fence for your yard with locking gates and keep them locked. A barrier fence is better than an electronic fence. Electronic fences do nothing to keep your dog from being stolen.
3. Never leave your dog alone in a car or tethered outside a store no matter how briefly you'll be gone.
4. Never leave your dog in the yard alone for a long time or at home alone overnight.
5. Microchip your dog.
6. Don't trust a boarding kennel that you have no references for.
7. Don't leave your dog alone in a hotel room.
8. Don't keep your dog outside in a doghouse.
9. Have a house alarm.
10. Hire only dog sitters who have excellent references and are bonded.

Let's start with a simple leash and collar. You would think that every person with a dog would have a leash and collar for it, but you'd be wrong. It is a law in every jurisdiction that your dog have a license that is evidenced by a dog tag, as well as a rabies tag as proof that your dog's rabies vaccine is current. Furthermore, it's mandated that the tags be visible on your dog when in public. There's no other way for you to comply with these laws than to attach the tags to a collar around your dog's neck.

I'm always surprised at the number of dogs I see out and about with their pet parents without a leash or collar or without any tags attached to the collar. This is too great a risk to take with your dog and subjects you to a fine and in some areas confiscation of your dog. Make sure the collar fits correctly and has a secure clasp. For the safety of your dog, you must also have identification tags with your telephone number and your dog's name. Even though your dog can be traced through the rabies tag and the dog license, this won't help if the town office or veterinarian office is closed when your dog is located and could delay your dog's return home.

Make sure the collar and leash are in good condition and check them periodically. The clasps on leashes and collars wear out and sometimes stretch. Before starting out on a walk with your dog, give the collar and leash an inspection to make sure that should your dog become frightened and lunge, the leash and collar will hold her. To ensure I do this regularly, on the day I give Sadie her flea and heart medication each month, I also check her leashes and collars. All of her collars have tags engraved with my name, my phone number, and her microchip ID number. That microchip ID number is registered, so I'll have a better chance of getting her back should she get lost or stolen.

Most state statutes that make it a crime to keep a lost dog specify

that the finder had access to some form of identification of the dog's owner, specifically information on a collar tag, a tattoo, or information written on the inside of the collar. No states require that a finder have a found dog scanned for a microchip.

These everyday precautions should be second nature to all pet parents. If your dog gets away from you and is lost, it will be some comfort knowing that at a minimum it has a tag on its collar.

Sadie also has a tag on her collar saying she has a microchip and what that number is. A microchip is about the size of a grain of rice and contains a unique identifying number that matches your dog to you. There's a lot of misconception and misunderstanding about microchips. I'm not a vet or a scientist, but as an overprotective dog mom I don't do anything that might harm my dog. I researched microchipping and decided it was safe and essential for my dog.

A microchip is not a radio receiver and has no connection to a locater satellite, nor does it function as a GPS. You can't track your dog through any computer program or Internet service by entering the microchip number to find her location. Shelters, veterinary offices, and most police departments have scanners and can scan the dog and contact the company where the chip is registered. The chip must be registered in order for your information to be accessed by a scan.

None of your personal information is stored in the actual microchip. Each chip has a unique ten-to fifteen-digit number that's associated with your contact information should your pet be lost. The microchip is worthless unless you have it registered. The American Kennel Club has a program called Companion Animal Recovery (CAR). You can pay for the registration when you buy the chip, and there is never an annual fee. CAR also provides a metal tag engraved with the microchip number for your dog's collar. This alerts the finder that they can call CAR with the registration number and locate the owner. A simple Internet search will give you a number of options for purchasing and registration of your microchip.

The majority of dogs are returned due to a collar with a clearly readable tag stating your name, telephone number, and the microchip number of your dog. Of course, this is not totally reliable, as collars come loose and fall off in any number of ways. They are also discarded by unscrupulous finders of pets who unlawfully keep the dog or sell it. Over time the information on tags fades or is worn off. Anyone finding a dog with a collar and a tag with clear information will be able to call you and facilitate the return of your dog, but should that fail a microchip is a permanent source of information confirming the ownership of your dog.

Dogs are stolen for almost as many reasons as anything else is stolen. Purebred dogs are stolen because they have monetary value and can be sold. Many people are willing to pay what they consider a substantial discount for a certain purebred dog and will ask no questions. Some purebred dogs are stolen and sold to puppy mills for breeding. Getting your dog spayed or neutered is not only a responsible pet parent duty, but it also might deter a thief from stealing your dog.

Certain breeds of dogs, such as pit bulls, are stolen and placed in fighting rings or used for breeding. Other run-of-the-mill mixed-breed dogs are stolen to sell to labs or fighting rings to use as bait dogs. Unfortunately, some dogs are stolen by abusers for the sole purpose of causing harm to the dog. Animal hoarders often steal dogs, and many missing dogs have been recovered when rescued from a large hoard.

Since dogs are considered property, and property laws are set individually by states, it's essential to know the laws in your particular state regarding lost or stolen pets. You should also do a quick search of the laws in a state where you'll be taking your dog for vacation in the unthinkable event she becomes lost or stolen while there.

Following is a list of some of the legal issues that arise when a dog goes missing.

- Does ownership of the pet transfer to the rescuer if they find it running at large and take care of it for a long period of time before the owner discovers it?

- Does the original owner have any right to damages when a private party or government agency seizes their dog, spays or neuters it, euthanizes it, or harms it?
- Does an innocent third party have any rights if they are a good-faith purchaser of a lost or stolen dog?
- Does a rescuer have a right for reimbursement for any medical treatment or other expenses incurred for the dog they assisted?

As with anything in the law, there are diverse answers to these questions based on many factors specific to the individual situation. All you need to do is watch a few episodes of *Judge Judy* to see that these and dozens of other issues you'd never think of can arise when your dog goes missing. You should become familiar with laws and ordinances where you live and what could happen if your dog is lost or stolen. Becoming aware of these things will help you create a plan if your dog is ever missing. Your county or city website will have a section listing the animal ordinances. Print them out and learn them. Your home state web page has a listing of your state code. Another great resource is the International Institute for Animal Law website (www.animallaw.com). It's easy to search by topic and by state, and the site has laws as well as current cases and legislation. All pet parents should have the phone numbers for animal control and/or the police or sheriff department near your home phone and programmed into your cell phone.

If you suspect your dog has been stolen, the first thing you should do is call the police. If you witness someone taking your dog from your yard, make sure you get every detail possible about the incident, including a description of the person; the make, color, and model of the car; and the license plate if possible. Treat the theft of your dog like the taking of any other personal property, only with more urgency.

Insist that the police department send an officer to take an official report and gather any evidence. Provide the officer with a photo of your dog and the microchip number.

It's not "finders keepers" when it comes to dogs in almost every jurisdiction. Think about it: If you "find" a bicycle that's not locked up, can you keep it? Of course not, and you can apply any common law or common sense concerning property without a heartbeat to dogs. One of the recurring cases on *Judge Judy* is when someone keeps a dog that doesn't belong to them and is subsequently discovered by the owner. What you do with a dog you find will depend on your own values and compassion; however, many states require that at a minimum you do all or some of the following:

- Call the owners if their name and phone number are on the tag.
- Ask people in the area where you found the dog if they know who owns the dog.
- If there is a dog license on the collar, call animal control or your county office that handles dog licenses to get the name of the owner.
- If you have no idea what your state law is, call the police department and ask to speak to an animal control officer about what you are required to do.

If you turn the dog in to the shelter, hopefully the owner will contact them before the holding period is up and the dog will be returned to the owner. However, the risk exists that they will not and the dog will get adopted by someone else or be euthanized. Owners only have a legal cause of action in such cases if they can prove the shelter broke the law in some way. For example, they let the dog be either adopted or euthanized before the holding period was up. In either of these situations, the owner would have a case against the shelter for civil damages, which at best in most jurisdictions would be limited to the "market value" of the dog. Do not assume this will be the case, though, and take the shelter to court with a competent attorney. Your dog is priceless, and while the court may not have a history of awarding emotional or punitive damages (monetary amount meant to punish the defendant), there is always a chance that your case could be the first.

If you do find a lost dog, taking a dog into your home and caring for it while simultaneously doing the above actions might be the best option. This, of course, has its own risks. What if you never find the owner? What if you get attached to the dog after a long period of time and then the owner appears? What about the harm to the dog if it becomes emotionally attached to you and its new life and has to be returned? I found a lost dog this past summer just roaming around my subdivision. I emailed everyone in the subdivision and put him on the Facebook page for lost West Virginia pets and my own page. After a day I took him to the shelter and asked them to call me if he wasn't claimed and would be in danger of being euthanized.

I couldn't wait to hear, so in a few days I called and was happy to hear that he'd been claimed. Someone who knew the family saw his picture and read on the Facebook page that I'd taken him to the shelter. I went to see the family, gave them some treats for the dog, and talked to them about getting him neutered and making sure he didn't get out again. One of the young girls whose dog he was just hugged me and told me how she'd cried and couldn't sleep. This is one lost dog story that had a happy ending. However, a Texas family had quite a different experience when their lost dog was turned in to the shelter.

In 2009, Jeremy and Kathryn Medlen's mixed-breed dog, Avery, escaped from their fenced-in backyard and was picked up by animal control. When the Medlens located the dog at a Fort Worth animal shelter they didn't have the eighty dollars required to claim her. A "hold for owner" ticket was placed on Avery's cage, and the Medlens left to secure the money. When Jeremy Medlen returned with his children and the money two days later, despite the hold, they were told Avery had been euthanized. The Medlens filed suit not for the money, but to change Texas law, which allows damage awards for sentimental value of personal property, but not for "live" property, such as dogs. Their suit in the Tarrant County District Court was dismissed, but the second court of appeals in Fort Worth overturned the dismissal and ruled in favor of the Medlens. For a brief time the citizens of Texas and the Medlens were hopeful the common law would be changed. Unfortunately, the case was appealed to the Texas Supreme Court and the decision handed down on April 5, 2013, was in favor of the animal shelter. The court held:

> *Under Texas common law, the human-animal bond, while undeniable, is uncompensable, no matter how it is conceived in litigation—as a measure of property damages (including "intrinsic value" or "special value . . . derived from the attachment that an owner feels for his pet"), as a personal-injury claim for loss of companionship or emotional distress, or any other theory. The packaging or labeling matters not: Recovery rooted in a pet owner's feelings is prohibited. We understand that limiting recovery to market (or actual) value seems incommensurate with the emotional harm suffered, but pet-death actions compensating for such harm, while they can certainly be legislated, are not something Texas common law should enshrine.*
>
> *We reverse the court of appeals' judgment and render judgment in favor of Strickland.*[10]

---

10. 397 S.W.3d 184; 2013 Tex. LEXIS 270; 56 Tex. Sup. J. 470.

In the end, the Medlens had no remedy for the loss of their dog and were left asking, "Why?" along with thousands of other Texans. Unless you live in one of the few states that have actually ruled in favor of noneconomic damage recovery, this is what you can expect if you sue for damages for the death of or harm to your dog.

Emotional damages for dogs are decided on a state-by-state basis, and the result is inconsistent at best and widely variant. The law is changing as our pets are recognized widely by society as family members. It most often depends on the facts of each individual case, a judge or jury that is willing to consider awarding emotional damages, and the law that the case is brought to court under. In asking for damages for the death of a pet, damages are more often awarded when the cause of death has been intentional and shocking.

A California appeals court decided that emotional distress was a valid claim even when the dog is cruelly and intentionally injured and survives.

In this case, the court found that California law does allow a pet parent to recover for mental suffering and noneconomic damages when a pet is intentionally and cruelly injured. In *Plotnick* v. *Meihaus*,[11] the plaintiffs were awarded $445,899.53 after their neighbor and his two sons injured their dog's leg in the midst of a property dispute. The Plotniks discovered an area of their fence that had been destroyed by their neighbor. While investigating it, their dog escaped under the fence to the Meihaus property and suffered a severe leg injury at the hands of Mr. Meihaus and his two minor sons. The court also awarded attorney's fees to the couple in the amount of $93,780, for a total of, as stated, $445,899.53. Interestingly enough, this amount was the *reduced* amount of damages after an appeal.

---

11. 208 Cal.App.4th 1590 (2012)146 Cal. Rptr. 3d 585.

A January 2016 Michigan case interpreted an existing law in favor of the owners of a dog. In this case the defendant, Ronald Hughes, a Michigan Department of Corrections Absconder Recovery Unit investigator, shot the owner's dog after entering her house by mistake to execute a fugitive warrant. In *Moreno v. Hughes*,[12] the plaintiff brought suit under a section of the Michigan law that defined damages available in lawsuits for loss of property. She asked for what the law calls "noneconomic" damages. That is, damages that are not tangible and have a certain value. In this case, she asked to be compensated for the pain and suffering she experienced as a result of this horrendous incident. The case was brought under federal law rather than a Michigan statute.

The court in this instance denied the police department's motion to deny these damages and limit the plaintiff's recovery only to the value of the dog. The court's decision stated that it is "beyond dispute" that compensatory damages under federal law 42 U.S.C. § 1983 may include noneconomic injuries. The court went on to say that the loss of a companion animal had different policy considerations than in traditional negligence claims. In fact, the court stated that, "[P]rohibiting recovery for emotional damages stemming from the loss of, or harm to, an animal caused by a constitutional violation would conflict with the compensatory and deterrence aims of 42 U.S.C. § 1983." Additionally, applying this law on the issue of emotional damages for injury to an animal would create inconsistency in civil rights actions since other states allow such damages. The court found that the determination of both compensatory and punitive damages must be left to the jury finder for each case, including this one.

These three cases are proof that the law is not set concerning emotional damages for companion animals. This is why pet

12. 2016 WL 212932 E.D. Mich. Jan. 19, 2016.

parents must not accept that the law in their state won't allow them to recover damages. Laws are interpreted by the judge in individual cases, and the intentional death or injury of a family pet must be brought to court where it can be determined on its own merit.

So, what if you do everything you can to find your lost pet and despite all your efforts you find out that it has been euthanized by the shelter or a vet, spayed or neutered, or harmed? Do you have a right to claim damages? The typical lawyer answer is, it depends. If you can prove that a person kept your dog knowing that it belonged to you, then the answer is yes. They can be charged with theft, prosecuted, and ordered to pay restitution. If you can prove they intentionally kept your dog for their own benefit, which can be difficult, you can sue them civilly for damages. People intent on keeping a dog will destroy any identification, but if your dog is microchipped you can at least prove it's your dog and get it back. Sometimes the best result in cases like these is just to get your dog back and be thankful. If it's a case of intentional cruelty, report the person to the police and have them arrested. As we've seen, results from a lawsuit are widely divergent, and even if you get a judgment, in many instances the defendant does not have sufficient assets to pay it. Even if they are charged with a crime and ordered to pay restitution, it is often difficult to collect even with the help of the court.

As mentioned previously, you can only have a cause of action against a government agency, such as a shelter, if they broke the law. The Medlens were able to sue the Fort Worth Animal Shelter employee because she broke the law by euthanizing the dog while it had a hold on it. In some states you have to file a notice first, informing any government agency, for example, a county shelter, that you plan to file a lawsuit against them. Most agencies are self-insured and, rather than spend money on a legal defense for a valid claim, will sometimes offer to settle with you. They will offer only what your state law allows for recovery, which in most instances is the economic value of the dog. Again, you can take them to court and hope for a verdict against the odds.

If you purchase a dog that turns out to be stolen and you were a bona fide third-party purchaser, or innocent third-party purchaser, which means you purchased the dog without notice that it belonged to someone else, you may get to keep it. Buyer beware can't be expressed enough in this situation. If someone offers to sell you a dog at a discount, has vague answers about where it came from, is in a hurry to complete the transaction, has no medical or birth records for the dog, or acts suspicious in any manner, run away. Sellers such as this should be reported to the police, as the dog has more than likely been stolen.

Innocent third-party purchasers are in a difficult position. They didn't do anything wrong, yet the lawful owner appears and wants the dog. Depending on how long they had the dog, both the new owner and the dog may have bonded, but the first owner has memories and attachment to the dog. The dog will also be bonded to the family and should be with his original family. No one really ever wins in this situation. If your dog is lost and subsequently purchased by an innocent third party, be prepared that in most instances, the legal remedy is that they get to keep the dog. If you can reach a solution between yourselves, that's usually the best course of action in these situations.

There are no good-Samaritan statutes in the United States that compel a person to offer assistance to a person or to a dog. Good-Samaritan laws relieve most people from lawsuits if they act in good faith to help someone, but end up causing harm. These statutes don't apply to property, and dogs are property. If you find a sick or injured dog and take it to your vet, do so because you want to and expect no repayment. The true owner of the dog has no liability to reimburse you. This is a situation where you have to let your conscience guide you, and in the spirit of kindness and goodwill do what you would want someone to do for your dog. A responsible pet parent should offer to reimburse you, but don't expect it. Shelters most often do charge a fee to redeem a lost dog, which varies from shelter to shelter even within the same state.

In 2015 there was an increase across the country in the number of dogs that were stolen. Most of the time it's only a misdemeanor. To meet the threshold for a felony, the property (the dog) must have a value of at least one thousand dollars under common and statutory law. While our pets are priceless to us, proving the actual value of a dog is often difficult unless it's a purebred dog with a purchase receipt. Then again, value is always diminished on any property due to age. In the case of our dogs, the longer we have them, the more valuable they are to us, not the court system.

Stolen dogs often disappear under the same circumstances as missing dogs, but thieves are bold and have been known to snatch dogs from an owner as they walked with the dog. Pay attention to your surroundings and be diligent of people who pay overt attention to your dog or whom you see in more than one place. Maybe they talked to you at the dog park and then you see them again while walking your dog somewhere else. It might be a coincidence, but it might not be. Trust your gut feeling and trust your dog's reaction to certain people. I'm not advocating paranoia toward every person who greets your precious pooch, but caution is not overrated when protecting your dog.

Know the law in your state concerning stolen dogs. In North Carolina it's a Class I felony to steal a dog. No value threshold needed. They have to pay a fine no less than the value of the damages, and the judge has the authority to impose a sentence of his own determination. It's interesting to note that the dog theft statute follows a long list of other prohibited thefts, and it's right below waste kitchen grease and right above portable toilets. That says a lot about the status our dogs get in the American justice system.[13]

Since stealing a dog is a crime, if the thief is caught, they will be charged and prosecuted. Part of a plea bargain or a conviction will include restitution. If you want damages beyond that, you will need to file a civil suit. As previously discussed, most courts limit the damages to a determined value of the dog. If it's a service dog, you can probably recover for the value of the services; if it's a run-of-the-mill mutt, maybe your adoption fee if you have a receipt. Damages are not easily obtained for a dog that was stolen versus a dog that has been intentionally injured or killed.

If your dog goes missing and you know or suspect that he was stolen, call the police immediately. Be as detailed as possible relaying all the information you have concerning the theft of your dog. You'll have to identify your dog if the police locate her. This is where a microchip is worth its weight in platinum. You have to be willing to press charges and testify in court. The police department doesn't operate as a lost-and-found department. Even for minor infractions an animal control officer is called out for, such as your neighbor's dog barking all night, they won't usually write a citation unless the person who complained is willing to promise to come to court and testify. In many scenarios you'd have a potential suspect to name to the police, but if your dog was taken while you were gone and you have no idea at all what happened, it becomes a difficult case right from the start. Many situations where your dog could potentially be

13. North Carolina Statutes, Subchapter V. Offenses Against Property. Article 16-Larceny. §14-81 Larceny of horses, mules, swine, cattle, or dogs.

stolen are preventable, but we don't have control over everything at all times.

David Toon and his fiancée Liz know this to be heartbreakingly true. Liz, a pharmacist in Mays Landing, New Jersey, returned from work to find her condo had been broken into and Luna, the little Yorkie she co-parented with David, was missing. Her first call was to David, during which she explained the situation at her home: a missing laundry basket (no doubt used to put Luna in) and an open balcony door. Nothing else was missing. He told her to call the police immediately and jumped in his car for the two-and-a-half-hour drive to New Jersey.

The police were just leaving when David arrived. They took a report, couldn't do any fingerprints on the exterior doors because it was raining, and said they'd be in touch. David noticed a small footprint on the pee pad in the kitchen and thought it must have been a child who broke in. The scenario made no sense.

Despite financial situations, pet parents rally their resources when it comes to getting their dog back, and Liz and David were no different. They offered a reward. They increased it. David searched for days, printing out maps, following leads, looking everywhere. One day he sat on the top of his car for seven hours at a basketball court because someone said a dog matching Luna's description had been coming there for a few days. She never appeared.

They printed posters, made signs, begged different media sources to cover their story. No Luna. A store reported that a dog resembling Luna had run inside and then back out, and they had a surveillance tape. David asked for it, but they said they could only give it to law enforcement. The police said they'd get it, but they never did. Dogs are very low on the priority list of busy police departments.

People prayed. A "Bring Luna Home" page was created on Facebook. Liz and David couldn't eat, they couldn't sleep. They received calls about sightings. They received scam calls saying someone had taken Luna to Nigeria. They heard about another dog, Katie, that had been stolen under similar circumstances. Justice Rescue, a dog recovery organization, had found her. David contacted them and begged them to take their case. Eight members of the organization traveled to New Jersey and canvassed the neighborhood, knocking on doors, questioning people. They found nothing, but promised to stay on the case.

At the time of this writing, Luna has been gone for more than two years. Saturday, September 28, 2016, will be her fifth birthday. Liz's and David's parents want them to let go and move on. Liz comes home from work every night and goes to bed. David goes to Mays Landing every weekend and searches. He understands his parents' concern, but he can't let go; Luna is their child. They planned a life with her, and as short as dogs' lives are, the months she's been gone have taken a massive toll on them and destroyed those plans. They hold on . . . they wait. There was no way they could have seen this coming, and there was nothing they could have done to prevent it.

In *Ace Ventura, Pet Detective*, Jim Carrey portrays a pet detective in Miami, Florida, who is hired to find the Miami Dolphins' missing mascot. Ace eventually found the mascot, but there were many mishaps along the way. There are real-life pet detectives who use sophisticated tactics to find missing pets. I met Corrin Culhane and Dawn Weichler through helping to find some missing dogs on Facebook. They have been volunteering to find missing pets for several years and have formed a business, On Your Tail Search & Rescue.

Dawn's two-year-old Siberian husky, Santi Amani, was stolen, and her other dog ran after the thieves. The thieves let Santi go, but never having been off a leash and terrified from the abduction, she ran wildly, was hit by a car, and died instantly. This was a profound tragedy for Dawn and a life-changing experience.

Dawn and Corrin receive calls from rescues and shelters that have foster homes that have lost a dog. They get frantic calls from transporters of dogs to shelters who have dogs run away at a rest stop. People whose dogs have been missing for a long time call them, because they can't believe they are gone forever or dead and are looking for any small glimmer of hope.

The company uses a variety of methods to find lost dogs, but just like police detectives, wearing down the soles of their shoes, talking to people, and putting up flyers is how many searches turn into happy endings.

Hiring a pet detective is a good option if your dog goes missing or is stolen. Be prepared to give them every piece of information you have leading up to the dog's disappearance, have a recent and clear photo, be willing to post a reward, and be as patient as possible.

With reasonable precaution your dog should never go missing or be stolen. Things happen quickly, and dogs can disappear in a matter of seconds. That's why constant diligence can't be over-stressed. Keep in mind the law views your dog as personal property. Don't expect law enforcement to rescue you from your own negligence or the court system to deliver an adequate remedy if your dog is stolen or suffers harm when out of your control. Until more states accept the standard that a pet is a family member, thus entitling pet parents to emotional and special damages, the best you can hope for is to recover economic damages or market value for your dog, which means nothing when you lose your canine companion.

Even when you're the best pet parent possible, things can go wrong. We all have to trust our dogs in the care of someone other than ourselves at times, and often that person is a veterinarian. What happens when your dog suffers harm from a vet's negligence? Are vets held to a higher standard than an ordinary person, which enables pet parents to recover damages similar to a medical malpractice case? Attorney Gail McMahon found out just how tough it was to sue a veterinarian when her show dog died as a direct result of a vet's actions.

Chapter 6

MEDICAL RIGHTS—
ROVER AND MED MAL
(Negligent Neutering and Beyond)

I f you had to choose a new doctor or find a specialist for an important medical issue, I bet you'd do a lot of research. You'd search the Internet, you'd ask friends. You'd do your homework, because you'd be putting your life in the hands of someone you must trust. We have confidence in our doctors, but even so, if it's something serious, most people get a second opinion. How much research did you do before choosing your dog's doctor?

Most likely you took recommendations from other pet parents or the place you adopted your dog, did some research online, maybe more, probably not. Did you know every state has a board of veterinary medicine where you can check the credentials of a vet before trusting them with your dog's care? I didn't. You owe your dog as much due diligence in selecting her vet as you do in selecting your own physician. The veterinary board will also have information about complaints filed against a vet. Even though I didn't have a clue when it came to any type of dog care, I was willing to learn and listen to the people who did know and was lucky to get the right vet for my dog. Taking time to research a vet beforehand could save your dog from a serious problem in the future or having to file a vet malpractice case.

I adopted Sadie at PetSmart from a local shelter. At the time, this particular PetSmart had a veterinary clinic located in the store. I agreed to take my dog to this vet since the adoption fee covered the cost of getting my puppy spayed and her initial vaccinations. The vet was wonderful. As a new pet parent with no experience, I appreciated all the information Dr. Paul gave me each time I took Sadie to see him. We made it through the series of shots and the spaying procedure, without any problems. The clinic was clean and the staff was friendly and competent. In my bliss as a new dog mom I thought all veterinarians must be as wonderful as this one. Unfortunately, there are as many incompetent and neglectful veterinarians as there are individuals in any other profession.

When you take your dog to a veterinarian for treatment you become a client and are bound to certain responsibilities, such as promising to pay the bill, following any instructions for your dog's care, and providing truthful information to assist in the diagnosis and care of your dog.

The veterinarian is also bound to certain responsibilities. These are set forth in the policies of the governing agency that oversees veterinary practice in the state where your vet practices.

Almost all states use the policies set by the American Veterinary Medical Association (AVMA) in some form. The AVMA provides a general guide of ethical responsibilities for member veterinarians, and they must abide by these standards for both their animal patients and human clients. AVMA membership is voluntary, but membership and licensing in your state agency is not. The AVMA's general guidelines are divided into three categories: professional ethics, criminal law, and civil law—malpractice cases.

Professional ethics are the standards of conduct veterinarians are expected to abide by. As a lawyer, I have a Code of Professional Conduct that I must follow or face sanctions from the Office of Disciplinary Counsel. Likewise, doctors must abide by the rules of the American Medical Association or they can be disciplined. Veterinarians are mandated to follow the standards set by the board in their state in addition to the basic principles of ethical and fair practice of medicine for animals they learn in veterinary school.

Criminal law applies when a vet commits a criminal act, such as animal cruelty, or if he fails to report animal cruelty or abuse. Veterinarians are mandatory reporters for any suspected illegal treatment of the pets they see. Just like schoolteachers and doctors, who are required to report abuse of people, vets must report abuse and neglect of the animals that come through their clinics.

Civil law applies to vet malpractice cases, but covers other issues that might arise between you and your vet, such as disputes over fees or collection of a bill owed to a vet. Additionally, veterinarians have an oath they swear to abide by. The oath (seen below) was first adopted by the AVMA Board of Delegates in 1969 and subsequently amended by the AVMA Executive Board in 1999 and 2010. The oath provides a general minimum standard for veterinarians and they promise to follow it the same as doctors and lawyers must with their own oaths when admitted to practice.

Being admitted to the profession of veterinary medicine, I solemnly swear to use my scientific knowledge and skills for the benefit of society through the protection of animal health and welfare, the prevention and relief of animal suffering, the conservation of animal resources, the promotion of public health, and the advancement of medical knowledge.

I will practice my profession conscientiously, with dignity, and in keeping with the principles of veterinary medical ethics, I accept as a lifelong obligation the continued improvement of my professional knowledge and competence.

AVMA Oath for Veterinary Practice

This is the minimum you should expect from your dog's medical provider and what you should use along with references and research to evaluate if a veterinarian is the best person to provide for your dog's well-being. All pet parents should possess a good knowledge of the policies of the AVMA to better understand the parameters of the veterinarian/client/dog patient relationship. The more you know about your vet and the standards he is mandated to operate under, the better you will be able to determine if your dog is getting proper care. The AVMA's national standards are implemented in various ways in each individual state's veterinary standards. These general standards include the following:

1. Licensing requirements in every state are different, but most states generally follow the national requirements with little variation.
2. Most of the licensing requirements are formatted from ethical principles for veterinary practice.
3. The principles deem it unethical for a licensed veterinarian to assist non-veterinarians practicing veterinary medicine.

4. Vets are not allowed to identify themselves as members of the AVMA or one of its specialty organizations if they are not members. This is an ethical violation.

5. Veterinarians are required to have continuing education to keep and renew their license. The amount of hours required is mandated by individual states.

AVMA Standards

These are important for pet parents to know, not to help you bring a lawsuit against your vet, but to help you select a vet who follows these principles and to better understand your relationship with your vet and how a practice should be operated. Membership in the AVMA is voluntary, and there are certainly good veterinarians who are not members but still follow the guidelines and abide by the rules of their state. If a vet disregards the standards set by his state board of veterinary medicine, he might be subject to disciplinary proceedings, but that alone is not enough for the basis of a lawsuit.

We found out just how lucky we were to have Dr. Paul when Sadie began having symptoms that suggested she had a heart condition. He researched, consulted with other vets, and tested her with a heart monitor over a twenty-four-hour period. (Actually, it wasn't quite twenty-four hours, because Sadie chewed the wires off before the time was up, but it was long enough to get a reading.) I was frantic, but his calm assurances and professional abilities gave me hope that all would be well. He referred us to the Virginia Maryland Regional Veterinary Hospital at the Virginia Tech Veterinary School. We were placed in the care of Dr. Jonathan Abbot, one of the few veterinary cardiologists in the country at that time. I did a lot of research about the potential heart condition Sadie was facing and about Dr. Abbot and was confident that he was more than qualified to take care of my precious Sadie.

There aren't enough accolades to heap on Dr. Abbot or the many Virginia Tech vet students who have cared for Sadie over the last fourteen years. She suffered from an "electrical problem" (easier to understand than the medical terms) in her heart. Like pistons running out of sync in an engine, her heart misfired in a similar manner. Scary? You bet. But Sadie was as much the perfect patient as I was the nightmare dog mom. After the initial diagnosis, and the decision to put her on a human medication, I still had to live with Dr. Abbot's frank, yet kindly delivered, full disclosure that they weren't sure this would work, but it was the best treatment available. If it did work, all would be well. If it didn't, Sadie would have a heart attack, and there was nothing I could do.

So, we returned home and were referred to a different local veterinarian who would be able to follow her condition along with Dr. Abbot and perform the routine ECGs (dog electrocardiograms) necessary to monitor Sadie's condition. I knew this vet because I had often watched his segment on the local TV station's noon news program. He seemed like a good guy. He kind of reminded me of Opie Taylor from Mayberry and someone I could trust my dog

with. Medically, while maybe off to a rough start, I set out to be the best caregiver possible for Sadie, to follow all the advice, and to be with her and stay positive. Sadly, not everyone and their dog have the excellent care or good results Sadie and I were fortunate enough to experience.

We were lucky, but how can you make sure you're getting an ethical, competent vet? You can't do too much research or ask too

©DAVID VOISARD '16

many people or organizations before entrusting your dog to a vet. We don't have crystal balls to see into the future, but before malpractice ever becomes an issue, simple prevention measures can lessen the possibility of becoming a victim. Knowing your rights and the veterinarian's duties and taking these additional steps will go a long way to ensure you performed due diligence before trusting a veterinarian with the life of your dog. You must be the advocate for your dog at all times, even when in the care of a competent vet. Here are some responsibilities of pet parents as your pet's advocate:

1. Make sure you have selected a qualified vet who is compassionate and has a genuine love for animals.
2. Don't be so quick to accept an initial diagnosis. Seek out a second opinion, see a specialist, or take your dog to one of the many wonderful clinics at veterinary schools.
3. Do research online to make sure you understand your dog's diagnosis and potential treatment.
4. Don't drop your dog off like dry cleaning. Stay and monitor her treatment. Ask questions. Don't agree to anything you're uncomfortable with or consider risky. Common sense and gut feelings are priceless resources here.
5. Immediately seek an independent second opinion if you suspect malpractice. If your dog has died, get the body to a veterinary college immediately for a necropsy (dog autopsy). Call them to find out how they want you to preserve the body. This is the last thing you can do for your dog so don't hesitate. Necropsies are not generally expensive.
6. You're entitled to and should get all of your dog's medical records, including all x-rays, surgical notes, and lab results.
7. If you have evidence and support that you and your dog are victims of malpractice, immediately find a lawyer with expertise in animal law or a very good medical practice attorney.

Despite your best efforts, negligence happens that results in malpractice actions. California attorney Gail McMahon loved her Maltese like a child. In addition to being the star of Ms. McMahon's life, Tootsie was a pedigreed Maltese show dog. Tootsie was only ten inches tall and weighed three and a half pounds, but Ms. McMahon's love for her was endless. Unfortunately, this beloved pooch had some serious health problems that led Ms. McMahon to seek the services of a vet with a stellar reputation as a surgeon, in particular for the surgery Tootsie needed. Ms. McMahon did a great deal of research before choosing this vet because Tootsie had a history of medical problems.

As a puppy Tootsie needed heart surgery. When she was about three years old she developed a condition known as laryngeal paralysis, a serious breathing disorder. Dogs who suffer from this condition are at risk for suffocation because the muscles that normally pull the airway in the trachea open don't work correctly. When the pet breathes, the walls of the airway don't pull open, which restricts breathing. The walls can be pulled into the airway opening, which can completely close it, and the dog will suffocate.

After consulting with the veterinarian, Ms. McMahon took several months to decide whether or not to subject Tootsie to the surgery. The vet gave her ample assurances of a successful procedure, and there was the chance her beloved dog could die without it. What is known in the legal field as "informed consent" (you agree to the treatment after you have been told the details) and "full disclosure" (the vet has informed you of every conceivable problem that might occur, no matter how remote) applies to veterinarians as well as medical doctors. Dr. Craig explained how the procedure would be performed and pointed out every conceivable problem and possible complications.

One was that Tootsie could develop aspiration pneumonia. This happens when food or liquid is aspirated from the stomach into the lungs. In people as in dogs that will receive anesthesia, it is essential that they have no food or water for a period of time prior to surgery, and Ms. McMahon made sure Tootsie did not eat or drink as instructed. Dr. Craig assured her that this was rare, and as a lawyer she was aware that even the most remote potential complication had to be revealed. She ultimately decided to move forward with the procedure. A date was confirmed for the surgery, the pretesting completed, and Tootsie was admitted to the clinic.

Following the surgery, Dr. Craig called Ms. McMahon to tell her everything went well and that even though Tootsie had experienced some minor surgical complications, there was nothing to worry about. Tootsie was placed in a cage in the back of the practice instead of in the special care unit where dogs who had surgery were routinely placed. No one ever explained the reason for this, and a large issue in the resulting lawsuit involved the lack of care Tootsie received because of where she had been placed. Dr. Craig told Ms. McMahon that Tootsie would be home in a few days. Tootsie never came home. Tootsie died shortly after a nurse discovered blood and fluids oozing from her nose and mouth.

How could this happen? How did it happen? What exactly happened? And the most heart-wrenching question of all, "Why did this happen?" The questions were endless, and there were very few answers. Ms. McMahon ordered a necropsy and started a quest to find her own answers. The necropsy results convinced her that Dr. Craig was responsible for the death of Tootsie. Dr. Craig's behavior after Tootsie's death did nothing to comfort Ms. McMahon or in any manner explain what happened to Tootsie. In fact, almost seven hundred dollars was charged on her credit card for Tootsie's post-op care—the very *lack of care* that contributed to, if not caused, her death.

Ms. McMahon filed a lawsuit against Dr. Craig for veterinary malpractice, loss of companionship, emotional damages, and other claims. She asked for seven thousand dollars in medical bills and one hundred thousand dollars for loss of companionship and emotional damages. The case was lengthy and spread out over several years, but in the end a dollar amount was awarded to Ms. McMahon only for medical bills and the market value of her dog. As reiterated throughout this book, dogs are considered property in most of the jurisdictions in this country. The case in chapter 5, where the plaintiffs received more than two hundred thousand dollars for the intentional injury to their dog's leg, was in the same state as this case, which shows there is no set standard for damages for animal cases. It sounds callous, but that's how it's done.

Battle lines were clear in the McMahon case, with large corporate support from the pet industry siding with Dr. Craig, and animal advocates siding with Ms. McMahon. The pet industry's interest was to keep veterinary costs low by making any recovery for loss or harm to an animal only for the market value of the animal and the cost of service. Animal advocates took a clearly opposite point of view, recognizing that Tootsie could never be replaced.

For a pet parent like Ms. McMahon, the cost of her dog and the medical bills are the least value for their loss. For me and other pet parents our dogs are everything. To the court system the only value is usually the cost of the dog and any damages suffered for medical bills. So the real question is, how does a court place a value on something intangible?

The short answer is that most often they don't. This court wouldn't determine or award that "priceless" value, and neither will most others. Emotional damages are claimed when the action of the defendant is so "outrageous" or intentionally cruel that the plaintiff suffers psychological harm. They often can't eat or sleep. Their world is changed because of the horrible event they witnessed. In this case, the court recognized that Ms. McMahon and other dog owners are attached to their pets, but this court interpreted California law not to allow this type of damage award. There were precedents (prior court decisions) where parents seeking emotional damages for harm to their children had been denied, so there was little chance a court would allow it for the owner of a dog.

Ms. McMahon's reason for suing the vet was never for money. Like many lawsuits where the action is so egregious and hurtful and there is little chance for recovery, they're filed to send a message and to make the public aware of the defendant's actions. Small comfort, but it's often better than nothing even though the time and money involved in bringing such a lawsuit usually takes a heavy emotional and financial toll on the plaintiff. Instead of suffering in silence, many pet parents find some comfort in making the negligence of the vet known, seeking justice for their companion animal.

What should you do if you believe a vet has harmed your dog, give up? Absolutely not. You should bring a malpractice case just as if it were for a person. In Ms. McMahon's case it got the public's attentions, went all the way to the California Supreme Court, and was supported by the ALDF.

In this case, the court was sympathetic to Ms. McMahon. This was the first time a California court of appeals had ever considered the question of how to evaluate the *true* value of a companion animal. The problem for the court that remains today is how to reconcile the value of a dog that is considered property in light of the fact that the dog means so much to the person and adds so much value to their life. Courts will hear an amicus brief, which is simply a supportive writing by an outside party that supports one of the parties in the lawsuit. In this case, the ALDF wrote an amicus brief in support of Ms. McMahon, but courts aren't obligated to give them a great deal of time or even consider them as any type of evidence in making their decision. In this case, the ALDF was only given ten minutes to present their point of view. They wanted the court to consider that the value of an animal killed through a negligent death can't be determined in a mere property valuation. Even though it wasn't a human who was killed, Tootsie was part of Ms. McMahon's family, and she was emotionally bonded to her. The loss of Tootsie would have a huge and detrimental impact on her life. The chief counsel for the ALDF reiterated what he had written in the brief:

"Although this lawsuit does not involve the death of a human, it does involve real loss—the loss of Ms. McMahon's companion animal, Tootsie. Ms. McMahon has sued the respondent veterinary medical providers for their role in Tootsie's death. The issues here focus on the changing evaluation of the damages available when companion animals, despite their status as personal property, are tortuously killed."

Courts across the country are increasingly finding that market value is not the appropriate measure of damages in cases involving the loss of a companion animal, particularly in veterinary malpractice cases. These courts recognize that longtime animal companions, like Tootsie, are a special kind of property, in that they cannot be readily replaced in the marketplace. Indeed, Tootsie cannot be truly replaced at all. Therefore, reliance on a market value measure is misplaced, as such a number would simply not provide adequate compensation to Ms. McMahon."[14]

Ms. McMahon never got to present her case to the Orange County Superior Court. The court dismissed the case without hearing arguments on the basis that dogs are personal property and therefore emotional damages and no recovery could be granted

---

14. 176 Cal.App.4th 1502, 97 Cal.Rptr.3d 555 Cal.App. 4 Dist., 2009.

beyond their monetary value. In order to expedite the case so a higher court could review it, both parties agreed to a legal compromise called a demurer, which was a judgment in favor of Dr. Craig.

The case then went to the Santa Ana State Court of Appeals, which also ruled in Dr. Craig's favor, writing that veterinarians only have a duty to the animal they are treating when they agree to treatment. They have no duty to the pet's owner, and Dr. Craig had no duty to avoid emotional distress to Ms. McMahon, in particular since she didn't witness the death of Tootsie; a bystander would have a better case. The justices felt that expanding the laws to include awards for emotional damages would be an economic disaster for veterinarians, pet insurance, and the pet industry in general. The opinion also said that such lawsuits would "burden the court system," and the court should be used for the resolution of "serious tort claims." (Tort is a lawsuit for damages.)

Of small consolation to Ms. McMahon, the final page of the nineteen-page opinion expressed a small amount of sympathy, writing that the court understood the "love and loyalty" a pet brings to its owner, however, California law "does not allow parents to recover for the loss of companionship of their children. [So] we are constrained not to allow a pet owner to recover for the loss of companionship of a pet."[15]

If you find yourself certain your dog has been the victim of a vet's negligence, by all means, file a lawsuit. Even if you can't win emotional damages or sentimental value for your canine companion, file a lawsuit with the help of a skilled attorney.

All states have malpractice statutes. Not all states include vets in their malpractice statutes, and that can be to your advantage. For example, Arkansas specifically includes veterinarians in its

---

15. *McMahon* v. *Craig*, No G040324, slip op at 2 (Cal. Ct. App. July 31, 2009).

definition of "medical care providers." This means that all veterinarians are included in the malpractice statute. The Arkansas law places a two-year statute of limitations (the amount of time you have to file your lawsuit from the date the incident occurred). However, if you are suing under a negligence cause of action in a bailment lawsuit, meaning you left your dog in the care of the vet and they were negligent, you have three years to sue.[16]

You can bring a lawsuit under a number of legal theories. It won't matter what cause of action (a lawyer's way of stating "this is what I am suing you for") you use if you get results that hold the veterinarian responsible for harm to your dog. Some of these are:

1. Breach of contract
2. Professional negligence
3. Bailment
4. Breach of expressed or implied warranties
5. Breach of fiduciary duty
6. Outrage
7. Fraud
8. Intentional or negligent misrepresentation
9. Intentional or negligent infliction of emotional distress
10. Violation of state consumer protection laws

Although these might sound like complicated legal jargon, they're very simple. Most of these causes of action are based on property law, which is good since animals are still considered property in most states. If you live in a jurisdiction where companion animals are still treated like personal property and you bring a lawsuit that applies to personal property, but it achieves the result you want, you will have a better chance of success. For example, bailment

---

16. Ark. Code. Ann. §16-114-201(2).

is an old term used when someone else agrees to be responsible for your property. If you leave your car in a parking garage, it's a bailment. Placing your coat in a coat check station at a restaurant; clothes at a dry cleaner; jewelry for repair; and dogs at a boarding facility, groomer, or veterinarian are all examples of bailment.

Bailment cases are much easier to win than malpractice cases because the standard is simple. You entrusted someone to care for your dog and return her in the same condition as when you left her. The bailee (person or facility keeping the property) failed to do so. Not all states allow bailment lawsuits against veterinarians, but with creative thinking your situation will most likely fit into one of the other causes of action. Any of the causes of action listed above can be an effective legal remedy for harm to your dog from an inept vet.

If you have a statute in your state that allows and recognizes malpractice lawsuits against vets, you've jumped a huge hurdle, but it doesn't mean your case will be easy. It also doesn't mean that you will receive any compensation for the love and companionship of your canine companion. Keep in mind, the value of your dog is the special bond that you share, but in court, even with a malpractice statute, your dog is still property and, as discussed in chapter 4, getting emotional damages is difficult at best in our justice system.

In order to bring a malpractice action in almost any jurisdiction you have to first set forth the basis for your case in addition to the fact that your dog has been harmed. It's important for you to keep all medical records, invoices, and other documentation of the treatment for your dog. You'll have to establish some facts up front.

1. First, you must show that the veterinarian had a duty of care for your dog. This means that the vet accepted the responsibility for the treatment of your dog. You took your

dog to the vet for treatment and he agreed to treat her. Keep in mind, just because you take your dog to a vet doesn't mean he has to agree to treat her.

2. The actions of the vet or his failure to act did not conform to the professional standard of care. Failure to act is extremely relevant if your dog was in a critical emergency situation.

3. The vet's failure to perform his duties according to the professional standard of care was the proximate (a lawyer word that just means it was the reason) cause of the harm to the dog.

4. The injury or harm resulted in damages to you, not just the dog. Of course you suffered emotional harm, but you will also be harmed financially and have other economic damages.

If you can establish these facts, you're ready to move on to making your claim public. Here are the steps for filing a lawsuit:

1. Start by sending a formal complaint to your state veterinary licensing board and any other entity that your vet belongs to, such as a county organization. You can find this on your state's website or through an Internet search. Make sure you comply with their procedure for filing a complaint. Keep emotions out of this complaint. It should be factual and as brief as possible, but still set forth all the pertinent details. Start a file on your computer and make paper copies of everything you send to or receive from the veterinary board. Remember, they have the power to discipline your veterinarian, including revoking or suspending his license.

2. You should have an experienced animal law attorney or a malpractice attorney. This attorney can also discuss whether there are any criminal statutes the veterinarian has violated and bring your case to the attention of the local prosecutor. Most lawyers realize there won't be a large monetary award

in veterinary malpractice cases, so they will most likely not be willing to take the case on a contingent fee basis, as doctor malpractice cases are handled. In a contingent fee case, you don't pay the lawyer anything if you don't recover damages. Otherwise lawyers are paid by the hour.

3. If you can't afford an attorney, at least have a consultation and discuss your options. Most attorneys offer consultations at no charge. You can retain the attorney only for negotiating a settlement with the veterinarian. Agree up front how many hours you can afford. This is much less expensive than going to trial.

4. Get a second opinion if you don't agree with what the attorney told you concerning your case or if he's not someone you are comfortable with. As an attorney, I treat every client's case as if it is the most important issue in the world, because I know that for my clients it is.

5. If you can't afford a lawyer, don't be afraid to take the case to small claims court yourself. Often called magistrate courts, in these courts, the amount you can sue for is usually limited. In West Virginia, it's five thousand dollars, but the amount varies depending on where you live. Small claims court is used to having people represent themselves and, despite what you see on *Judge Judy*, usually forgiving of mistakes pro se (without a lawyer) plaintiffs make. You can ask for a jury trial depending on your state, but most often you will only be trying to convince the magistrate judge, not an entire jury.

Whether you handle your case yourself in small claims or magistrate court or hire a lawyer, you will need evidence to prove your case. That file you start when you file the complaint with the veterinary board is where every important piece of evidence must be placed. How many times have you placed something you were going to eat within reach of your dog and come back to find an empty plate? The dog looks guilty, and you know she ate that roast beef, but the empty plate isn't evidence that your dog ate the roast beef or if there was ever roast beef on the plate. Photos of your dog eating the roast beef would be necessary to prove your case beyond a reasonable doubt.

The same sort of standard is relevant with evidence for a court case. A good rule is to keep everything. It's easy for your lawyer to get rid of it later if it's not needed, but it's hard to go back and get evidence that's lost or destroyed. You need to preserve factual evidence to show:

1. How your dog was before the vet's treatment.
2. What happened from the treatment.
3. How you were damaged by this.

It's irrelevant if you can collect emotional or sentimental damages. Your bond with your dog is what you've lost if she has died as a result of the treatment, so make sure this is part of your case presentation. You need to show that your dog and your life together were "whole" before the treatment. That if it weren't for what the vet did to your dog, your life, and her life, would still be the same. A picture really is worth a thousand words for this type of evidence. Photos, a short video, anything that shows the close bond the two of you shared or that she had with the entire family is considered evidence and is important.

If your dog survives but had pain and suffering from the treatment, needed extra care, and has residual problems, you must provide before-and-after evidence.

As a trial attorney I've used a tool that most trial lawyers use in cases for personal injury and other civil cases. It's called a "Day in the Life" video. It's simply a video recording of how difficult a person's day is after they are injured. With the ease and availability of video on our cell phones and digital cameras, it's easy to create one of these. You can put together scenes of great times with your dog and what your life is like now. It doesn't have to be long, but it needs to get the point across. If your dog is injured, but survived, you can make a video of any hardships she has had to deal with since she suffered harm. These videos are very convincing to juries.

Start a phone log and record every person you talk to and a summary of the conversation. If you live in a state where only one person has to know a conversation is being recorded, record them. You can use them in your court case if a witness contradicts what they said previously with what they testify to on the stand. These recordings can also be useful in negotiating a settlement with your vet.

Your dog's medical records prior to the treatment are a crucial part of your case. Perhaps this was a routine procedure, such as a dental cleaning, and your dog was given too much anesthesia. If she had a healthy life prior to this treatment, her records will show it. If she had some particular medical condition and the vet was advised of it prior to treatment, the records will show that.

Evidence of what happened from the procedure will be in the medical records. Get the medical records from the negligent vet immediately. If your dog dies or is injured this might be the last thing on your mind. Ask for the records before you leave their office. You paid for the service and are entitled to the records. Refusing to give you the records is not permitted by the veterinary board, and if this happens you must include this in your complaint. If you ask for them before leaving the practice, they might tell you they aren't complete. Insist on them anyway and tell them to send you the completed copy later. In the case for Tootsie, the vet actually didn't put the truth in the records, then when the lawsuit was initiated she changed them. It's important that you get the records immediately.

I always advise pet parents to take someone with them if their dog is going to have surgery, is in a medical emergency crisis, or any type of treatment requiring anesthesia. This is because in times of emergency and grief we are scared and don't think clearly. If you have a friend with you, they can remain calm and help you remember to get the records and other things.

Keep in mind that even if the veterinary board sanctions your vet and the court awards you a significant amount of money, this will not ease your deep sense of loss if your dog has died due to the negligence. Chances are you will feel that void forever. If your dog was harmed, she may still have physical limitations, and money won't correct the physical damage or erase any suffering she's experienced. The goal of any lawsuit is to make the person bringing the lawsuit "whole" again, but this rarely happens. The best you can hope for is some satisfaction that you've done all you can to make it known that a veterinarian caused harm to your pet and hopefully prevent it from happening to others.

Your damages will be economic (money you've spent), emotional damage you have suffered, sentimental value of your dog, or punitive damages. Evidence for economic damages include the vet bill, cost of any prescriptions or medications, additional treatment your dog requires, any special food, or other expenses related directly to the vet's negligence. If you have retained a lawyer to file a lawsuit or negotiate a settlement, ask for attorney's fees. Courts often grant the person who wins the lawsuit the amount of money they had to spend for legal representation. If the worst happened and your dog died, any cremation expenses or other costs directly related to her death are also considered economic damages. If you had to miss work, lost wages are also included in economic damages. Subsequent corrective veterinary care, travel expenses to see a specialist, and any other expense you incurred as a direct result of the vet's negligence are included in economic damages.

Emotional damages are difficult to determine. Within emotional damages is a set of particular economic damages for expenses you've accumulated to deal with grief and resulting problems from the loss of your dog. There are two kinds of emotional damages. Intentional infliction of emotional distress is the legal term when someone hurts your dog on purpose. This could be purposely hitting her with a car, shooting her, or any number of acts intentionally performed. This cause of action is rarely if ever used in a veterinary malpractice case. Negligent infliction of emotional distress is when a negligent action causes emotional stress to a person. Malpractice by nature is a negligent action, and when it happens to your companion animal it causes emotional harm.

Every piece of evidence of your dog's life prior to this malpractice action is important to prove emotional damages. Was your dog a therapy dog? Did she participate in Reading Education Assistance Dogs? Get statements and records from any doctors or grief counselors you saw after your dog's death. Did you depend on your dog for security? Explain what a terrible impact this has had on your life. Losing sleep, anxiety, a profound sense of loss, and other conditions brought on by the loss of your dog are emotional damages. If the case goes to trial, expert witnesses in the field of grief, and in particular the loss of a pet, can help prove your case.

Sentimental damages are different from emotional damages. What you felt for your dog and her value to you in particular are sentimental damages, or the sentimental value of your dog. The law regarding sentimental value is constantly changing, cases are often decided on an individual basis, and they are widely different from state to state. Seven states—Alaska, Florida, Hawaii, Idaho,

Kentucky, Louisiana, and Texas—allow noneconomic (sentimental) value to be recovered in the loss of a companion animal.

It might seem impossible to place a value on your dog because she'll always be priceless in your valuation. Here's where a lawyer can be of great assistance. By examining verdicts of other cases within your state and other jurisdictions, a lawyer can get a good idea of what's "reasonable" and won't be considered excessive by the court.

If you decide to represent yourself in small claims court, you can easily research online and make this decision before filing your lawsuit. Even in states where they use the standard of "value to the owner" in awarding damages for the loss of personal property, they often do not include family pets in this standard even though pets are classified as personal property. It's a murky area of the law at best, and it's changing all the time. However, evidence speaks for itself and can be persuasive. A thorough and compelling collection of evidence can be crucial in the decision-making process of the jury or a judge. If the law is unclear and has been decided in different ways, evidence is the key for a ruling in your favor.

If you remember the Medlen case from chapter 4, the Texas courts went back and forth in their decisions of whether the Medlen family could recover sentimental value for their dog that was wrongly killed at a county shelter. The Texas Supreme Court ruled that dog owners could recover noneconomic damages for their dog. They cited an 1892 case that was way before its time when it stated that dogs "were of special value to the owner."[17]

An Indiana case, *Henning, et al.* v. *Nicklow*, allowed sentimental value damages for the loss of a pet. In this case the dog owners sued police officers claiming deprivation of their Fourth Amendment

---

17. *Heiligmann* v. *Rose*, 81 Tex. 222, 16 S.W. 931 (Tex.1891).

right of unreasonable seizure of property when police officers shot and killed their dog Misty. The dog owners sued to recover damages for the value of Misty as a companion animal. The court held that the dog owners' testimony as to the value of Misty "as a companion, pet, and watchdog" could be used in determining the "market value" of the dog at the time of loss.[18]

Hawaii is perhaps the most liberal state in awarding sentimental value damages for pets. In *Campbell* v. *Animal Quarantine Station*, 632 P.2d 1066, 63 Haw. 557 (Haw. 08/26/1981), the Campbell family sued the Animal Quarantine Station when their dog, Princess, died from heatstroke while being transported in the defendant's van. At the trial court level, the family was awarded the value of the dog, and one thousand dollars for "serious emotional distress." The defendant appealed the case, but the Hawaii Supreme Court ruled in favor of the Campbells, reasoning that it has long been the law in Hawaii that dogs were personal property and that plaintiffs in Hawaii could recover damages for emotional distress for the negligent loss or destruction of personal property.

Punitive damages are the only damages a court awards that aren't intended to reimburse you for what you've suffered and lost. They are intended to punish the defendant. Punitive damages are only awarded in cases where the conduct of the defendant is outrageous and so beyond normal conduct that the judge or jury feels that awarding them is necessary to punish the defendant and send a message to others who might take similar actions. They're not granted often in civil cases, but it happens. If your vet did something so egregious it's completely beyond any acceptable standard, punitive damages should be asked for in your lawsuit. Punitive

18. *Henning, et al.* v. *Nicklow*, Slip Copy, 2009 WL 3642739 (N.D. Ind. Oct. 30, 2009) (NO. 1:08-CV-180).

damages go a long way in sending a clear message to your vet and others that they will be held accountable for negligence.

Even if you've hired a lawyer and your case is ready to go to trial, there's another alternative that might give you more satisfaction. Mediation, or alternate dispute resolution, is an effective way to settle a lawsuit without a trial. Mediation is mandatory in many states before a case actually goes to trial. During this process you, your attorney, the defendant's attorney, and the defendant go before an impartial mediator appointed by the court. In some jurisdictions you are permitted to have private mediation. In these cases, your lawyer and the defendant's lawyer agree on a mediator and the cost of the mediation is either split between the parties or paid by the losing party.

Mediation usually begins with the mediator gathering all parties in one room where the lawyers give an opening statement, each lawyer presenting his client's side of the story. You may present evidence, just as in court, but usually there are no witnesses. Then one side stays with the mediator while the opposing side goes to another room. After the mediator talks with one party he goes to talk with the other party. This back-and-forth usually goes on several times. Each time both parties learn a little bit more about what the other side is thinking and what they want for the settlement.

During your talks with the mediator, you can tell him things and tell him not to tell the opposing side. They will abide by your wishes. It sounds confusing, but mediation is very successful in settling cases out of court. It's informal, and you can be more relaxed and open about your feelings and what you really want from the case. If your veterinarian's insurance company will be paying any proposed settlement, someone from the company must be available in person or by telephone. They do not participate in the mediation.

If a settlement is reached, an agreement is drawn up and signed. If the veterinarian agreed to pay you money, you will receive a check within a set amount of time. If you want an apology from the vet and haven't heard one, you can ask for it, and this often goes a long way in healing.

Sometimes there is no resolution and nothing is lost except some time and the case continues to trial.

Courts are beginning to realize that our canine companions fulfill a specific and irreplaceable role in our lives. More and more the legal system is starting to recognize that a judgment for emotional or sentimental value is appropriate when the award is not excessive, but reasonable when considering the role of the pet in the plaintiff's life.

As more jurisdictions move toward the view that companion animals do not neatly fall into the category of personal property, more decisions will be handed down awarding sentimental value for canine companions, emotional damages for pet parents, and a great understanding will prevail that the market value of a dog is not the same as for a painting or other inanimate object. Awards in veterinary malpractice cases will increase substantially from merely the costs of the veterinary bills and what you paid for your dog, to a more substantial amount intended to compensate you for your loss.

Pet parents aren't always in court as plaintiffs. What happens if you get sued because of something your dog does? What if she bites someone and causes harm? The Sanders family in Missouri never dreamed they would be defendants in a lawsuit due to the action of their beloved yellow labrador, Phineas. However, not only were the Sanders sued, the case received national attention, and thousands of supporters like me followed every action of the case on social media. National media swarmed into the small Missouri town that had been torn apart over the alleged actions of one family dog. The family's long public and emotionally draining journey started with two little girls playing in a suburban backyard and an alleged dog bite.

Chapter 7

DOG BITE!
(Do Dogs Really Get One Free Bite?)

Labrador retrievers top the list almost every year as one of the best choices for a family dog. They are loving, intelligent, active, and loyal. So when Patrick and Amber Sanders chose a yellow labrador puppy for their family pet, they had no idea what was ahead of them.

Until that fateful June 2012 afternoon, Phineas lived a normal puppyhood and grew into a beautiful three-year-old cherished family member. On that day, Phineas was playing in the backyard with Lexi Sanders and her seven-year-old neighborhood friend. The friend fell on Phineas and claimed that he bit her. Subsequently, the girl's mother said that Phineas had bitten the girl on two previous occasions that had never been reported. The girl was taken to the hospital and the "bite" was photographed and treated.

After the animal control authorities were involved, Phineas was seized and a sixteen-month ordeal began. In July of 2012, Phineas was sentenced to death by the town's mayor, Gary Brown. He ruled that Phineas was a "dangerous dog" under the town's Dangerous

Dog Ordinance because of the unsubstantiated allegations that he'd bitten before this incident. The Sanders appealed and hired local attorney Joe Simon. Not an experienced animal attorney, but convinced of Phineas's innocence, Simon took the case pro bono (for free), and it became his mission to get Phineas exonerated and back home with his family.

As the protracted legal battle inched along, Phineas was first housed in the local fire station basement, where he was not getting adequate care or exercise. Mayor Brown, who had not only ordered the death sentence and deemed Phineas "vicious," also vigorously denied these accusations and claimed that he'd walked Phineas on many occasions. The firefighter who disputed this was fired. Why the mayor would walk a dog he deemed dangerous and vicious was a question that was never answered, and not one witness had ever seen Brown walking Phineas.

Phineas was next moved to a local kennel, where he escaped through a hole in the fence. Finally, a local vet took Phineas in and the family was allowed to visit. Things did not quiet down, though. Hearing after hearing was held and rescheduled with no results. This small Missouri town was deeply divided, and the story spread across the nation and the world thanks to social media. Billboards went up all over the area with a giant picture of Phineas pleading, "Don't let Salem, Missouri, kill me."

Attorney Simon did his research and filed hundreds of pages of motions and memorandums to the court. He interviewed witnesses and spent hours with the Sanders family and as much time with Phineas as allowed. Emotions ran high, with the local citizens pitted against one another. The largest contingent of citizens and millions of people on social media demanded the mayor's resignation. The judge initially ruled that Phineas must be euthanized, as he had bitten someone before, and therefore was a dangerous dog.

The Sanders, their supporters, and attorney Simon did not give up. They requested a new hearing, citing newly discovered relevant evidence. A forensic dog bite expert was retained—just like CSI, a dog bite expert can tell if a specific dog caused a bite. At the new hearing, detailed testimony and forensic data were presented as proof that Phineas was not the dog that caused the bite, because his teeth simply did not match the bite marks. Additionally, there was no testimony that Phineas had ever bitten anyone in the past.

With time running out for Phineas, attorney Simon and the Sanders contacted the Lexus Project, a nonprofit organization started after a greyhound named Lexus was sentenced to die in Rhode Island for killing a Pomeranian puppy. Lexus was doing nothing more than her canine instincts compelled her to do. For a typical greyhound, long-haired small animals are prey, so when she saw the small dog running in a dog park, her natural instinct kicked in. Despite expert testimony and no record of any aggressive behavior, Lexus was scheduled for death.

Due to the volunteer efforts of two attorneys, Lexus was released and allowed to be relocated out of the state and the Lexus Project was born. They've intervened on behalf of dozens of dogs. Many of the dogs they assist are those that breed-specific legislation (laws specifically designed to ban and/or impose sentences on specific breeds of dogs perceived to be naturally aggressive) is directed at or dogs that have been declared dangerous. Labradors, however, are not included in any breed-specific legislation, and the only thing they're often accused of is loving and excessively licking their pet parents. The mayor's determination to have Phineas killed and the judge's agreement were vigorously challenged.

Finally, the Dent County judge reversed his previous ruling. On October 25, 2013, the court ruled that it would be a "manifest injustice" if Phineas was put to death and that he should be returned to the Sanders family immediately. Thousands of

Phineas's supporters rejoiced, and the news spread rapidly on social media. Only one problem—Phineas was missing. Despite the impossibility, Phineas had vanished into thin air. The stunned Sanders family, while happy and relieved over the ruling, had no idea if they would ever see their beloved dog again.

Phineas went missing from the veterinary clinic on October 11, 2013. There were no signs of a break-in. There was nothing missing from the clinic: all the drugs, money, and every dog was accounted for. There were no clues, and nothing was recorded on any of the surveillance cameras. The initial jubilation over the judge's ruling was tempered by the fact that Phineas was gone and no one seemed to know where he was. The billboards all over Dent County had a new urgent plea: "Where is Phineas?" Everyone close to the case was stuck in a bittersweet limbo waiting for even the smallest piece of news that could lead them to Phineas.

Then the Sanders received an anonymous letter stating that Phineas was safe and was in the care of a person who was supportive of their case. They said they'd taken Phineas in the event the court's decision had gone the other way. He was being cared for and he was in good hands.

Phineas was at a safe house, where the family was able to visit him and give him the good news in person. They didn't bring him home right away, as they were receiving threats as the controversy kept going. Pat and Amber Sanders eventually brought Phineas home.

One dog, one bite—a huge problem that's repeated daily throughout the United States. While Phineas's story eventually had a happy ending, the lives of many people were changed forever. One thing blaringly lacking in this case that could have simplified everything was good old common sense.

An interesting result of this case was the election results in Salem, Missouri, in April of 2014. Jim "Doc" Tune, the veterinarian who housed and cared for Phineas during the legal proceedings, was urged by the many Phineas supporters to run for mayor against Mayor Gary Brown, who had signed the death warrant for the dog. Although Brown had been an incumbent mayor for many years, Doc Tune won the election, and the dogs and people in Salem rejoiced.

As long as we've had domestic dogs there have been incidents of dogs biting people. If your dog bites someone, the situation can quickly get out of control and become a matter of life and death for your dog. If you have a certain breed of dog, including and leading the pack pit bulls, rottweilers, or Dobermans, your dog will be in immediate jeopardy due to the influx of dangerous-dog and breed-specific legislation (BSL) in recent years. Such legislation is nothing more than dogscrimination, but if it's the law in your jurisdiction, you must overcome the presumption that your dog is dangerous or exhibits aberrant qualities attributed to her breed. Below is a list of the dog breeds most often targeted in breed-specific legislation.

1. American pit bull terriers
2. American Staffordshire terriers
3. Staffordshire bull terriers
4. English bull terriers
5. American bulldogs
6. Doberman pinschers
7. Mastiffs
8. Dalmatians
9. Chow Chows
10. German shepherds
11. Presa canario
12. Dogo Argentina
13. Wolf hybrids

In many areas, in addition to the breeds listed, mixed-breed dogs that resemble one of these breeds are also banned and subject to stricter scrutiny than other dogs.

A typical BSL statute prohibits the ownership and/or regulation of certain breeds deemed dangerous within a designated jurisdiction. That's a legal way of saying that one town may prohibit certain breeds of dogs, but one five miles down the road won't. As of January 2016, nineteen states have laws banning breed legislations. They are:

- California
- Colorado
- Connecticut
- Florida
- Illinois
- Maine
- Maryland
- Minnesota
- New Jersey
- Nevada
- New York
- Oklahoma
- Pennsylvania
- Rhode Island
- South Dakota
- Texas
- Utah
- Virginia
- Washington

If you live in a state that prohibits BSL that means there can be no such law passed anywhere in your state. Your town can't decide on its own that it will enact a local BSL law because state law has power over local law. Most BSL laws are local, meaning specific to a city or county. Ohio is the only state that has a statewide BSL statute, and all municipalities and counties in Ohio are subject to this state law and prohibited from exempting out of it or making any changes on the local level.

Besides outright banning ownership of specific breeds, BSL also regulates ownership and control of dogs where they are permitted. The regulations are passed in an effort to ensure public safety from dog bites, although there have been no proven studies to confirm this. Regulations can include:

1. Mandatory spay/neuter
2. Mandatory microchip

3. Liability insurance
4. Prohibiting ownership by convicted felons
5. Muzzling the dog in public
6. Prohibiting them from certain public spaces such as parks and dog parks

It's not just owners of dog breeds included in BSL who are opposed to such regulations. The American Bar Association, the Animal Legal Defense Fund, the Center for Disease Control, the Humane Society of the United States, and the American Society for the Prevention of Cruelty to Animals are only a few of the many organizations that don't support such laws. Even President Barack Obama, in August 2013, said that BSL laws are not effective, do nothing to improve the safety of the public, and are most often a "waste of public resources."

Although BSL has gotten a lot of publicity in recent years, it's not new. In 1989, Denver, Colorado, passed BSL for the purpose of reducing the number of dog bites in the city. However, from 1995 to 2011 Denver had a higher rate of dog bites than any other city in the state. A National Canine Research Council study concluded: "Breed-discriminatory Denver County, with a population of about twice that of breed-neutral Larimer County, had more than seven times as many dog bite–related hospitalizations during the same seventeen-year period."[19] The Netherlands repealed their national BSL after fifteen years because they found that it didn't reduce the number of dog bites, which was why they had passed it in the first place. In Florida, Miami-Dade County's BSL banned only pit bulls (which are technically not a breed) in 1989. It didn't reduce dog bites, but created excessive legal expenses from the numerous court proceedings it generated. Legal expenses have

---

19. www.nationalcanineresearchcouncil.com.

also risen in jurisdictions that have BSL when disabled persons are denied housing because their service dog is one of the prohibited breeds. As discussed in chapter 3, it's illegal to discriminate against persons who require service dogs. Municipalities have been challenged in court when they ban a person from housing contrary to the Americans with Disabilities Act due to the breed or presumed breed of their service dog.

One of the most maddening aspects of BSL is that in many jurisdictions if your dog even vaguely *resembles* a prohibited dog, you will be judged under the conditions and specifications of the BSL laws. BSL has been largely unsuccessful in reducing the number of dog bites in jurisdictions where it's implemented.[20]

Even if you don't live where BSL is the law and no specific breeds are prohibited, if your dog is one of the "presumed" dangerous-dog breeds and she bites someone, be prepared to refute in court the presumption that she is a "dangerous dog." There has been so much publicity about breed-specific legislation that the breeds it targets are usually presented in a negative context. This detrimental publicity makes the general public wary of such breeds and drives local law enforcement and animal control officers to treat these dogs unfairly.

Most states have laws that specify what behaviors or incidents lead to a dog being labeled "dangerous" or "vicious." The most universal standard is if the dog has bitten before. Known as the "one-bite rule," it originated in English common law when the determination was made that each animal a person owned was exonerated from liability for the first bite. How they kept track of this is beyond me. Did each animal owner and farmer have "Bite Books" where they recorded what animal bit which person on what day and a short description? Did animal-to-animal bites count? I can't see this system being at all accurate or even working.

---

20. Ibid.

However, we use this standard today, in particular to determine the degree of "punishment" a dog will receive if she bites someone. If a dog has a record of biting someone she can face very severe penalties, including death. Pet parents need to be aware that allegations of previous biting must be proven, but they are often falsely alleged in order to have the dog that bit euthanized. Sadly, this is particularly true if you have one of the dogs on the BSL list. Emotions run high on both sides of a dog bite incident, and often the truth is not only bent, it's stretched beyond feasibility. In the case of Phineas, there was no proof that he had ever bitten anyone, yet that allegation lingered throughout the court proceedings.

This sounds like a sound principle on paper. No previous bite, no problem. Let's say you have a docile dog who's having a bad day and nips the mailman. Your dog never bit anyone before, so you say you're sorry and that's the end of it. Not so fast. Everything legal is often just a "maybe" premise, and this is no different. It seems pretty clear that if your dog hasn't bitten someone, you won't be liable for the first bite. Maybe. Your dog won't be considered

dangerous or vicious in most jurisdictions if she hasn't bitten anyone, but if you "knew or should have known" that your dog had a tendency to be aggressive or bite, you can still be charged with keeping a vicious dog and held responsible for the person's damages. The one-bite rule also only applies to actual bites. So if your dog knocks someone down and you knew she had a tendency to do this, you may be held liable. If you deny being responsible for any injuries the person suffered from the fall, the case most likely will end up in court and the judge or jury will have to decide if you "knew or should have known" your dog would do this. Factors that can be considered to prove you had knowledge of the alleged behavior include:

- Barking at strangers
- Jumping on people
- Threatening people: growling and snapping
- Frightening people: running along the fence and barking at people
- Fighting or lunging at other dogs
- Fight training
- Complaints about your dog
- Beware Of Dog sign

As to notices of a dog on the property, such as the Beware Of Dog sign, this in itself is not an indication that you knew your dog was dangerous. A sign will most likely prevent someone from entering your property and it could prevent bites to a trespasser and the resulting legal nightmare, even though a dog is most often given the benefit of a doubt when biting someone on her owner's own property. On the other hand, a good attorney will do everything possible to show that because you posted the sign it's evidence that you *knew* your dog was aggressive.

Where the bite occurred is also a factor in determining the severity of the punishment and the amount of any fine if applicable. A dog that's loose or "running at large," as the law refers to them, is subject to stricter penalties. In West Virginia, if your dog is running at large and bites someone, you don't get to quarantine her at home for the required ten days. As most statutes refer to them, dogs running at large are dogs that are not controlled by the owner with a leash. Loose dogs receive more severe punishments, which often include euthanasia. Bites that occur on the dog owner's property receive less scrutiny and more lenient consequences, as the dog is presumed to be protecting her territory and not attacking. This is a general presumption and given different weight in deciding the case depending on the circumstances.

A prevalent factor in determining what punishment a dog receives for biting, sometimes even when it's a first bite, is the severity of the victim's injuries. Almost every state gives more stringent punishments for any bite that causes serious injuries. Additionally, in some states a severe injury not only results in a strong punishment, but often is enough to have the dog declared "dangerous" or "vicious" and sentenced to death. The severity of the injury is often assessed by these factors:

1. Medical bills over two thousand dollars
2. If plastic surgery is required
3. Broken bones
4. Length of recovery
5. Permanent scarring or disability

The average dog bite (if there is such a thing) doesn't usually result in injuries this egregious. While writing this chapter, a neighbor's dog bit me, which is the second dog bite I've experienced. Maxi, my neighbor's dog, had previously attacked my dog Sadie while we were walking one evening. Her owner and I separated the dogs and no one was hurt. I liked Maxi and believed she needed more socialization.

The night Maxi decided to bite me I was bringing treats for her to the house. When the front door opened she ran out. I got down to her level with the treats and she bit my arm. I was stunned. Her owner was frantic as he grabbed her and yanked her back in the house. When I got home I was more upset to see that her tooth had put a hole in a favorite jacket, but I did have a small puncture wound. Since I couldn't remember when I'd had a tetanus shot, I went to the local urgent care.

When I told them why I was there, I was given a "Dog Bite Incident Report" to fill out. This is standard at any medical facility that treats a dog bite. I thought nothing of it, got my tetanus shot, and went home. Later I was called by animal control for more information, and my neighbors had to quarantine their dog for ten days.

I could have reported the previous attack on my dog, but I didn't. This dog had a lot of recent trauma in her life. She'd been placed at my neighbors when a relative could no longer care for her. After spending five years with one person who was home all the time, this dog was not used to a busy family that left her alone far too often and never gave her a chance to socialize with people or other dogs. I gave my neighbors the name of a good dog trainer/behaviorist who could address these issues with them. I believe they are spending more time with the dog, and on a recent walk we met up with Maxi and her dog mom. She was calmer and didn't lunge at me or Sadie, but we kept our distance.

Another mitigating factor if your dog bites someone is if she was justified in biting, or in simple terms, maybe the person asked for it. Just like human justification for killing someone to defend and protect your own life (self-defense), there are times when a dog bite is justified. If your dog attacks someone who's attempting to harm you, it's justified. If someone is intentionally harming your dog, hitting her or kicking her, for example, and she bites them, it's justified.

One thing is for sure, as a pet parent you must know the dog bite law in your state and your community. Dog bite laws vary from county to county and sometimes from town to town. Dog law sections in state codes are not usually very long. I advise every pet parent to become familiar with their state law and all county or municipal ordinances that govern dogs in any or all of the following ways:

1. Make a copy of your state code animal law section as well as your city and/or county ordinances and read it, highlight it, memorize it!
2. Gather the names of two or three attorneys or law firms in your area that handle animal cases. If you ever need legal counsel for any issue with your dog, you'll be prepared.
3. Make it a priority to know the state political candidates' views on animal issues in your jurisdiction. We think to question politicians on everything from clean air to health care, yet not about how their voting and background could affect our companion animals.
4. Be active in the local shelter. Know the structure of your county or city animal control division. If you hear of abusive tactics, take action to have them corrected. If you hear of great jobs being done, let them know.
5. Attend county commission or city council meetings when animal issues are on the agenda.

I believe that while I share my life with my dog, it is not an insular existence. While she is part of the great world, what governs her is like a parallel, but separate, universe. Many things

I experienced while writing this book convinced me of this. It's similar to having a loved one move to a foreign country and you just can't understand the customs and laws. You have to "learn to speak the language" of dog law, and the most important laws are the ones governing biting. These are the laws that can inflict the harshest punishment and loss for you and your dog. All dogs will bite in the wrong circumstances. This situation can become a completely different event when presented by an attorney in court. The best solution is keeping your dog from being in a situation where she might bite someone. It sounds impossible, but here are some simple steps that can go a long way to avoid your dog biting someone.

1. Always keep your dog on a leash in public places.
2. Be aware of people, children in particular, approaching your dog. If a child comes quickly toward your dog, place yourself between the child and your dog.
3. Don't take your dog into large crowds or where fireworks and other frightful events are possible.
4. *Never* leave your dog alone tethered to a fence, pole, or other object while in public.
5. Have a fenced yard with gates that can be securely locked from the inside.

Reducing the chance that your dog will be near or around frightening circumstances and people that might provoke her are good starts to preventing dog bites, but an understanding of why dogs bite is imperative. A friend gave me a beautiful poster of a German shepherd and the caption was, "People shouldn't bite." This is true, but people have many choices for expressing fear or reacting to provocation. Dogs do not. They can run away, but when they are provoked, threatened, or frightened they often bite. It's not the end of the world if your dog bites someone; however, it could be the end of your dog's life if you don't respond quickly.

Dogs bite for as many reasons as people lose their tempers. Dog bites account for almost 90 percent of all reported animal bites.[21] Attorney Ken Phillips represents dog bite victims full-time. Dog bite statistics on his website state that between 2001 and 2003 there were four and a half million dog bite victims per year in the United States, according to data collected by the Centers for Disease Control. Considering that approximately seventy-five million dogs live in the United States, that's only about 16 percent of the total number of domestic dogs. Despite horror stories of unleashed pit bulls randomly attacking a child and severely mauling them, this almost never happens. Men are bitten by dogs more than women. (Seems cats prefer to bite women.) The greatest number of dog bite victims are friends, acquaintances, or members of the dog owner's family. Sixty-one percent of dog bites happen at home or a familiar place. A relatively small percentage of bites are inflicted by errant stray dogs. This means that most bites leave surprised pet parents shocked by their loyal canine companions and often wondering whether they can ever trust them again. This is a misconception, because under the right circumstances all dogs will bite. Biting is a normal means of canine protection and defense. Knowing this, I find it surprising that less than 25 percent of the domestic dogs actually bite people each year.

So, why do dogs that have never shown any aggression before bite when it's not justified? We all know what it feels like to be extremely stressed, but we have many ways to express our anxiety. Dogs often bite as an expression of stress or fear. When a dog bites out of stress or fear it's referred to as provocation. A good

---

21. www.dogbitelaw.com/dog-bite-statistics/dog-bite-statistics.

definition of provocation relating to dogs is when a person's action immediately causes a radical change in the dog's behavior.

Below is a list of some of the things that cause dogs to stress and may provoke them to bite.

1. Excessive and out-of-the-ordinary noise. Fireworks and loud music, such as at an outdoor concert, fair, or other event with crowds and noise. Gunshots, backfire from cars, and sirens are also frightening to dogs.
2. Active children whom the dog is not acclimated to, particularly if the child is pulling the dog's ears or trying to take something out of its mouth.
3. New and unfamiliar places, such as hotels. Most hotels that allow dogs require that if you're going to leave the dog in the room you must secure them in a crate and place a tag on your door signaling to the maid a dog is in the room. Some hotels allow room cleaning with a crated dog and some don't. It's foreseeable that a dog would consider a chambermaid a trespasser and bite them.
4. Teasing—a dog will eventually reach a threshold of no patience and bite.
5. Pain from an undiagnosed injury or illness.
6. Stranger invasion of the dog's space by hugging or other touching.
7. Unintentional injury to a dog, such as stepping on its tail or paw.
8. Taking food or toys away from a dog.
9. Startling a sleeping dog.
10. Physical threat or harm to the dog's owner.

Stressors vary widely from dog to dog. Many dogs are fearful of thunderstorms and will quiver and try to hide from the noise. It's imperative that you know your own dog and what triggers stress in him. Adopted dogs may have had terrible experiences before they were rescued. They often carry these memories with them and react to similar situations and people aggressively. I learned this while my dog Sadie was a puppy. As mentioned previously, Sadie has always had a fearful reaction to people limping or those using crutches or in wheelchairs. She also barks furiously and growls at men in ball caps with glasses. I have no idea why, but she will growl, start barking, and then hide behind me.

I'm the only person Sadie has ever bitten and it was very lightly when I attempted to remove a knot in her hair. I know her triggers and how she reacts, so I avoid them as much as possible. You can avoid a potential biting incident if you learn what stresses your dog and protect her from circumstances where this might occur. People need to understand dogs better and realize most biting issues are the result of human behavior and mistakes. Most bites don't signify that the dog can never be trusted again. After a first bite almost all dogs could remain at home and have long, happy, and bite-free lives if their pet parents would learn what causes them to become stressed and do everything possible to reduce it.

In the event that your dog bites someone, here are the steps you should take to make the incident as easy to deal with as possible. If your dog bites someone, it will be a complete shock; however, you must remain calm and take action immediately.

Two things have to be done immediately and almost simultaneously: Make sure the victim is okay, and remove your dog from the scene as quickly as possible. Put her in the house or another room of the house, a crate, or your car if you are at a dog park. See that the victim goes for medical treatment if necessary.

Don't yell at your dog or discipline her. I'm not a dog trainer or behaviorist, but I've learned that getting aggressive or physically punishing your dog if she bites is the wrong thing to do. There are two reasons for this. First of all, aggression creates aggression, and that's the last thing needed in a biting situation. Secondly, you don't want the victim to get the impression that this is common behavior for your dog or that you are blaming your dog. This sounds like legal advice because it is; don't admit guilt on any level. Sympathy and expressions of comfort are fine, but say nothing that will indicate guilt or responsibility.

If the victim is a stranger, exchange information. If there are witnesses, get their names and contact information. Take pictures of the victim's injuries with your cell phone. Even if you won't be liable for their medical bills, offer to pay for any medical expenses. This is not an admission of liability, but it goes a long way to prevent any thoughts of a lawsuit immediately. This is particularly important if the bite is superficial.

Don't blame the victim even if the bite was the result of a clearly egregious act from the victim. Why? You simply don't want to aggravate the situation. Everyone has heard the warning given to criminals from watching movies and television: "Anything you say can and will be used against you in a court of law." This is true. It's better to keep your remarks conciliatory and neutral during the aftermath of the bite. If someone is at fault, there will be a time and place to make that known. Keeping calm, rational, and nonjudgmental can make a dog bite episode much easier to deal with.

Tell the victim that your dog is up to date on his rabies vaccination. There should be a tag issued by the county or municipality on your dog's collar that shows this.

If this happened on your property, put your homeowner's insurance on notice. If the victim goes to a doctor's office or the emergency room, they'll have to fill out a report that will be sent to your local police department and animal control. I advise clients to inform the authorities before they get the report. Sometimes the police are called to the scene by the victim or a bystander.

In that case, be cooperative and provide your information and a statement of what happened.

In every state, you'll be required to quarantine your dog for a period of time. This is commonly from ten to fourteen days even if your dog's rabies vaccination is current. If your dog is not currently vaccinated for rabies, the confinement period can be up to six months. Where and who supervises the quarantine varies from state to state. In West Virginia, the owner is permitted to quarantine the dog at home if it's a first bite, she was not running at large, and she has been vaccinated. The owner is also allowed to quarantine the dog at home if she wasn't vaccinated, but must do so for six months. However, if the owner doesn't want to quarantine the dog at home, for whatever reason, or any of the other conditions apply, the dog must be quarantined at a licensed veterinarian, not the local shelter. The veterinarian is permitted to charge the owner a reasonable fee for boarding.[22]

The law in your state will determine where the dog will be housed during the quarantine and who will monitor her. Local ordinances are sometimes different than the state law, so make sure you know what applies to where you live. Know your rights concerning this. This is important because local rules vary and local favoritism and bias can play more of a role in dog bite cases than the law allows.

For example, we have a case in West Virginia where the local animal control officer, who also happened to be the director of the shelter, immediately seized a dog from owners when a bite occurred. The dog had never bitten before. The dog was not running at large. A neighbor child had entered the yard uninvited and went straight to the dog and tried to take a ball out of her mouth. The dog jumped up to get the toy, which resulted in an

---

22. West Virginia Code § 19-20-9a(c). ˙

injury to the child's lip that required seven stitches. The animal control officer came to the dog's home the next day, threatened the owners, and took the dog. Not knowing their rights or the law, the owners were helpless.

The dog was kept at the local shelter in an outside kennel not for the required ten days, but for twenty-nine days. It wasn't until local animal advocates, attorneys, and veterinarians intervened that the dog was released. The local prosecutor reached an agreement with the family's attorney that the dog had to stay in the jurisdiction until the owner was served with a criminal complaint for harboring a dangerous dog and the case was decided in court. Before the animal control officer would release the dog, the owners had to pay two hundred dollars for the "boarding fee." Even though West Virginia law only allows a veterinarian to charge a rate of fifteen dollars a day for boarding when the owner refuses to quarantine an unvaccinated dog, these desperate pet parents paid it. This case is discussed in detail in chapter 8, as the illegal seizure in the "Tinkerbelle case," as it became known, was only the beginning of a long court battle that garnered national publicity and is being cited in jurisdictions across the country in dog bite cases.

Throughout any dog bite incident, you must remain calm. After all information is exchanged and the victim and witnesses are gone, contact your veterinarian for your dog's current medical records. You might need these. If all indications are that the victim is going to sue you or insist that your dog be euthanized, contact a lawyer immediately.

Be prepared to at least cover all medical expenses incurred by the victim. Additionally, they may claim lost wages for any time away from work or expenses for services needed in relation to their injury, such as housekeeping or lawn services. Get copies of invoices for anything you're asked to pay for, as well as receipts signed by the victim. It's always better if you can work this out between both parties and end up with an executed release of all future claims from the victim. In order to do this you might need an attorney to negotiate the release and any claims that seem outrageous. The victim can sue you in civil court, but unless criminal charges have been filed, the damages should be limited to the actual costs from the incident.

Criminal charges might be filed against you for any number of reasons that are set forth in your state code. The most common one from a dog bite incident, as in the Phineas and Tinkerbelle cases, is "harboring a dangerous dog." The burden of proof is on the plaintiff (victim) to prove each and every part of your state's criminal code specifications about your dog.

The worst result of a criminal case is if a court orders that your dog must be euthanized. Appeal this decision until you can no longer appeal it. Remember Phineas and the ultimate vindication that brought him back to his family. Think of Tinkerbelle and the long wait to get her freedom. Trust the system and a good lawyer.

There are many considerations after your dog has bitten someone even after all the legal issues have been resolved. You may feel uneasy about your dog and unsure if you'll ever feel at ease with her again. Each case is as individual as the dog, the dog's family, and the community where you live. In the West Virginia incident mentioned previously, where a first-bite dog was illegally seized then sentenced to death, that family knows without a doubt that their dog will be a target of animal control officers and local law enforcement as long as she lives there. They steadfastly worked with their attorney preparing for the appeal, knowing they would most likely not get her back home, as they were more concerned for her safety. She was returned to her rescue, a much different dog after the entire time in a shelter, but will eventually find a new home and put this behind her. This might be the best option in many cases where local bias is prevalent against certain breeds.

The Sanders, who owned Phineas, chose to move after the ordeal and took Phineas with them. This happens much more than you'd think. Things change after your dog bites someone, and most often it's not for the best. People have strong opinions and align with one side or the other, which can make things difficult for the dog's family. If your situation ended up in court and you prevailed, it's not uncommon for local law enforcement or animal control officers to feel that their authority was usurped and many pet parents, like the Sanders, to feel on edge.

You have difficult decisions to make following a dog bite. Find ways to manage your dog's behavior so she doesn't have the opportunity to bite again. Analyze what happened and consult a dog trainer/behaviorist for assistance in modifying stressful situations and triggers for your dog. Modifying your dog's reaction to situations that cause her to be aggressive is not a simple task and requires a long-term commitment.

Pet parents often feel that they can't take the risk of a dog bite happening again and they re-home the dog. This isn't as easy as it sounds. There are literally millions of dogs that have never bitten that need homes, which greatly reduces the chance you can successfully find a good home for your dog. Many rescue groups won't accept dogs that have a biting history, and shelters that will take them often euthanize them.

If your dog is young enough, one option is to place her in a training program that will accept a dog that's bitten, such as government programs for drug- or bomb-sniffing dogs, law enforcement K-9 units, or cadaver search dogs. Relatively few dogs can't be rehabilitated after a first bite when pet parents successfully make their dog's world one that is comfortable and easy to tolerate, thus eliminating the possibility of a second bite.

No matter what the outcome, and in almost every jurisdiction, once your dog has a record of a first bite, if she bites again she has a slim chance of escaping the dangerous-dog designation. If your dog ever bites again, she will be subject to higher penalties under statutes applicable to dangerous dogs. That first bite is never really forgiven and sets the stage for severe consequences should it happen again. Sometimes, despite the bite being the first time the dog has bitten, or the bite not classified as severe, things can get out of control and elevate even a first bite to a tragic situation in many jurisdictions. In Manatee County, Florida, this was heart-breakingly proven true in March of 2014.

Karen Erskine is a nationally known dog trainer. In December 2012, she was visiting a friend in Florida with her two Australian shepherds, Buck and Bill. While Karen and her friend were out, someone broke into the house, which frightened the dogs and they escaped. Witness reports of what happened next were varied, but one or both dogs bit a thirteen-year-old boy on his bicycle. Local law enforcement was called to the scene and they entered the house without a search warrant, a seizure warrant, or even a probable cause warrant and seized the dogs.

The dogs were held at the Manatee County Animal Shelter for four hundred and four days. A protracted and heated legal battle ensued that gained national attention and thousands of supporters on social media. The Lexus Project got involved, but in the end the county killed Buck and Bill even though they had never bitten before, there were exigent circumstances that caused their behavior, and whether the victim's injuries were "serious" was never ruled on.

But what happens if your dog is bitten? Do you have the right to exercise the same legal options on behalf of your dog as a two-legged victim? Yes, in almost every state you do. Since dogs are still mainly classified as property in the American justice system, you have the right to sue the owner of a dog that attacks and harms your dog, just as you would for the destruction of any other piece of property. These cases are usually brought into small claims court, where the value of damages is typically limited to five thousand dollars. Here's a list of what you can recover for:

- Veterinary bills and any other damages to your personal property destroyed.
- The original amount you paid for your dog if your dog is killed or must be euthanized.
- Medical bills for injuries you suffer while protecting your dog.
- You can seek emotional damages, although recovery is not a certainty.
- You can ask for punitive damages if the owner was aware of these propensities in their dog.

If the attacking dog is already listed as a dangerous dog, the owner may be charged criminally with harboring an aggressive dog and be ordered by the court to pay restitution to you without filing a civil lawsuit. The attacking dog's owner may also be charged with other violations of local and/or state law, such as leash laws.

Insurance of one kind or another usually pays the awards plaintiffs win in court for car accidents, property damage, and other tort claims. While getting veterinary coverage insurance is commonplace, insurance companies are not so quick to cover damages caused by dogs for tangible property damage, such as damage to a rental property, or any injuries caused by dog bites. More than one-third of all homeowner claims paid in 2014 were for dog bites, according to the Insurance Information Institute. Many insurance companies actively pursue ways to deny these claims by refusing to sell insurance to homeowners with dogs, refusing insurance to homeowners with dogs included in breed-specific legislation, or writing an exclusion of coverage for dog bites. This trend is detrimental to homeowners who are dog owners, as well as the victims of dog bites. Victims can't recover from a person who doesn't have the money to pay them. Potential homeowners can't get a mortgage if they can't get insurance to cover the home, and the reason for denial is often the dog.

Some insurance companies will cover dogs included in BSL by charging a higher premium. They'll ask a series of questions similar to what you provide concerning your driving history for automobile insurance. Just as the rate increases with the number of driving infractions, it increases with dog bite incidents. Some insurance companies offer a discount if you can show proof that your dog has had behavior modification training.

I called Allstate to query about homeowner's insurance with my dog Sadie. I asked the customer representative if Allstate would write homeowner's policies for any type of dog. He told me no, and said that they excluded pit bulls, rottweilers, Doberman pinchers, Siberian huskies, Akitas, and many terriers. He asked me what kind of dog I had, and I told him she was a shepherd mix. He thought this over for a minute and asked me what kind of mix and I explained that Sadie had a cocker spaniel mom and a German shepherd dad. I could hear the computer keys clicking, and after a few seconds he told me that Allstate would be happy to write a policy including Sadie because German shepherds and cocker spaniels were not excluded. An Internet search or a phone call can answer all your questions about protecting your pooch's potential problems with insurance.

Pet parents can also purchase an umbrella policy, which is a separate policy that covers things excluded in your main policy. There are insurance companies that offer canine liability policies that are written for the sole purpose of insuring dogs for damages caused by them, such as injuries and other losses. The Federation of Insured Dog Owners is a relatively new organization that offers these policies for *any* breed of dog. It's no mistake that the company's acronym is FIDO. Policies start as low as seventy-five dollars per year per dog plus a membership fee. This unique company was started by dog lover Deborah Turner and is available in California, Florida, Iowa, Michigan, New Hampshire, North Carolina, Pennsylvania, Utah, and Wisconsin. They do not discriminate against any breed, realizing that it's the *behavior* not the *breed* that factors into dog bites. The website www.dogbitequote.com has great information for pet parents and information about the policies, which offer coverage up to seventy-five thousand dollars.

A dog bite is a serious and often life-changing experience. We live in a society ready to file a lawsuit for the slightest reason, and dog bites are no exception. It doesn't have to be the end of your world or your dog's life, though. Make sure you know the laws in your state and any local ordinances. Take the precautions described in this chapter and other sources. Socialize your dog and your chances of getting sued for a biting incident are greatly reduced.

Dog biting is not the only reason dogs end up as defendants in court. Canines commit "crimes" unknowingly, despite the best efforts of the pet parents, and often it's right in your own hometown. What happens if your dog ends up in the legal doghouse? Will your dog need a lawyer?

While your dog rules in your world, cities and counties have numerous dog rules in the form of ordinances and laws that you must know and keep your dog from violating. Kelly and John Anderson found themselves facing this predicament, and that's how I wound up in court in Charleston, West Virginia, defending three of the sweetest beagles I'd ever met.

Chapter 8

CANINES IN COURT
(Running Afoul of the Law)

When you're a sole practitioner lawyer, you usually have to take any case that comes through the door just to keep your practice going. However, when I opened the door and three beagles and two people walked in, I had my doubts. The Andersons' dogs had been charged with a canine crime, and they were positive the dogs weren't guilty. They arrived home to find a summons stuck in their front door detailing the charges against their dogs, and that's what brought them to my door. Their crime: excessive barking after 11 p.m. during the City of Charleston's mandatory reduced noise level, an infraction of City of Charleston Code Section 10-6-Animal Nuisances.

It shall be unlawful to own any animal, including a dog or cat, in a residentially zoned district, which by frequent or long-continued noise shall disturb the comfort or repose of any person within the vicinity of such animal, or shall by the nature of their maintenance or by the numbers of the same create an offensive odor so as to be objectionable to surrounding residences. The

*provisions of this section are to be interpreted consistently with
any city noise ordinance.*

A neighbor two houses down accused the beagles of barking
continuously during the night when she was trying to sleep. She also
claimed that they barked when she came home for lunch during the
day and the Andersons weren't home. A Charleston animal control
officer was assigned to her complaint. He took notes, listened to
her lengthy recriminations against the beagles, and went to the
Andersons' house to meet them. They discussed the situation and
explained that this neighbor complained about everything on their
small residential street, including kids and people having parties
that caused excess cars to be parked on the street.

The Andersons took the animal control offer to the backyard
to meet the dogs and they didn't even bark when he invaded their
territory. The Andersons pointed out that the dogs didn't spend
nights in the backyard, so it would be impossible for the neighbor
to hear them barking since they slept in the family room. He
assured the Andersons they had nothing to worry about and told
them he'd get back to them when he finished his investigation.

Over the next several weeks, the officer went to the Andersons'
street at all hours of the night and day. He sat in his van and listened.
He had a tape recorder with a time stamp feature ready to record the
boisterous beagles. He interviewed homeowners on all sides of the
Andersons' home, including the person between the Andersons and
their accuser. They said they never heard the dogs. The complaining
neighbor kept calling the police department demanding that something be done. The officer listened more carefully, cruising the street
before, during, and after his shift. He heard nothing. No barking. No
whining. No noises of any sort coming from the Andersons' backyard.

Finally, he went to report to the neighbor, who had logged
dozens of calls to the police department by this time. He told

her he found no evidence of the dogs barking during the noise ordinance time, and, in fact, he'd never heard the dogs bark at all. Beagles are not generally known to be quiet dogs, but these dogs were the exception.

The neighbor was livid. She made threats and promises of retaliation to the officer and the city if he didn't give a citation to the Andersons. So, as ridiculous as it sounds, the officer caved in and wrote a summons to the family's dogs for excessive barking in violation of the statute cited above. However, on the back of the ticket he wrote: "I found no evidence of these dogs excessively barking or actually barking at any time. However, in deference to the complainant's many calls to the police department and other city departments, I am issuing this citation so the matter might be decided in court."

I'd never handled a case like this and decided to approach it like any other case by presenting the best evidence possible in court, and that would be the beagles. After my initial meeting with the Andersons, I went to meet the beagles. Just as the animal control officer had reported, they didn't bark at me. I found them to be sweet and loving as well as very quiet.

Not satisfied, I did my own surveillance to see if the beagles were barking. I even walked up to the fence one afternoon and they sniffed at me and wagged their tails, but they didn't bark. I drove around the neighborhood to see if some other dogs were perhaps the culprits and the neighbor was mistaken as to where the barking was coming from. I didn't find any other dogs outside on that day and could only assume that if there were any other dogs on the short street, they too must stay in the house at night.

About three months after the Andersons first came to see me, they met me at city court for our hearing with the beagles in tow, as I'd requested. City Court is a confusing melee even on the best days. Police officers, defendants, witnesses, plaintiffs, and lawyers were all crowding to get through the security screening. In the midst of all the chaos the three beagles remained calm. Tails wagging, they were taking it all in, but they weren't barking despite the circumstances they had been thrust into.

No one was used to seeing dogs in city court, so they were getting a lot of attention. In fact, it was enough to make the city judge take note. She began sorting through all the case files on her bench until she came to ours. She called me up to the front of the courtroom and asked me why I had three dogs in court. I told her they were my best evidence and would be witnesses to speak on their own behalf, which brought laughter from the crowded gallery. I went back to stand against the wall with the Andersons and the silent beagles.

When it was our turn, I called the animal control officer to the stand first and questioned him about his investigation: what he discovered about the beagles barking, and what the note on the back of the summons meant. Through it all, the dogs remained silent.

At the conclusion of his testimony, I asked the court to take notice of the three dogs accused of this crime and that not one yip had been heard from them during the entire proceeding.

I then asked that the case be dismissed for lack of evidence, in particular that there was no barking from the dogs in this extreme situation, where most dogs would be frightened, yet they remained calm *and* quiet. The judge agreed and the case was dismissed.

As with anyone wrongfully accused, the Andersons subsequently brought a civil suit against the complainant for their damages, which included my fee and lost wages from work for meetings and court. You are almost always entitled to attorney's fees in a civil case you win, and it's no different if your dogs are wrongfully accused.

This was my first experience in court concerning dogs, and it was an easy case. The difficult ones are when the outcome can mean life or death for your dog. Simple noise ordinance violations are a nuisance, but the penalties are usually small and don't end in a criminal record for the pet parent.

There are five levels of laws in every state that govern the behavior of dogs and subsequently the lives of their pet parents:

- **Federal**—The predominant law is the Animal Welfare Act (AWA), however, it doesn't apply to companion animals. It sets forth the minimum standards of care and treatment for certain animals bred for commercial sale, transported commercially, or exhibited to the public. The AWA also sets regulations for animals used in research and testing. Wholesale breeders, dealers, exhibitors, and research labs are covered, but not small retail breeders and pet shops selling only domestic pet animals.
- **State Legislation**—These are laws that cover the entire state in a general sense, because other political subdivisions are often allowed to amend them as long as their local laws don't change the general purpose of the state code.

- **County Ordinances**—These countywide laws are usually created by the county commission, which is made up of elected citizens who reside in the county.
- **Municipal Ordinances**—These laws apply to a particular city and are not applicable to property located outside the city limits. They originate with the city council and are often on the local ballot during elections for citizen approval.
- **Homeowner's Association** (HOA)—While HOA rules don't carry criminal penalties unless it's a law in effect by one of the above entities, you can be fined by your HOA if you break their rules concerning dogs. HOAs are not permitted to write rules that exempt homeowners from any other laws or ordinances in the state that cover dogs.

So what's a pet parent to do if a state law has different requirements or standards from their local laws and they seem in conflict? In legal terms, this situation is called "preemption," which means a higher law has precedence over a lower local law. If the two laws are not in conflict, there's no problem and both laws must be followed. If, however, the lower law tries to regulate something the higher state law already regulates, then the lower law has been preempted and you must follow the state law. State laws usually give great deference or authority to local units to regulate dogs. But laws that deal with complex and far-reaching issues, such as rabies quarantines and dangerous dogs, may be exclusively up to the state to regulate. Your local government may be able to help you sort out the conflict in laws. If following the lower law has led to further problems for you or if you feel following the local law may contradict the state law, consult an attorney. An argument of preemption may help to invalidate a local law that stretches the municipality's authority to regulate. This is more common than you'd think, as local authorities often pass laws after a specific incident in their jurisdiction that

©DAVID VOISARD '16

are much more restrictive than a higher law's restrictions, which tend to be broader.

Local ordinances and state laws dealing with dogs attempt to strike a balance between protecting people and respecting owners' rights. On each level, except for federal law, you as a pet parent have a voice in whether these laws get passed or voted down by lobbying or making your opinions known in public meetings, such as city council or county commission meetings.

As pet parents you must pay attention to the agendas of your state legislature, county commission, and city council. Ask candidates if they have a dog and what their views are on issues affecting dogs in your community. You can also contact your representative in any of these government agencies as well as attend your annual HOA meeting and make your opinions known. Social media is an excellent way to get the word out about pending legislation, and as a pet parent it's important to be informed and active in any animal legislation issues. Pet parents must become involved to ensure that local governments create ordinances that attempt to meet the needs of all its citizens, four-legged and two-legged.

The large national animal welfare organizations, including the Humane Society of the United States, the Society for the Prevention of Cruelty to Animals, the American Society for the Prevention of Cruelty to Animals, the American Humane Association, the Animal Legal Defense Fund, and others, are actively involved in tracking legislation and getting important laws passed. They have representatives who will assist you in getting laws passed to protect animals and can be contacted on their websites. The Humane Society of the United States has a state director in almost every state, who is there to assist the public in animal issues.

State laws cover many items and are located in each state's code, and as noted previously, these can be found online on your state's website. All state codes cover criminal animal abuse and neglect, setting forth the penalties and the conditions that denote abuse and neglect. Mandatory spay and neutering laws are usually at the state level and apply to the entire state.

Rabies vaccination is a state law in every jurisdiction. It's also used on the local level as a requirement for licenses, boarding in a kennel, using public dog parks, and a myriad of other things.

Abuse and neglect, dog bites, killing dogs, hoarding, and other state statutes impose criminal sanctions on pet parents on the state level. Each state differs, so make sure you're familiar with the ones in your state.

State laws also regulate dogs riding in vehicles. The most common is prohibition of dogs riding in the back of an open pickup truck. Not only is it dangerous, it's illegal in many states. According to the Humane Society of the United States, nationwide, approximately one hundred thousand dogs are killed each year because they jump or are thrown from the truck in an accident. California and New Hampshire have statewide statutes restricting or banning dogs in the back of trucks. Similar statutes are also in effect on a local level in Miami, Florida; Dade County, Florida; Indianapolis, Indiana; and Cheyenne, Wyoming.

Louisiana Governor Bobby Jindal vetoed a bill that would have made it illegal for an unrestrained animal to ride in the back of a pickup truck on interstates and highways. His reason for the decision was that he didn't feel it was necessary to explicitly state this within the state's animal welfare legislation.

At least eight states have laws requiring owners to kennel or tether dogs or other animals that ride in a vehicle's open areas, usually a truck bed. States with restraint laws include Connecticut, California, New Hampshire, Massachusetts, Nevada, Washington, Oregon, and Rhode Island. Fines range from fifty dollars to two hundred dollars.

In 2009, the Maryland Legislature failed to pass a bill banning dogs from riding in the back of pickup trucks due to strong lobbying from farming organizations.

Many local and state governments regulate how dogs can be carried in pickup beds instead of making it completely illegal. California, for example, requires dogs in the open back of a pickup to be either in a cage or cross-tied to the truck unless the sides of the truck are at least forty-six inches high. The laws don't apply to cattle or sheepdogs being used by farmers and ranchers. Violators can be fined fifty dollars to one hundred dollars for a first offense and up to two hundred and fifty dollars for a third offense.[23]

The majority of states have implemented mandatory spay and neuter laws to address the overpopulation of homeless animals.

23. Cal. Veh. Code 23117, 42001.4; N.H. Rev. Stat. Ann 644:8-f.

County shelters across the nation are overburdened with unwanted animals. The goal is to decrease the number of unwanted animals that become homeless and create overcrowding in shelters, decrease the risk to public health and safety, and reduce the cost to local governments for impounding and destroying animals. Violations are punishable both civilly and criminally, with fines being the most common penalty for not complying with the sterilization requirement.

Mandatory spay/neuter laws are predominately set by state legislatures, although city councils and county commissions in some areas also have local laws. These laws require that you spay or neuter your dog within a certain period of time or qualify for one of the exceptions.

States with mandatory spay/neuter laws have a much lower population of unwanted animals. Most laws set affordable spay/neuter fees at designated clinics, making it easier for pet parents to comply with the laws. Exceptions to the mandatory sterilization are available in most jurisdictions for a variety of reasons.

One such exception is in the San Mateo, California, city ordinance that requires all dogs and cats over six months old to be spayed or neutered unless the owner buys a permit allowing an animal to be kept unaltered. Before an unaltered animal permit is issued, the owner must sign a statement promising that the animal will not be allowed to breed until a breeding permit is issued. Violators can be fined one hundred dollars for a first offense and up to five hundred dollars for subsequent offenses.[24]

If you live in a state that has a mandatory spay/neuter law, you must get your dog spayed or neutered according to the specific requirements of the law or face civil and/or criminal prosecution and fines. If you adopt an animal in one of the thirty-four states

---

24. San Mateo County Ord. Code 6.12.030.

that have mandatory spay/neuter laws, the shelter or rescue is required to provide for the sterilization of all animals they transfer or adopt out so your dog will be compliant with the law when you bring her home.

In Oklahoma, failing to have an animal sterilized is considered to be either a public or a private nuisance.[25] So, an unneutered dog in Oklahoma will get the owner a fine and potentially a civil lawsuit from a neighbor, which can include veterinary bills and other costs, should Rover become the father of the neighbor dog's puppies. Additionally, the pet parent can be charged with a crime and fined.

Approximately seven states consider the failure to have a dog or cat sterilized to be a misdemeanor. A fine is the usual penalty, but Louisiana may impose a sentence of up to thirty days imprisonment. The fines vary widely, ranging from twenty-five dollars to five hundred dollars, and may include the cost of prosecution, enforcement, and court costs.

Some states, such as Rhode Island and New Jersey, increase the fine for each subsequent violation. Also in Rhode Island, the fines for agencies and organizations, often called "releasing" agencies, such as shelters or rescues, range from fifty dollars to five hundred dollars per violation. Upon conviction of three or more offenses, they can have their license to operate temporarily or permanently revoked.

Here is an example of what consequences can occur when you live in a jurisdiction with a mandatory spay/neuter law and you decide to ignore the law. Let's say your neighbor's dog, which they have a breeding permit for, turns up with seven puppies and at least half of them coincidently look like your unneutered dog. The

---

25. Oklahoma Statutes Annotated Title 4: Animals. Chapter 3. Dogs and Cats. §499.10.

neighbors aren't happy and they let you know by suing you. What are the chances of the neighbors winning? They're actually pretty good. First of all, your dog broke the law by running at large, and you broke the law by not having your dog neutered.

There's a phrase used in legal actions saying you must come before the court with "clean hands," or in this case "clean paws." This means you can't have done something wrong and then want to sue someone or even try to defend yourself even though you're deemed innocent until proven guilty. If the neighbor had let their dog roam free, they would not have "clean hands," and this fact could be used in your defense. Additionally, if the neighbor dog had not had a breeding permit, again, they would not have "clean hands" and would also be subject to legal penalties. If your dog had been cited before for running at large, you would not have "clean hands," and this could be used in their defense. In both cases, neither dog would have "clean paws," and its actions can be used against it. What are your defenses in a case like this?

First of all, you have no defense against the violation of the mandatory spay/neuter law unless you had an exception. For the purposes of this contrived example, we'll assume you had no exception. You'd be found guilty of violating the law and in this mythical jurisdiction your fine is five hundred dollars, plus you must get your dog neutered and pay for the procedure.

Additionally, you're charged with a misdemeanor crime of "dog running at large." Unless you can prove the neighbor's dog came into your yard, you'll be found guilty of this as well. The fine for this crime is also five hundred dollars, since your dog has been charged before.

Now, what about the neighbor? They too will be charged with violation of the mandatory spay/neuter law unless they had an exception. For this example, they do have an exception.

They applied for and received a breeding permit for their pure-bred cocker spaniel who now has a litter of puppies that are half German shepherd. The neighbors don't get charged with breaking the law, nor do they get fined.

The civil suit comes to court and you really have no defense. During discovery (the period of time in a lawsuit for investigation before trial) the neighbors' attorney asked for an order to take a DNA sample from your dog. Think of it as a "pawternity" determination test. (Yes, canine CSI is alive and well in our courts today!) It proved conclusively that your dog is the father of the puppies. You lose, and the neighbor is awarded damages, which include veterinary costs for their dog, care and expenses for the puppies, and loss of future earnings from the sale of purebred cocker spaniel puppies because their dog had a difficult time giving birth to these puppies, will never be able to have any more, and is now spayed. Your neighbor asked for and was awarded punitive damages as well. You are now facing several thousand dollars in damages awarded to your neighbor.

This isn't as far-fetched as it sounds. In almost every jurisdiction, if the female dog was on her own property in compliance with the state's law for female dogs' confinement during heat, you'd be liable. In some states female dogs in heat are considered "attractive nuisances." An attractive nuisance can be anything that is enticing to a person to see closer and is not properly safe-guarded. A swimming pool is an attractive nuisance, and in most states must be surrounded by a locking fence. States that deem female dogs in heat as an attractive nuisance have laws stating they must be contained indoors. If you live in one of those states and break this law, you will be fined.

County commissions promulgate a great number of ordinances that apply throughout the entire county and all the cities within that county. Depending on the state, individual cities may write exceptions, usually limited only to making the law more stringent for their individual city. That ordinance will apply only within that city's boundaries.

Municipalities' ordinances cover very specific items, such as behavior in dog parks, picking up your dog's waste, barking, fencing, tethering, leash laws, the number of dogs you can own, rabies vaccination, reporting dog bites, which breeds aren't allowed inside city limits, license requirements and any taxes imposed on dogs, public areas where dogs are prohibited, selling dogs in public, owner liability for damage or harm caused by their dog, and many other laws.

There are definitely crossover regulations on each level of dog law ordinances, which makes it even more important for pet parents to know all the laws in their area. For example, if your city has breed-specific legislation, it might only apply within the city limits. Also, it's rare to have a noise ordinance, let alone any regulation that relates to dogs barking in areas outside the city limits.

Most dog laws are enforced and investigated by the animal control officer for the jurisdiction where the infraction occurs. In some jurisdictions there are ample officers, but more often than not there aren't sufficient numbers for rigorous enforcement of all the incidents involving animals in their area to be dealt with adequately. This is no excuse for not knowing and obeying the law. So, what is a pet parent to do if their dog is charged with a crime and, like the Andersons, they know she is innocent?

Depending on the severity of the punishment, pet parents might want to start by consulting a lawyer experienced in animal matters. Most dog crimes that are infractions of ordinances are misdemeanors with minimal fines; however, if a subsequent violation of the same law brings stiffer penalties, it's important to fight for exoneration of your dog. You *must* contact a lawyer if the charge against your dog calls for her to be impounded or she was seized when the incident occurred.

Many pet parents don't know the laws pertaining to seizure of their dogs. In a panic state after your dog is charged with breaking a law, pet parents are scared and feel they must comply with the law and what the animal control officer or the police officer tells them they must do. This is not always true. Many states don't even call for seizure of a dog after a biting incident, let alone for barking or running at large. When dogs are running at large they are often taken to the shelter, but are quickly returned to their owners if they have a microchip or collar with identification. Before you let anyone take your dog off to a shelter where you have no idea what conditions she'll be held under, make the officer show you where it's in the law. Overzealous animal control officers may pick up dogs that are not subject to confinement. Your dog could remain locked up for the weekend and there would be nothing you could do. This is one of the dangers of dogs getting free from leashes and out of yards without collars or microchips.

More likely than not, when you do retrieve your dog, she'll be dirty, frightened, and hungry. Can you recover from the city or county for its wrongful "arrest" of your innocent dog? Probably not. The law acknowledges only injury to you, not your dog, but if your dog becomes sick or is injured because of the wrongful stay at the animal shelter, you may be able to sue successfully.

You have a chance of winning a lawsuit against the city or county only if the shelter was wrong to pick up your dog or kept it after you tried to bail it out. If your dog just got caught running around unleashed and the shelter didn't break any of its own rules about notifying you or releasing the dog when you paid your fine, you've got nothing, legally, to complain about.

The case of Tinkerbelle has had far-reaching consequences as more than just a dog bite case. This case is also an example of illegal seizure, where the dog was illegally seized after an alleged biting incident. Our statute requires the *owner* quarantine the dog for the ten-day period. If the owner doesn't want to keep the dog at home for this, then our statute says a veterinary office will be asked to hold the dog and they may charge fifteen dollars per day. However, in this particular county, they seized the dog and then charged the owners two hundred dollars to get the dog out. The shelter held the dog much longer than the statute required, but only charged for ten days.

The owner was charged criminally for harboring a vicious dog. It's a misdemeanor, but if the owner is found guilty and the dog is declared vicious, the court may order the dog to be euthanized by the animal control officer.[26] In this case, the owner was found not guilty and the dog not vicious. A pit bull mix, she'd never been aggressive or bitten anyone before. That should be the end of the story, but it isn't.

The prosecutor of this particular county for unknown reasons decided to bring a separate action to have the dog destroyed. Despite having no evidence, and I mean *none* at all, the judge ordered the dog to be killed. Once again, the dog was seized and languished in the shelter for almost a year before the appeal could be heard in the state supreme court.

Despite a clear West Virginia Supreme Court ruling in Docket No. 11-0745, *Durham* v. *Jenkins*, that demands "satisfactory proof," Tinkerbelle remained a prisoner. Even the animal control officer stated on television that he didn't find the dog "aggressive." (He was fired shortly after that.) Tinkerbelle was in peril of losing her life. One of the rumored reasons for the decision to kill Tinkerbelle was that the victim's family didn't want her in the community anymore, even though their child was a trespasser on

---

26. West Virginia Code §19–20–20.

Tinkerbelle's property when the alleged bite occurred. Everyone was perplexed, as dozens of people from across the country and as far away as Australia offered to adopt Tinkerbelle, but neither the prosecutor nor the judge would consider it.

The appeal was heard before the West Virginia Supreme Court of Appeals on May 12, 2001, to a courtroom packed with animal advocates, including me. When the decision came down later that summer, I got a call from the lawyer who had presented the argument—Tinkerbelle was saved! The court had reversed the county court's decision in a three-to-two vote. Later that day, Tinkerbelle was released from the county shelter and the most amazing scene was captured by local media. The shelter workers cried as they kissed her good-bye. This was one dog who should never have been seized, let alone kept prisoner for almost a year.

There are thousands of cases like this. Local politics play a big role in the administration of justice in some jurisdictions. Personal prejudices are carried over into political positions with power, and sadly they're often directed against dogs. A good animal law attorney will be priceless if your dog is charged with a canine crime in a jurisdiction where this kind of behavior is prevalent. A lawyer can appeal unjust decisions and get the attention of the media when laws are applied unfairly.

Many people, particularly in rural areas, think nothing of chaining/tethering a dog outside in all weather conditions, with no reprieve from the confines of the chain. Thirty-three states have laws that prohibit chaining, including two jurisdictions in Arkansas; one in Arizona; six in Florida; eight in Georgia; New Orleans, Louisiana; two in Missouri; three in North Carolina; one in Ohio; one in Oklahoma; eight in Texas; and Kanawha County, West Virginia, where Sadie and I live.

Dozens of other communities limit chaining by the amount of time a dog must be off the chain and other conditions, such as the length and weight of the chain, as well as access to food, water, and shelter. Some jurisdictions require the use of a trolley on a line so the dog has more freedom to move about, and the use of a swivel so the dog won't get tangled in the chain. Violations for tethering include fines ranging from fifty dollars to five hundred dollars, depending on the jurisdiction and if there were previous violations. Criminal sanctions often apply and are misdemeanors. If chaining a dog results in serious injury or death, it's a felony and the penalty may include jail time.

Just like you'll get a ticket for driving without a license, your dog can get one for walking on a public street without a license. She can actually get a ticket for being anywhere without a license. The law requires that you get a license for your dog and that your dog wears the license at all times. Here are five good reasons to get your dog licensed.

1. It's the law.
2. If your dog is lost, having a license greatly improves your chances of getting her back.
3. The cost of the license is less than the penalty for being cited for having an unlicensed dog. In some cities it's a misdemeanor criminal penalty as well.
4. A license is verification that your dog is up to date on her rabies vaccination.
5. License fees help fund local shelters.

Licenses generally cost from five dollars to twenty dollars, depending on where you live. Charging higher license fees for unspayed/unneutered dogs is common in all states that have a mandatory spay/neuter law. Some cities require special licenses for certain dogs, such as guard dogs, and charge a slightly higher fee. The licenses in New York City, as in all other jurisdictions, must be renewed every year. In King County, Washington, for example, licenses for unaltered animals cost sixty dollars, but owners also get a twenty-five-dollar voucher, accepted by most local veterinarians, toward the cost of spaying or neutering. You can get a reduced license fee if any of the following factors apply:

- Disabled or older people are sometimes given free dog licenses. Free licenses may be limited to dogs that have been spayed or neutered. Some cities also require that household income be below a certain amount.
- You may be able to buy a "lifetime license," valid for the dog's lifetime, not yours. Pennsylvania makes such licenses available if the dog has some kind of permanent identification, such as a tattoo or microchip.
- If you have a lot of dogs, you may be able to (or be required to) get a kennel license that covers all of the dogs—a sort of volume discount.
- Licenses for specially trained guide, signal, or service dogs are usually free.

You'll be required to provide some type of documentation that makes you eligible for the discount you're seeking, such as vet records for vaccinations, microchip information, or others. Everyone applying for a dog license must have a rabies vaccine on file from their vet. You'll be given a rabies tag from your vet, and that number must be on your application. Most jurisdictions require veterinarians to state whether the vaccinated dog is licensed or not. Dogs don't have to have a license until they have all their vaccines and rabies shots; thus you don't need licenses for puppies.

If you don't license your dog and you never get asked to show the license or your dog never gets lost, bothers the neighbors with barking, gets picked up by animal control for running at large, or bites someone, then nothing will happen. However, the fines for not having a license are much higher than the fee for being legal and obtaining one. Fines can be as much as two hundred and fifty dollars, and in jurisdictions where it's a misdemeanor you may also be required to do community service.

In Seattle, Washington, the fine is one hundred and twenty-five dollars (9.25.050 of the Seattle Municipal Code) and they have a zero tolerance policy for failure to renew or obtain a dog license. In Kern County, California, the fine for an unlicensed dog is three hundred and seventy-five dollars. In Maine it's a one-hundred-dollar fine if you don't license your dog.[27]

The fine isn't the most serious potential problem if your dog isn't licensed. Unlicensed dogs that are picked up and taken to the shelter are often the first to be euthanized. Believe it or not, there are still some states that make it a crime to steal a licensed dog, but it's not a crime to steal an unlicensed dog.[28] Dogs can't get their license on their own, and pet parents must make sure they are responsible for obtaining a license, which is a most important safeguard for your dog's health and safety.

My court trials are often boring cases. The jury enters the box eager for something they can relate to, ready for an exciting CSI case, and it doesn't happen. However, dog cases that make it to court might prove to be much more interesting with the onset of canine CSI. DNA not only is being used to solve crimes humans commit, but is used as evidence in crimes your dog might be charged with.

There's even a canine CODIS (Combined DNA Index System) database used to combat the crime of dogfighting. The Missouri Humane Society; the ASPCA; the Louisiana Society for the

---

27. Maine Revised Statutes Annotated. Title 7 Chapter 721. §3924.
28. Mich. Comp. Laws 287.286b.

Prevention of Cruelty to Animals; and the University of California, Davis, Veterinary Genetics Laboratory joined together to create a database of DNA samples for dogs that are seized in fighting operations. DNA is collected from blood samples or cheek swabs and compared to the samples in the database to track dogfighting rings. The database is used solely for prosecuting criminal dogfighting cases, and only law enforcement professionals who investigate and prosecute these cases can contribute samples.

One big area where DNA identification is used is in defense against breed-specific legislation cases. Your dog might *look* like a prohibited breed in your city and you get charged with breaking the BSL restrictions. Your dog will probably even be confiscated and taken to the shelter in an area where such breeds are specifically prohibited with no exceptions. A DNA test will prove whether your dog is the prohibited breed or not. If your dog's DNA doesn't prove she is one of the banned breeds, she is exonerated and should be returned to you.

In the West Virginia case discussed previously, Tinkerbelle was ordered to death simply because she was a pit bull and the judge said pit bulls were inherently dangerous and vicious. Actually, she was a mixed-breed dog, but the judge wouldn't allow any DNA evidence in the case. When the West Virginia Supreme Court handed down its decision, they made it clear that a dog can't be ordered to be killed simply based on breed.

DNA can also be used as defense in dog bite cases. If saliva can be swabbed from the victim's bite area immediately at the scene, you can have a DNA test done for your dog to prove her innocence. Similarly, dental impressions can exonerate your dog, as was done in the case of Phineas, the wrongly accused lab in chapter 7.

It seems extreme, but pet parents have used DNA to exonerate their dog when they've been accused of not picking up their dog's poop. A DNA test costs less than one hundred dollars. DNA tests can be used to deny paternity in cases where your dog visited the neighbor dog and they are suing you.

Dog shaming has become popular online in recent years. You see morose-looking dogs with a sign around their neck proclaiming their crime, everything from I LIKE PLAYING IN THE MUD to I ATE MOM'S CELL PHONE. While these signs and the accompanying photos are amusing, your dog being accused of a real crime that threatens impoundment is not.

As seen in the previous chapter, dogs aren't always defendants. Though dogs are considered personal property, they also own personal property, such as toys, leashes, bedding, food, and other accessories. They are consumers of goods and services just like their pet parents. What happens if one of their possessions is defective and harms them? What remedy does a dog have if a groomer or dog sitter hurts them?

Samson was a beautiful St. Bernard who, through no fault of his own, became a litigant in a civil lawsuit that brought about great changes. He didn't choke on a defective toy or get scalded by a groomer. His damages started just by being born.

Chapter 9

CONSUMER CANINE
(Fetch and Return)

S amson was a rapidly growing St. Bernard when Bob spotted him at a mall pet shop. You know the ones with the glass cage storefronts that look like waterless aquariums for dogs. They're specifically designed to evoke sympathy for the puppies enclosed, first catching your attention and then your wallet. Thankfully, these puppy mill peddlers have been outlawed in many states, but on that day this one was in full swing.

Bob couldn't tear himself away from the large puppy that was barely able to turn around in the small space. He asked that the puppy be taken out for him to look at, and it was quickly transferred to a bonding room. These puppy purveyors are slicker than used-car salesmen, and Bob was living proof. A man known for his frugalness, Bob never bought lunch or morning coffee, but before he knew it he had handed over several hundred dollars and was carrying the large puppy through a crowded mall to his car, since trying to walk him on a leash was impossible. Bob named the puppy Samson.

Samson soon became a happy member of Bob's home. He was a loving dog that liked to play and had a good attitude and a sweet personality. Samson seemed healthy and had a great appetite, but it soon became evident that something was wrong. Instead of running with anticipation for his walk when Bob got his leash, Samson slowly walked toward Bob and didn't have much enthusiasm for chasing balls or even the cats. The rides in Bob's convertible, which Samson had loved, became an ordeal, as he couldn't jump in the car or get comfortable on the seat. It was clear that Samson was experiencing discomfort.

The veterinarian performed tests and took x-rays, which revealed that Samson was suffering from hip dysplasia even though he wasn't even a year old. Hip dysplasia is caused by a subluxation (dislocation) in the hip joint. This creates abnormal wear and erosion of the joint and, as a result, arthritis and pain develop. It's a genetic disease that affects specific breeds of dogs more than others.

Samson required a triple pelvic osteotomy (TPO). This method is used in dogs usually less than ten months of age. It involves surgically breaking the pelvic bones and realigning the hip joint, restoring the weight-bearing surface area, and correcting the dislocated joint. The vet explained that it was a major surgery and very expensive, but if the surgery was successful Samson could be restored to his active self with therapy. Bob's veterinarian didn't perform the surgery Samson needed, so he recommended the teaching hospital at the Ohio State University College of Veterinary Medicine in Columbus, Ohio.

The veterinarian's report confirmed his belief that Samson most likely inherited this from one or both of his parents. If a parent has hip dysplasia, then the animal's offspring are at greater risk for developing it. If there are no carriers of hip dysplasia in a dog's lineage, then it is highly unlikely he will contract the disease. If there are genetic carriers, then he is at risk to contract it.

Since Samson was purchased from a pet store and Bob had no information about his parents, there was no way of knowing if his genetic heritage included hip dysplasia. The vet believed that Samson most likely came from a puppy mill. Since puppy mills don't provide regular vet care or keep records, there's no way to know what health problems the offspring could suffer. Puppy mill puppies like Samson can appear happy and healthy, as if they came from a reputable breeder, but usually only for a short while. The list of health problems puppy mill dogs may face is long:

- Epilepsy
- Kidney and heart disease
- Joint disorders such as hip dysplasia
- Endocrine disorders (diabetes, hypothyroidism, hyperthyroidism)
- Blood disorders such as anemia or von Willebrand (blood doesn't clot)
- Deafness
- Blindness .
- Eye problems such as cataracts, glaucoma, and retinal atrophy
- Shortened or missing limbs
- Respiratory disorders
- Matting
- Mange
- Mites
- Scars
- Periodontal and gum disease
- Nail overgrowth or growth into the paw
- Missing teeth
- Heartworms
- Intestinal parasites

After getting such devastating news from the vet, Bob first went to the pet store. Bob had received a guarantee when he purchased Samson that promised to cover any major medical expenses during the first year that weren't caused from an accident, neglect, or other reasons that could relate to the actions of the owner. Armed with the vet report, Bob approached the pet store and asked that they cover Samson's medical expenses. They refused, so Bob decided he needed a lawyer and Bob came to me, paperwork in one hand and Samson's leash in the other. After greeting Samson, I listened to Bob's story.

He told me how and why he became Samson's dog dad and how much he cared for him. He explained how Samson had begun showing signs of being in pain and what the vet had told him. He felt the pet store should be responsible for Samson's surgery because they'd given him a health certificate that stated Samson was in excellent health, had come from a good breeder, and would make a great family pet with no foreseeable medical problems.

The pet store's "guarantee" was a document that looked like an award of some type, with hearts around the edge and the repeated phrase, "We sell love." It listed the names of Samson's supposed

parents, when he was born, and his breed. Other papers included a health certificate signed by a veterinarian and a registration application should Bob want to register the dog.

I looked the pet store up on the secretary of state's website and noticed that the incorporator, the president, and the treasurer were all the same person: the veterinarian who had signed Samson's health certificate. This was an interesting turn of events. My suspicions were the same as Bob's vet: that Samson was a puppy mill puppy.

I looked at the rest of the documents, which included a bill of sale, a sales receipt, pamphlets about taking care of a new puppy, some type of registration paper for Samson from an organization I had never heard of, but it was the guarantee I'd looked at first that was of great interest. The official-looking paper that looked like an award certificate. Despite the decorative paw prints and the clever sales slogan it clearly created a contract. The simple message said the seller guaranteed the health of the dog during the first year after purchase. It had a couple of official-looking seals and was signed with great flourishes by the pet store owner, who had also signed the health certificate as the veterinarian who examined Samson. Additionally, being the seller, the store owner, and the veterinarian certifying the health of Samson created a conflict of interest and was grounds for legal action.

A guarantee is a legal contract and enforceable in court. Bob's guarantee was very clear that the pet store was issuing a "warranty of merchantability" for Samson when they sold him by issuing a health certificate and other assertions they made. Warranty of merchantability is a legal term that means what the seller is selling is what they represent the item to be and will suit the purpose the buyer is expecting. In common-law jurisdictions, an *implied warranty* is presumed, and it doesn't matter whether the seller has promised certain things verbally or in writing. The product sold, even a live animal, must be fit for the intended use. In the case of a companion animal, they must be able to lead a normal life without major health problems.

To be "merchantable" the item you buy must reasonably conform to an ordinary buyer's expectations. In Bob's case, he had no reason to believe that Samson wouldn't be a healthy puppy that would thrive. The pet store, though, went a step further and provided a guarantee, which only made the implied warranty stronger. The Uniform Commercial Code Article 2, Section 31, is the law in the United States, and it is often referred to as a warranty of fitness. This code is adopted into the statutes of every state. It applies to all sellers, such as vendors at flea markets or private individuals, and the warranty of merchantability applies only to professional merchants, which in Bob's case was the pet store.

I told Bob that I'd contact the pet store owner/vet and tell him that he must honor the guarantee. I explained that the pet store was responsible for all of Samson's medical bills; lost wages from Bob's job for the time to take Samson to the vets for exams and for the surgery; his out-of-pocket expenses, including the travel to Columbus, Ohio; and any other expenses incurred as a direct result of Samson's medical problems, including my fee.

I made a trip to the pet store and looked around. I was pounced on by a salesperson and given the heartrending sales pitch that thousands of people fall for in these stores. I asked to see the owner and a manager stepped forward. She told me the owner was a veterinarian and didn't really come to the store often and offered to help me. I gave her my card and asked her to have him call me. I repeatedly tried to call him at the store and at his practice, but he never answered or returned my calls.

I sent him a certified letter clearly explaining Samson's medical problem, the anticipated expenses, and that he had a duty to honor his guarantee and pay for these expenses, as well as my legal fees. I told him to put his insurance company on notice that we intended to file a lawsuit in the event that he did not honor the guarantee. I enclosed copies of Samson's vet report and medical records. Before I received the certified mail receipt back, the vet/owner called me.

After profuse apologies for being "too busy" and neglecting to return my call, he explained that his guarantee actually meant that the store would provide another dog for Bob and take Samson back. All Bob had to do was give him a week or two to obtain another St. Bernard puppy and then bring Samson in and make the exchange. I couldn't believe what he was saying, so I asked him to repeat it, and yes, I had heard him correctly.

I told him this was totally unacceptable and reminded him that his guarantee said repeatedly, "We sell love." How on earth would a replacement dog be fair and reasonable compensation by depriving the buyer of a dog they were in love with?

He said he understood, but that was the store's policy and other people had accepted it with no problem. (This is the defense of, "We've been doing it for years and you're the first person who complained," which is always a lie.) I asked him if he had children, and he said yes. I asked him, if one of his children became ill and his pediatrician offered him the same deal, that he could receive a substitute child, would that be okay with him? He told me that was an absurd example and of course not. I completely agreed with him, but it was the same deal he was offering Bob.

I asked where this dog swap provision was in writing or posted in the store, and he said it wasn't, but that was their policy. Then I ended the call with the phrase we lawyers love: "Well then, doctor, we will see you in court."

We sued the vet as owner of the pet store, individually as the veterinarian who certified that Samson was in good health, the corporation, and "other unknown parties" who were down the chain of ownership of Samson, including the unnamed puppy mill where he was born. Our claims were breach of contract, (you didn't keep your promise), breach of implied warranty (the dog isn't what you indicated he was), breach of express warranty (your health certificate was false), violation of the West Virginia code section that mirrored Uniform Commercial Code Article 2, Section 31, negligence, fraud, and unjust enrichment (you received money you were not entitled to).

The complaint was served by process server to the vet at the pet store on a Thursday afternoon. The next day I got a call from the insurance company lawyer. They wanted to settle the case rather than bear the publicity and expense of a trial; however, they wanted us to admit they didn't do anything wrong. They wanted a compromise of our valid claims. This is very common in lawsuit settlements, however, and the decision is ultimately made by the plaintiff or the person who suffered harm. We couldn't ask Samson his opinion, but Bob was quick to tell me, "No. I want these people to admit they were wrong." I agreed.

We began to prepare for trial, drafting Interrogatories (a set of written questions the defendants must answer under oath) and a Request for Production of Documents (all the paperwork about Samson and other things such as tax records, business records, records of other lawsuits and complaints). We asked for everything we could possibly think of that was allowed by the Rules of Civil Procedure.

Then we waited for the thirty-day time period the defendants had to answer us. Instead of getting any answers or documents we got a phone call. The defendant's insurance company wanted to settle with us and they had no conditions. I could draft the agreement and they would review it and write a check. I drafted an agreement and it was over. They paid every expense for the medical bills, physical therapy, lost wages, miscellaneous expenses, and my fee. Samson had a successful surgery and enjoyed a great life free of pain with Bob's family.

As for the pet store and the vet, a big scandal occurred about two years after this when the owner was charged with animal neglect and the store was closed. The story, complete with photos of dogs crammed into crates without food or water and the puppy mills where they got their dogs, was in every newspaper and on every local television station.

This example is to show all pet parents that you have rights for fair compensation as a consumer for products that affect your dog's life and even when the "product" *is* your canine companion. Pet parents must be advocates for their dogs in every instance, but even more so when your dog's health is in jeopardy through the fault of someone else.

Buying a pet from a pet store is risky business, and it's even worse if you purchase a dog online. Suing a so-called Internet "breeder" can often be impossible. They frequently vanish after the sale, and you have no one to cover expenses if your dog becomes sick or, even worse, arrives at your airport destination deceased. The Internet is full of sad stories of thousands of people who were scammed by Internet dog peddlers. If you do decide to purchase a dog from an Internet site, be sure to take these precautions.

- Check the secretary of state's website in your state to see if the seller is licensed to do business in your state and make sure they have an Agent for Service of Process listed. If you have a big problem and file a lawsuit, this is the person you'll serve the complaint on.
- Look them up through the Better Business Bureau to see what their rating is and if there are any complaints about them.
- Do a thorough Internet search for comments from other buyers. Be prepared, though; you will most likely find only complaints.

- If they claim the dog will come with AKC registration papers, ask for the name of the parents and check to see if they are registered with the AKC.
- Get *everything* in writing ahead of time. Have them fax or email the document to you for review.
- Make an appointment to go see their kennel and the parents of your dog. If they refuse or continually have excuses, you can be confident they get their puppies from puppy mills.

Fighting an Internet breeder is difficult at best and impossible most of the time. The Humane Society of the United States (HSUS) filed a class action lawsuit against Purebred Breeders, LLC, in 2011 along with many other pet parents who had purchased sick pets from this company. The case was dismissed in September of 2012 because the court ruled the HSUS had not proved their case. HSUS is one of the biggest animal advocate organizations in the world and was unsuccessful in suing an Internet breeder, so what chance would an individual purchaser have?

Buyer beware in any Internet dog purchase. Enter into the transaction totally aware you most likely will not be successful in recovering any expenses, getting your money back, or returning the puppy. For most pet parents, though, returning the puppy is not an option. Love of dogs and empathy toward a puppy that got a bad start in the world with puppy mill parents make most people keep the puppy to give it a better life. They end up paying medical expenses that can run into thousands of dollars. Some lawsuits just aren't worth pursuing, and Internet breeders might be one of them.

Our big animal organizations have resources most pet parents do not, and just as the vet/store owner had to pay me because Bob was successful in filing a lawsuit, if you lose, you have to pay. For example, HSUS paid Feld Entertainment fifteen million seventy-five thousand dollars in 2014 to settle fourteen years of unsuccessful litigation against Feld, owner of Ringling Brothers Circus. The ASPCA paid nine million three hundred thousand dollars to the same company as settlement of their unsuccessful lawsuit. Just think how much good that money could have done if it had been spent to help animals in need. Pet parents should take a lesson from these two lawsuits. You can avoid pursuing a costly lawsuit you most likely won't win against an Internet dog seller by not buying a dog from anyone online.

Last year my neighbors approached me about their attempt to buy a Great Dane puppy from an Internet breeder. They had many emails back and forth, fell in love with a photo of a puppy, and sent the five-hundred-dollar deposit. Later they paid the remaining one thousand dollars plus over seven hundred dollars to have the dog sent to them. They never received the dog. The lawsuit was destined to be unsuccessful, and I did not accept it.

In chapter 6 we covered veterinary malpractice and what to do if a vet harms your dog. Veterinarians aren't the only ones who provide services to our dogs, though, and the others are just as responsible if they cause harm. Every year several hundred dogs are injured or killed from negligent personnel at groomers and pet boarding facilities.

Barbers and beauticians have to be licensed in every state in our country. However, the dog equivalent, a dog groomer, does not have to be licensed in most states. Each individual state determines if a groomer must have a state professional license and sets forth the requirements that must be met to obtain a license. In states without license requirements, usually no special training is required. Similarly, individual state law determines whether the grooming facility must be licensed and subject to periodic inspections. You may see official-looking certificates on the wall, but most likely they are from an online school or a certification that can be purchased online or created by the "groomer." If there is a technical or vocational school that offers dog-grooming certification, certain states require that they be licensed.

Certification is not the same as licensing. You can get certified by any number of Internet schools and you'll never even touch one dog hair. Many groomers are self-educated through online courses or videos. You can also get certification by attending seminars where no hands-on training is offered.

Certification through a national organization that requires hands-on training and yearly continuing education is a good indicator that your groomer has adequate training. The National Dog Groomers Association of America (NDGAA) provides this training in various locations across the United States. The training takes place over two days. The seminars cover the basics of pet grooming and styling. On the first day, instructions and demonstrations are given for grooming standard breeds. The second day participants demonstrate their skills to a board of NDGAA certifiers. A written exam and demonstration of acquired skills lead to certification.

Licensing requirements are more stringent than certification. For example, Connecticut has required dog groomers to be licensed since 1970. The Connecticut regulations apply to groomers as well as grooming facilities. Groomers must obtain a license from the agriculture commissioner each year. The annual fee is one hundred dollars, and the groomer must obtain approval from the commissioner to transfer the license to a different location if they move. In order to obtain a license the groomer must prove that they have complied with the department of agriculture's regulations and the zoning regulations at their location.

Connecticut's regulations for dog-grooming facilities (not for groomers) can serve as a guideline for pet parents when selecting a grooming facility. Here's what is required of grooming businesses in Connecticut: state law requires the agriculture commissioner to develop regulations for grooming facilities addressing issues of sanitation, disease, humane treatment of animals, and protection of public safety.[29]

Connecticut Regulations for Grooming Establishments

1. A grooming facility established in a home must be in a room that (1) is separate from living quarters and at least 12 feet by 12 feet in size, (2) has a separate outside entrance, and (3) has adequate lighting and ventilation.

2. The facility's walls and ceiling must be painted, paneled, or made of other suitable materials. The floors must be covered with a nontoxic, easily cleaned, water-impervious material.

3. A grooming facility must be equipped with at least a bathtub, a grooming table, hot and cold running water, a dryer, clippers, combs, brushes, and shears. All equipment must be sterilized after each use and kept in sanitary condition.

4. Drying cages must be (1) kept clean and sanitary and (2) large enough to comfortably contain the dog. The regulations recommend the following dimensions: 22 to 24 inches wide, by 24 to 28 inches high, by 30 to 34 inches deep.

5. Grooming facilities that keep dogs for grooming for longer than four hours must have an indoor or outdoor dog exercise area. The exercise area must measure at least 3 feet by 8 feet, with a covered top. Dogs cannot be kept overnight unless the facility meets certain kennel licensing requirements.

6. The groomer must keep the grooming area, and exercise area if necessary, disinfected, clean, and sanitary at all times.[30]

---

29. CGS § 22-344.
30. Ct. State Agency Regs. §§ 22-344-26 to 31.

Pet parents must visit a grooming facility before booking an appointment. Drop by the grooming business and check it out. If dogs are unattended, you don't want to bring your dog to this business. If any of the above six requirements is not evident, keep looking for a better facility.

Colorado has extensive regulations for dog groomers and grooming facilities. Colorado's statutes are more detailed and cover a wider range of topics. In Colorado, an owner must give permission for the groomer to tether their dog. There are stipulations that the dog can't become entangled with another dog or object. The tether or grooming loop, as they are often called, must be attached (1) to the dog with a well-fitted and non-tightening collar or loop and (2) at the other end to a permanent, solid attachment. All tethering chains or grooming loops must have a swivel. Grooming loops, tethers, or muzzles may be used only under "constant direct human supervision." Tethers and grooming loops are dangerous and only a well-trained groomer should use them.

The regulations also require, for example, that the groomer annually keep an animal incident file, maintained for three years, at each facility, which covers[31]:

1. Injuries sustained while at the facility that required veterinary contact;
2. Severe illnesses;
3. Seizures;
4. Veterinary treatment plans;
5. Death; or
6. Escape

---

31. 8 Code Colo. Regs. § 1201-11c-15.

Although a groomer's license may be required, some states still have no educational requirements for a pet groomer. Michigan requires pet groomers to have a domestic animal pest management license if they provide flea baths for clients; however, the state does not require a license for groomers. New York and Massachusetts have laws requiring groomers to be licensed. "Lucy's Law" (California Senate Bill 969) failed to pass. It was named for Lucy, a mixed-breed female dog who had five of her nipples shaved off at a Palm Springs, California, grooming salon and also suffered a dislocated hip.

Placing your dog in the care of a groomer who most likely has no professional training, is not certified in canine first aid, and might possibly be working as a dog groomer until something better comes along is a frightening prospect. Dogs have suffered serious injuries and some have even been killed at grooming facilities.

Some dogs suffer from heat exhaustion as a result of being left unattended in front of dryers. In one such incident, a Lhasa apso died in a drying cage at a California Petco. Two Yorkshire terriers died from overheating when a Connecticut salon's dryers failed to shut off. In an affidavit, a veterinarian who tried to save one of the animals reported that the dog had the worst case of heatstroke that she had ever seen.

Groomers drop dogs from tables and they suffer dislocated joints, broken legs, or head injuries. They've left dogs unattended while attached to a tether or grooming leash on the grooming table and many dogs have been strangled by stepping off the table.

A California couple sued PetSmart when their English bulldog, Rita, died during a grooming session. A necropsy stated the cause of death was strangulation. The plaintiffs believe the dog was strangled while her nails were being clipped and she was attached to a short tether. PetSmart sent the couple a check for two thousand dollars and offered to give them another puppy. The offer was refused and they filed a lawsuit.[32]

PetSmart calls its groomers "Pet Stylists" and requires that they meet any state requirements as well as go through PetSmart's twelve-week, four-hundred-hour training. Yet, in Charleston, West Virginia, a dog jerked free from a groomer when out for a walk and was hit by a car and killed. Petco offered to pay the vet bills for a California woman's shih tzu, Joey, for injuries suffered at the hands of a dog groomer. When the woman went to pick Joey up, he was walking on three legs. A veterinarian exam showed that Joey had a dislocated hip. Petco offered no explanation for what happened to Joey and refused to pay the bills when they learned they totaled almost seven thousand dollars. That case is still in litigation. If your dog has a strong behavioral reaction to grooming, it's imperative that you *never* leave her in the care of a groomer whose qualifications you don't know thoroughly.

Listed above are the standards you need to look for in the *grooming facility*, but the cleanest and best-equipped dog salon might have groomers with no training or experience. More states require that the business be licensed and meet certain requirements than the groomers. Here are some important things to do and know before you pick a groomer for your dog.

- Find a groomer who makes house calls so your dog is in a familiar setting and the groomer is under your supervision.
- If that's not possible, ask to be present during grooming— that doesn't mean watching from behind a glass wall. Dogs can be hurt so quickly that you might possibly never make it to your dog's aid in time to assist.

---

32. Kathleen Miles, "PetSmart Sued for Puppy's Death after English Bulldog Was Allegedly Strangled," The Huffington Post, 9 Apr. 2012.

- Know if your state law requires groomers to be licensed and what the requirements are, such as professional training and membership in the National Dog Groomers Association.
- Check to see whether the groomer you are considering is a graduate of a training program and then check out the training program to see if it required hands-on experience and was not just an Internet certification.
- Find a groomer with experience. Groomers who have many years of experience working with animals will be more confident in their skills and limitations and should be more comfortable with animal behavior than those who have less experience. Taking part of any "Grand Opening" discounts for grooming is not a good idea.
- Request references from other pet parents.
- You can ask if any animals have been injured or have died in the salon's care, but don't count on them to be truthful. Check with the Better Business Bureau to see if any complaints have been filed against the facility.
- Request that your dog be hand- or air-dried. Cage dryers can malfunction and inadvertently be left on.
- Be sure to tell the groomer of any health issues that your dog has.

Another option is a mobile grooming service, which is becoming popular in many areas. Cyndee's Cruisin' Critters near Altoona, Pennsylvania, is one such service. Cyndee has more business than she can handle most weeks and performs an important service to elderly dog owners living in nursing homes or assisted living facilities and disabled pet owners who can't take their dogs to a salon.

Mobile grooming services such as Happy Tails Mobile Dog Salon in the Charlotte, North Carolina, area are large vans or pull-behind trailers completely outfitted as a grooming facility with their own water systems. Jill Young used her lifetime love of dogs and seven years of experience as a groomer to launch her mobile grooming business. Jill's van has a table that adjusts in height to accommodate the size of the dog. Dogs never need to leap down from the table. She blow-dries the dogs by hand and doesn't use dryer cages. There are no distractions like in a salon, such as other dogs nearby and people coming and going. There's no need to take the dog clients for a walk (when many accidents happen at grooming facilities), as they are handed over to the pet parent when the grooming is complete. While mobile services are more expensive, most customers gladly pay the price because it's safer and more convenient.

Another option is to use grooming services at your vet's office if they're offered. Your dog is acquainted with the employees there and is familiar with the place. If your dog is fearful of going to the vet, this might not be a good idea, but once she realizes she is not going in a treatment room, things might be okay. In the worst-case scenario, if there is some type of accident and your dog needed medical attention, your personal vet would be right there.

You can also learn to groom your dog yourself. Take a grooming class at a local technical or vocational school. Your dog trusts you, and no one knows your dog better than you. Most of us can't afford an in-house dog salon like the family mentioned in chapter 5, but it's easy to find a suitable place at home for your dog's personal salon.

You did all your homework. You found out if your state required a license and what training was required. You visited several salons and took the checklist from this chapter with you. You asked for references. You checked the Better Business Bureau as well as the training schools you saw on the certificates during your salon visit. Everything is to your satisfaction and you take Rover for a grooming. What do you do if he is injured?

The first and most important action is to get your dog to a vet as soon as possible. Take pictures at the salon if it's not an urgent medical incident. I'd take pictures before the treatment. Even if everything goes perfectly, nothing is lost from a minute or two of taking photos that could become very important should something happen. Unless your dog has an egregious injury and you need to get to the vet immediately, get some necessary information. Notify the owner if they are on the premises and get names, contact information other than the place of business, and statements from the groomer and any witnesses.

You are entitled under bailment law to have your dog returned to you in the same condition (less the clipped-off hair and knots or mud) as you delivered her to the groomer in. She should not be limping, be bleeding, have trouble breathing, or anything else she wasn't experiencing when you took her to the groomer. She should not wince when you hold her or when she gets into the car. Nothing about her physically should be different except being cleaner and less straggly.

If your dog had only injuries, send a certified letter to the owner of the facility with the vet bills and details of what happened to your dog and that you expect the vet bills to be paid or reimbursed to you within ten days after receipt of the letter. Make certain your dog will not experience any further problems from her injury if you decide getting the vet bills paid is enough.

If your dog died as a result of the groomer's negligence, have a necropsy performed. Send a similar letter asking for reimbursement of vet bills, cost of the necropsy, any final expenses such as cremation or burial, and fair market value for a new dog. You might not want another dog immediately, but get the money now.

In either case, if your letter is ignored, you are told they won't be responsible, or you feel compelled to send a message to the business and seek further damages for your dog's pain and suffering as well as your own stress and emotional damages, get a lawyer and file a lawsuit against the business, the individual groomer, the corporate company if it's part of a chain, and any person or entity even remotely involved in your dog's death or injuries. If you chose to handle this yourself (not a good idea), file a lawsuit in your county's small claims court. Make a list of witnesses you'll call, including the treating veterinarian, and gather photos, medical records, and anything else to document what happened.

Find out if there have been any other injuries, deaths, or blatant negligence at this salon. Even when you check thoroughly, information often remains hidden.

Social media and local news stations are priceless when you need to get the word out about a negligent grooming facility or any other dog service business that harms your dog. Not only does this attention make your personal case stronger, it often prevents harm happening to other dogs. Be persistent in contacting your local television stations, as these stories serve a valid public purpose in warning other pet parents, and the coverage will help in getting a settlement offer for your case. Often other victims come forward after social media and local media spread your story.

Boarding facilities that harm your dog may be sued in the same manner. They too are required under the legal action of bailment to return your dog in as good condition as you left her there in. State laws and local ordinances have guidelines and requirements for boarding facilities. Make sure you know what these are and that the facility you are entrusting your dog to is in compliance with them. Thoroughly check out a boarding facility looking for many of the same things you look for at a groomer. If your dog has to take medicine, it's best to take your dog to a boarding kennel that has vet tech on staff and be very clear about the frequency and dosage. Leaving clear and detailed instructions, providing your dog's own food, and making sure your contact number is correct are all ways you can minimize the risk of harm when boarding your dog. Even then, there are no guarantees.

A family in West Virginia learned this in a tragic way. They'd used this particular boarding facility previously and had no problem. However, this time an inexperienced kennel worker who was not a vet tech gave their eleven-year-old shih tzu an overdose of insulin. They rushed her to the local veterinarian, but despite their efforts she died.

The family was devastated. The vet froze the dog's body until the family returned from their vacation. That's when they contacted me. I suggested they get a necropsy at Virginia Tech Veterinary Hospital. The necropsy found only one possible cause of death, the insulin overdose. This family is still in shock, grieving, and unsure of how they want to handle this. They are strongly concerned that this should never happen to another dog again. Letters to the business have not been responded to. We are planning a lawsuit, as there is a two-year statute of limitations, but the family is waiting until they are emotionally stronger to deal with it.

Pet sitters are often a good option if you must leave your dog behind when traveling. Pet sitters are not regulated by any government agency or covered by any state animal laws. Always hire an experienced pet sitter and check them out thoroughly, including a criminal background check, and get references from previous clients and previous employers. Pet parents need to get valid identification from a pet sitter and verify every piece of information the pet sitter provides. You can't be too careful since you'll be trusting this person with your dog's life. A pet sitter should be insured and bonded. If you find someone you really like and they are not bonded, offer to bond them. It's not expensive and is worth it. Agencies usually have all their sitters bonded.

Pet Sitters International (www.petsit.com) is the largest organization of pet sitters in the United States. They offer certification through in-home study and information for pet sitters to keep up to date and assist them in setting up their own business. Pet Sitters

International began the first pet-sitter-specific criminal history verification program in 2013. It's called the Locator Designation Program and, according to the website, checks many different sources for criminal history. However, they do want pet parents to perform their own background check. If your dog is hurt, lost, or dies as a result of a pet sitter employee who is bonded and insured, your damages will be covered. Things happen, and it's good to know if any damages to your home or your pet occur, you will be covered.

The following are a few examples of what can happen to your pet when being cared for by a pet sitter. In each case, the sitter was insured.

- While on a walk with an insured pet sitter, a client's dog drank water that was contaminated and became very sick. **Total paid: three thousand one hundred and eighty-seven dollars.**
- A pet sitter left a client's puppy out of its crate between visits. While out, the puppy ingested hand warmers and required veterinary care. **Total paid: five thousand thirty-four dollars.**
- A pet sitter placed dogs in the client's garage to keep warm. The dogs ingested antifreeze. They died. **Total paid: three thousand twenty-four dollars.** [33]

The Pet Sitters International website offers great information for pet parents on choosing a pet sitter and the important questions to ask a potential pet sitter.

---

33. www.care.com/pet-care-p1087-q32706720.html?null&_qs=1 (www.petsit.com/stuff/contentmgr/files/36/8455f8809adedc12554c4b70a9714101/misc/beonguardbutbeinsured.pdf).

The best arrangement with a pet sitter is to have them stay in your house with your dog. This way your dog remains in familiar surroundings and isn't left alone at night, which is never safe for your dog. Provide clear written rules and instructions for the sitter and check in every day.

If you hire a pet sitter who is an employee of an agency, the agency should have business liability insurance and the employees should be bonded. If there is a problem and damages occur from the pet sitter, you have the right to sue the pet sitter (who may have limited assets) as well as the employer. Pet sitters provide services the same as another person or business that cares for your dog, and you have the right as a consumer to be compensated for any loss that occurs.

Pet parents are a large and powerful group in the pet product industry. Americans spent more than sixty million dollars on their pets in 2015. Our dogs benefit from an endless number of pet products. These products all are subject to the laws of other items in commerce and must be "fit" for the purpose they're sold for and intended for as set forth in the Uniform Commercial Code. Dog products, such as toys, beds, houses, grooming aids, leashes, collars, and others, are not regulated or overseen by any government agency, including the Federal Drug Administration.

Unfortunately for dogs and their owners, manufacturing of pet toys relies on the honor system. Conscientious companies have safety standards to ensure their products are safe for our pets. However, the processes of less scrupulous companies are sometimes no better than trial and error. In some cases, even errors (discovered through consumer complaints) are ignored. Among the most familiar hazards are choking and stomach obstruction. Small pieces of toys as well as particles that can be chewed may be ingested and cause choking. Companies have used toxic materials and coatings that pose a risk of poisoning. The Consumer

Product Safety Commission only regulates pet toys that can be proven to put *consumers* (people, not dogs) at risk, therefore dogs being harmed by products intended for them are not on any government regulatory radar.

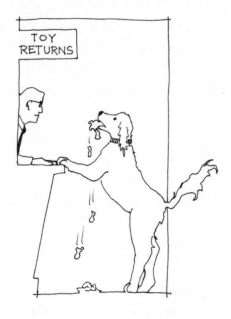

Private organizations have lobbied for years for the creation and implementation of uniform, mandatory industry standards for pet products, but there's no sign of it happening in the near future. Many dog products are on the market and bear tags proclaiming AKC approval; however the American Kennel Association has no research laboratories or testing facilities to determine if any pet product is safe. An AKC-approved sticker doesn't mean they approve it, only that it was featured and utilized at AKC dog shows. They merely license their name and it is used in any number of misleading ways.

So what's a pet parent to do to ensure they provide only safe toys for their canine companion? Since the manufacturing of pet accessories remains self-regulatory, it's good to know which companies follow the only standards available, and those are the standards for the manufacturing of children's toys. Worldwise, founded in 1990, is a company that grew out of pet parent's frustration for safe pet products. They create eco-friendly, safe products for dogs at their California company while simultaneously calling for better government standards for pet products.

While private organizations, such as the American Pet Products Association (APPA) and the American Pet Products Manufacturers

Association (APPMA), are involved with various government agencies, they are private organizations with no regulatory authority as to the safety of pet products. APPMA represents more than one thousand pet product manufacturers, importers of pet products, and suppliers of products for non-pet livestock as well. They sponsor a Global Pet Expo every year, during which the newest products for pets are on display with hundreds of pet product vendors and product manufacturers on-site to demonstrate. Research has shown that toys aren't just a luxury for dogs, they contribute to their physical and cognitive development.

If your dog suffers harm from a pet product, you have a right to bring a lawsuit under a product liability tort action. This means you believe you can prove the product was defective and that defect makes the company liable for your dog's harm and other damages.

You may also bring a lawsuit under your state's code provision of the Uniform Commercial Code. It's easy. Dog toys are made for one purpose: for dogs to play with. The manufacturer knows this, therefore they are liable if the product is not suitable for that purpose.

Uniform Commercial Code § 2-315

Implied Warranty: Fitness for Particular Purpose

Where the seller at the time of contracting has reason to know any particular purpose for which the goods are required and that the buyer is relying on the seller's skill or judgment to select or furnish suitable goods, there is unless excluded or modified under the next section an implied warranty that the goods shall be fit for such purpose.

So, if you purchase a dog toy that is not fit for the purpose of a dog playing with it, which includes biting, chewing, throwing, and tugging on it, as well as any other normal activity a dog would engage in with a toy, and your dog is harmed, you are entitled to damages, including vet bills. If your dog dies, you are also entitled to fair market value of your dog and possibly emotional damages, as discussed previously. Additionally, every state has its own consumer protection laws that may allow other causes of action in a product liability lawsuit.

For example, Maryland has the Maryland Consumer Protection Act, Md. Code Ann., Com. Law. § 13–101, *et seq.* ("MCPA"). In 2012, Dawn Stanley brought a lawsuit against the retailer and the manufacturer of a popular dog chew, Nylabone. Ms. Stanley filed a product liability case and pled in the alternative under the MCPA as well as for negligence, fraud, breach of implied warranties, breach of express warranties, strict liability, and unjust enrichment.

Ms. Stanley purchased a Nylabone double-action chew toy for her French bulldog, Booker, based on the many claims the manufacturer made of the safety and effectiveness of its product.

Shortly after receiving the toy and playing with it for several days, Booker began throwing up. He was rushed to an emergency veterinary hospital and returned home. After trips to a number of other clinics, exploratory surgery was performed and the vet found that a piece of the Nylabone had lodged in Booker's small intestine. Several of Ms. Stanley's claims were dismissed, and the retailer, Central Garden and Pet Corporation, was dismissed from the case. However, the claims of unjust enrichment and fraud were allowed to go to trial.

Before trial, Ms. Stanley's attorney received an offer of settlement from Nylabone. She accepted it, as it covered the veterinary bills and was enough to pay the lawyer. Corporations and their lawyers will wear you out in litigation that they could easily settle initially. Happily, Booker is now a healthy six-year-old.

Pet parents should read the case,[34] as it gives great information on what you must prove to win a pet product liability case and what to expect. The travesty of this case is that a simple Internet search brings up dozens of cases against Nylabone for similar incidents, yet the product is still on the market.

Pet parents do have an online independent resource as well as all the search engines and independent reviewers of dog toys and accessories. The All Creatures Great and Small website (www.benderplace.com/allcreaturesgreatandsmall) has a "Product Alerts" page that lists any product that may be harmful to animals. Don't wait for a recall. Before you purchase a product for your dog, research the company, check reviews, and inspect the item thoroughly for potential hazards.

No dog pet parent has forgotten the huge dog food recall of 2007. I was traveling with Sadie for book signings and events. My dad called me early one morning while we were just outside of Orlando, Florida, to tell me about the dog food recall and to make sure Sadie didn't have any of the recalled food. I turned on CNN and the story was big news. I watched as the names of the affected brands scrolled across the screen and let out a sigh of relief.

The night before, after a long nine hours on the road, I thought Sadie and I both deserved a treat. I wanted to run into Kmart to grab a few things I'd forgotten, and since it was so hot I took Sadie with me. No one asked me any questions as we made a quick dash to the cosmetics department and then to the dog food area. I went to the dog food section for one of Sadie's "junk food" treats. I had it in my hand and for some reason changed my mind and put it back on the shelf. I decided to get her a fast-food hamburger instead, as she considered them an extra-special treat and it certainly had

---

34. www.gpo.gov/fdsys/granule/USCOURTS-mdd-1_11-cv-02401/
USCOURTS-mdd-1_11-cv-02401-0.

been a long day. As I watched the brands in the recall scrolling across the screen, I saw the brand of dog food and that particular flavor I'd held in my hand the evening before.

Pet parents panicked as the days of the recall stretched on with more and more brands being added to the tainted list every day. Dogs were getting sick in record numbers, and before long numerous deaths were reported. Grief-stricken pet parents were on the evening news, veterinarians were interviewed, and dog food company executives issued statements of apology with promises to investigate the problem.

The recall involved one hundred eighty brands, most of the biggest names in the pet food business, and dozens of the largest retailers in the United States and Canada. More than one hundred class action lawsuits were filed for death and sickness of pets that ate the tainted food. The end result was a payout of twelve million three hundred fifty-seven thousand two hundred and seventy-seven dollars divided between twenty thousand two hundred and twenty-nine claims from the United States and Canada, according to information provided by the claims administrator, the accounting firm of Heffler, Radetich & Saitta LLP in Philadelphia.

The recall also led to the criminal prosecution of the American company ChemNutra, Inc., and its owners. The owners pleaded guilty to distributing adulterated food and selling misbranded food. Despite the widespread grief their actions caused thousands of pet parents, and the serious illness and deaths of hundreds of pets, their crimes were only misdemeanors.

Unlike dog toys and accessories, dog food is subject to regulation by government agencies, including the FDA, the United States Department of Agriculture (USDA), and the Federal Trade Commission (FTC). The Federal Food, Drug, and Cosmetic Act (FFDCA) requires that all animal foods, like human foods, be safe to eat, produced under sanitary conditions, contain no harmful substances, and be truthfully labeled. In addition, canned pet foods must be processed in conformance with the low-acid canned food regulations to ensure the pet food is free of viable microorganisms.[35] The USDA is involved with regulations concerning pet food labeling and identification and the approval of pet food ingredients. The FTC works to prevent misleading advertising, and pet food manufacturers must conform to the FTC's general-truth-in-advertising standards.

Pet food is also regulated at the state level, and the regulations differ from state to state. Pet foods come under even tighter control at the state level, where each state can have its own Feed Control Laws and Regulations, Food and Drug Acts, and Weights and Measures Acts. It is important to note that state feed laws regulate the distribution of a pet food everywhere within that state. Pet foods are subject to the same regulations, whether they are sold by a veterinarian, feed store, or grocery store.

Yet with all these controls we still have pet food recalls. Pet parents should be familiar with Dog Food Advisor (www.dogfoodadvisor. com), an informative website about dog food. The website not only reviews and rates dog food, but also posts timely and up-to-date recalls and advisories. It's a great source of information if you're thinking of changing your dog's diet or if you suspect your dog is sick from a food you purchased. You can sign up on the website to receive recall alerts by email so you'll always be aware of any recalled food you might have purchased. The Truth about Pet Food (www. truthaboutpetfood.com) is another excellent website for pet parents. The site tracks and reports on lawsuits against dog food companies.

Consumers, human and canine, have a right to feel confident in the food they eat. If you suspect your dog is ill from a manu-factured food, your first step is to take your dog to the vet. Save

---

35. Title 21 Code of Federal Regulations, Part 113 (21 CFR 113).

the suspected food for testing if your vet confirms the food is most likely the source of your dog's illness.

Pet parents can definitely sue for damages from defective dog food. Individual lawsuits are expensive and often unsuccessful. However, class action lawsuits where numerous dogs have been injured or have died get the attention of the company, which is then more often than not willing to settle. In March of 2014, Diamond Pet Foods settled a class action lawsuit.[36] Depending on which settlement class the plaintiff was categorized in, payments ranged from two-dollar coupons to payment in full for all veterinary bills. A total of slightly more than two million dollars was allocated for the settlement.

As in any lawsuit, documentation is important to prove your case. Keep records of your dog's symptoms, vet records, out-of-pocket expenses, veterinary bills, and other pertinent data. Start by sending a certified letter to the legal department of the dog food company. Often they will be willing to settle with you individually. These settlements often require that you sign a release with clauses denoting that the company did nothing wrong, confidentiality, and you agree that this will be settlement in full and you can never bring a lawsuit later even if in the future your dog develops consequences directly related to the dog food illness. Many pet parents whose dog has endured pain and suffering are unwilling to take the money offered and put it behind them. Making the public aware is important to avoid further illness or death to other dogs, and even when a settlement is offered, it is often rejected.

Dog food companies also sue each other. In May of 2014, Purina filed a lawsuit against Blue Buffalo, accusing them of false

---

36. *Marciano* v. *Schell & Kampeter Inc. d/b/a Diamond Pet Foods, et al.*, Case No. 2:12-cv-02708, in the US District Court for the Eastern District of New York.

advertising, unjust enrichment, and disparagement. The case is making its way through the court. According to the American Pet Products Association, the pet food industry had a market of more than twenty-two billion dollars in 2015. It's actually a dog-eat-dog ultra-competitive business, and pet parents must protect their canine consumers for oversight and mistakes that could mean life or death for their dog.

While dogs are consumers of goods, they are also consumers of services, and this is even more true when you take your dog on the road with you. Safety is of greater importance when your dog is in unfamiliar surroundings. I had never taken Sadie to stay in a hotel, but then we got a book contract and Sadie decided she needed to be included in the contract in more ways than one.

Chapter 10

TRAVELING TAILS
(Reservations for Rover)

It was late, and I was weary of reading the contract my publisher had sent to my agent for me to review and sign. I was so happy that someone actually wanted to publish my book, I would have signed it without reading it, but she cautioned me not to do this. I decided nothing would happen to me or my publishing contract if I waited until morning, so I placed it on the floor beside my bed then turned off the light.

Sadie jumped off the bed, showing sudden interest to the document on the floor. She began sniffing and pawing it and pushed it around until all six pages were separated and under her paws. Then she sat on it and looked at me. Suddenly it dawned on me; this contract didn't say anything about Sadie going along with me on the book tour, and without Sadie there would not have been a book. However, the only trip I'd taken Sadie on was a disaster, with her throwing up in my Mercedes before we were twenty miles from home. So while I realized that she needed to be part of our book publicity, I knew nothing about traveling with a dog.

Before Sadie, I confess when I looked at vacation rentals I intentionally skipped over all the ones with paw prints, designating that dogs were welcome. It's hard for me to admit, but back then I never gave a thought to traveling with a dog, and now here I was trying to figure out how I could get my publisher to allow my dog to go with me to who knew where! I knew my town had certain rules and regulations governing Sadie's behavior, but what about other cities? How would I know what we could and could not do in New York or Pittsburgh? And did decent hotels really allow dogs to stay with you, or did they have to stay in a kennel down in the lower levels of the hotel?

If I couldn't stay in a hotel with Sadie that had room service, how would I be able to get my meals? Would Sadie be allowed in a taxi? Would I be able to take Sadie into stores or have to miss out on all the great shopping in the cities where book signings were scheduled? Of all the questions, what troubled me the most was worrying about the consequences for both of us if we happened to run afoul of the law in a strange city. What if I ended up in jail and Sadie in the pound for doing something we didn't know was illegal? There was no way I would let that happen, so I did some research. Every pet parent must know the laws of their travel destination: the rights they have in public spaces with their dog; what liability, if any, hotels, cities, and transportation systems (taxis and airlines) have if your dog is harmed; and what to do if you're in a strange city and become tangled in a legal nightmare.

As I traveled with my dog, the first thing I quickly learned was that not all accommodations that allow dogs are equal. Some of the terms that hotels and other establishments use to denote that dogs are allowed include: pet friendly, pets welcome, and pets allowed. (I haven't seen "pets tolerated," but I have experienced it!) There is a world of difference from place to place of what pet friendly actually means, and it has nothing to do with the words chosen to note

©DAVID VOISARD '16

it. You need to know the rules of your hotel in order to avoid any unforeseen legal charges for damages or other things.

You would think that a hotel or resort that touts itself as pet friendly would be just that and your dog would be treated kindly, perhaps receive a welcome treat, and be permitted to accompany you in most areas of the property. Sadly, this isn't true. I've arrived at pet-friendly hotels to be greeted rudely by desk clerks who clearly don't care for dogs. They have tried to shove me and Sadie off to a room other than the one in our reservation confirmation, telling me that only certain rooms allow dogs. That is not what their website or corporate advertising touted.

In cases like this you have a legal right to stand your ground unless this stipulation was clearly stated in their advertisement and is in equal-sized print as everything else on your confirmation. Ask to see the manager and be firm that you want the room you reserved. If it's a national chain, call the 800 number, particularly if you are a member of a rewards program for that hotel, and get them to intervene for you. You create a contract with the hotel corporation when you make a reservation. The hotel makes an offer (their advertisement and all amenities, including pets allowed). You accepted this offer when you made your reservation and gave good consideration (your deposit). The hotel is obligated under contractual law to provide what you contracted for (room and conditions offered). Offer plus acceptance equals contract. Any first-year law student, business person, home buyer, or just about any adult person knows this, but sometimes hotel management gets a case of amnesia.

Hotels that claim to welcome dogs often have the most ungracious, ridiculous, and sometimes plain unacceptable rules for dogs once you get there. Again, unless this was clearly advertised and you accepted it, you are not bound to it. These restrictions range from not allowing dogs in any common areas of the hotel or resort, specific entrances for dogs, and certain eviction if your dog barks. If you're reprimanded for breaking any of these rules, ask where this is on the corporate website and where you agreed to these terms. Again, if this is not on their website or reservation form, be polite but firm that you did not agree to this.

I realize there is a valid concern and there are questions about what you do if they refuse to follow the reservation confirmation or drop the silly rules that were never disclosed. Sadly, there are only two choices as you stand there with Rover and your luggage: you can stay or you can go. This isn't as easy as it sounds. If there are no other accommodations nearby that accept dogs and you're tired from driving a long distance, you most likely will have to stay. If you've done everything suggested above, make sure to lodge your complaint with the hotel reservation center and speak to the on-site hotel manager so a claim down the road can't be met with the, "You should have said something," defense. Before leaving, insist that it be put in writing why you left and that your deposit be refunded.

Now if your Rover is a big rottweiler or similar breed, you might get the deposit back rather quickly. Even if you have a barking rat terrier in your arms, I'm betting the deposit refund will be handed over right away. However, many times they will refuse. In this case get it in writing why they refused your refund. You can use this later when you write a letter to the corporation customer service department demanding your deposit back *and* a certificate for a free night in the future or enough hotel points for a free weekend or whatever you feel you deserve. Take a photo of any signs at the front desk and lobby that say anything or nothing about dogs. This will be valuable when you make a claim with the hotel.

One blatant indication that a hotel is truly not pet friendly is the size of the deposit they require, and these deposits are almost always unilaterally nonrefundable. If the deposit for your dog is more than the cost of your room, this hotel clearly is *not* pet friendly. I encountered this at a Wyndham property in Georgia on our book tour. It cost fifty dollars more than my room fee for Sadie to stay there; the room fee was one hundred and fifty dollars, and Sadie's fee was two hundred dollars. I had to be in that area for a book signing and a television appearance, so my publisher paid it. Had it been just me and Sadie, I would never have paid it. Unfortunately, unlike usury laws that don't allow unreasonable interest to be charged, hotel pet fees clearly are not covered by any law yet.

Again, I go back to the pets-are-personal-property designation in our country. Would a hotel charge me extra for an unusual amount of luggage? And what do they clean that room with that actually costs two hundred dollars? The truth is, nothing. I've asked in many different hotels how a room that a dog had occupied was cleaned differently. The answers went from, "Not at all," to showing us various bottles of spray cleaners, but no one told us anything that would amount anywhere near the fee most hotels charge. Not one hotel said they used a special machine to fumigate the room, clean the carpets, or anything else after a dog was a guest.

The earliest chain of hotels to welcome dogs universally was the Motel Six chain; they still welcome dogs and don't charge a fee. There's an urban rumor out in the dog world that Omni Hotels only became pet friendly after Oprah Winfrey threatened to leave when they said her cocker spaniels couldn't stay with her. I do know from personal experience that Omni has treated Sadie like a princess at each of their properties we've stayed at. La Quinta, a family- and dog-friendly chain, has no restrictions on the size of your dog, and they also don't charge a fee. I discovered La Quinta after a most ridiculous incident I encountered while traveling with Sadie.

Our publisher had made a reservation for us in Raleigh, North Carolina, at a hotel that's part of the Marriott Corporation. We checked in, no problem, until we were walking away from the desk. The clerk said, "Miss Lawson, you can't bring your dog in the front door, and she's not allowed in the elevator." I looked at the various signs behind and on the front desk and carefully reviewed the handful of papers I'd just signed. Not one word about this anywhere. So I asked, "Why?"

Clearly confused, she said she'd have to get the manager. A few minutes later, a man appeared in a corporate logo golf shirt and she told him I wanted to know why dogs weren't allowed in the front door or the elevator. He told me it was corporate policy. I asked where this corporate policy was noted on the website or my reservation. He began to stutter and said, "I mean, it's our policy here, and you should've been given an agreement to sign before you got your key."

He reached behind the desk and handed me a document and began tapping a pen on the counter, waiting for my signature. He tapped. I read. I looked at Sadie. He handed me the pen and I told him I wouldn't be signing it.

At the time, I had my right arm in a sling recovering from a dislocated elbow, a large wheeled duffel bag with enough clothes and shoes for two weeks, Sadie's luggage, and our cooler with food. I asked the manager how I was to get all this to the third floor. He said I could take Sadie up the stairs, then come back and take my things in the elevator. I asked him how I was going to do this since one of their rules was that you couldn't leave your dog alone in the room. He had no answer. I asked him what the purpose of this rule accomplished and he told me it was to protect people who were allergic to dogs, as they only allow service dogs in the elevator.

Really? "If you're allergic to dogs, wouldn't you also be allergic to service dogs?" I asked him.

He had no answer for me on that one either and didn't offer to help with my luggage, but he did agree to return my money. So we went out the front door and down the street and were warmly welcomed at a lovely La Quinta that asked no questions, had no restrictions, provided us a lovely suite, a place for Sadie to play outside, and even allowed her to eat breakfast with me.

Stonewall Resort in West Virginia has a clause in the pet agreement you're required to sign stating that if any other guest complains about your dog you will be asked to leave with no refund. Make sure you read everything you sign in a hotel agreement that is presented to you when you arrive. More often than not these may be contrary to what you read on the hotel website.

If you don't see a pet policy on a hotel's website, don't despair. Often hotels will allow dogs if you ask. I've stayed at several hotels with Sadie that didn't advertise they allowed dogs, but when I called and explained my situation they agreed to welcome her, and it wasn't reluctantly. Each hotel did charge a reasonable fee, but they were congenial to both me and my canine companion.

Every state, county, town, city, or municipality has ordinances that govern the behavior of dogs. Earlier we covered some of those ordinances that are for residents and property owners. However, even if you are a visitor, just like traffic laws, you must obey the local laws that govern dog behavior. If in doubt, do some research before you go or ask a knowledgeable source in the area you will be visiting. A hotel concierge, a local chamber of commerce website, the town website, and dog travel websites are all great sources for this information.

The most prevalent dog law in the United States is the leash law. I don't know of any city in the United States where it's legal to let your dog run free. Some dog parks have leash-free areas, and some cities and public parks have an "under your voice control" provision. It's important to check the area you're in so you don't inadvertently break any law. Keep in mind that dog bite laws are much stricter for dogs that are running at large, so despite how well your dog listens to your voice, I would never allow my dog off her leash in a strange city.

One of the great American dog writers, Ted Kerasote, bemoans the American leash laws for dogs in his book *Pukka's Promise*. He believes they prohibit dogs from being dogs. Kerasote's book explores diverse methods of extending the lives of dogs, and he believes one way is to let dogs have more free running time. In general, he believes if we go back to the basics, when dogs had more freedom, they got more exercise and were healthier because they were reveling in their natural instinct, just being dogs.

He points out how other countries have successfully managed "city dogs," those lovable street mongrels that run throughout cities all over the world. For example, in Western Europe there are free-roaming dogs in most major cities without causing a crisis. There's no attempt made to corral or contain dogs, and the cities manage quite well. Kerasote's belief that dogs require running free much more than urban restrictions permit is probably correct, but leash laws are usually strictly enforced. Leash laws curtail dog bites to some extent and also protect dogs from becoming hurt in traffic, getting lost in a strange city, and other dangers.

Certain areas have leash laws on a restricted basis. For example, some United States beaches now have an area they call a "dog beach." In these designated areas dogs are allowed to run leash free. Of course owners are responsible for their dog, and the entity that governs the beach usually assumes no liability for injury to your dog. You could still be held liable if your dog caused injury to another dog or property on the beach.

On the BringFido website (www.bringfido.com) you can search for pet-friendly accommodations, attractions, beaches, hiking trails, restaurants, tours, events, and more around the world. In addition, the site provides local beach laws for some beaches. However, it's still necessary for you to check the beach restrictions for dogs. These can most likely be found on the website for any pet-friendly vacation rental company near your destination beach,

the town's website where the beach is located, or on signs posted on the beach. Many beaches impose strict and often large fines for breaking their rules. Ignorance of the law is no excuse.

For example, at Caswell Beach on Oak Island, North Carolina, you'll be fined one hundred dollars if you or your dog walk over the dunes, twenty-five dollars if you don't carry a waste bag and pick up after your dog, and twenty-five dollars if your dog isn't on a leash. Yet on Carmel Beach in California, dogs don't have to be on a leash at any time, and you can even build a fire on the beach if you want to cook a hot dog for you and your dog to enjoy!

Below are some of the common restrictions for dogs on beaches.

- Time of day. Many beaches do not allow dogs on the beach during warm months (May or June to September in most areas) from 9 a.m. to 5 p.m. This is to protect the dog from heatstroke and other heat-related health problems.
- Picking up after your dog. Waste disposal bags are usually located at beach entrance areas.
- Leash restrictions. Some beaches only allow dogs off-leash during certain time periods, other beaches never allow it, and some allow it all the time.
- The number of dogs one person may have on the beach, usually one dog per adult.
- Aggressive breeds are often banned even in places without breed-specific legislation.
- Leaving dogs unattended.
- Requiring a collar with current tags, including ID and rabies.
- Age restrictions, which usually pertain to banning dogs under six months old.
- Female dogs in heat are not permitted on most beaches.
- Having an adequate supply of water with you for your dog.

- No spiked collars on dogs.
- Rules change depending on the time of year. They're generally more lenient from September to the end of May and stricter from June until August in many states.
- Some beaches require permits, which include paying a fee. Dewey Beach in Delaware charges ten dollars for an eight-day pass and five dollars for a weekend. Residents can buy a lifetime pass for their dog for thirty-five dollars. Check ahead so you'll be in compliance with any local fees.

As expected, there are the unusual, funny, and interesting local beach laws for dogs. Long Beach, California, has a city ordinance that regulates the behavior of *children* on the beach and how they treat dogs.

The City Code of Long Beach,[37] which covers the designated beach area where dogs are permitted, states: "Children shall be accompanied by an adult and shall not run, shout, scream, wave their arms, or otherwise excite or antagonize dogs." Pet parents might have a difficult decision whether to take the dog or their child to the beach!

At Laguna Beach Dog Park in California, professional dog training is not allowed on the beach, and you aren't permitted to have a picnic on the beach. Maybe not a silly rule after all, as it prevents dogs from crashing picnics or disrupting your picnic with begging! At Clearwater Beach in Florida you're not permitted to bathe your dog in any public beach or swimming area with soap.

Cape San Blas, Florida, is known as one of the friendliest dog beaches in the state. Dogs are allowed on the beach at any time of the year, any time of the day, and there are no leash requirements. Additionally, nearby Apalachicola Sailing Adventures offers sailing trips up and down the coast that your dog is welcome aboard. To make it even more attractive to pet parents, there are nine pet-friendly restaurants in the area. They post a list of good-dog-etiquette rules with one that is quite amusing: "Do not let your dog visit with other beachgoers or dogs unless welcomed (meaning, talk to those around you)." There are no size or breed limitations, and most rental agencies in the area are equally pet liberal.

Know the law at your destination before you leave. Beach laws differ not only from state to state, but from beach to beach within the same state. Most beaches have their rules and any city ordinances posted, but you can't count on that.

Besides leash laws, there are certain other local laws that are common in most cities and only require a little bit of common sense. In addition to leash laws, dog owners are universally

---

37. Section 6.16.310 Dog Beach Zone. ORDINANCE NO. C-7859 K.

required to pick up their dog's waste. Most metropolitan areas have imposed fines if you don't pick up after your dog in a public place. However, many cities also have legislation that applies to private property as well because of its impact on the environment. Most parks and cities have containers with waste bags, but to be safe pet parents should always have their own supply.

In 2013, New York City decided not to replace the faded and aging signs advising dog owners to pick up after their dogs. Nonetheless, you'll be fined two hundred and fifty dollars if you're caught not picking up your dog's poop. The Center for Watershed Protection refers to errant dog parents who don't pick up poop as "bad dog walkers." Their research claims there are sixteen million such dog owners in the United States. Fairfax County, Virginia, also has a two-hundred-and-fifty-dollar fine, and in Dallas, Texas, it's a Class C felony and a five-hundred-dollar fine.

In England they call it "dog fouling," and the penalties are huge. In Rochdale Borough the council set a maximum fine at one thousand pounds, which is about eighteen hundred US dollars. The borough's website has a Dog Fouling Card you can download to report culprits. In Paris, the Incivility Brigade will fine you the equivalent of fifty dollars if they catch you. Even though it's been illegal in Paris not to pick up after your dog since 1982, Parisians seem to think it's the job of the street cleaners and the law is largely ignored. Don't let your travels be marred with a fine for something a responsible pet parent should always do. A local person might be able to get away with something that you as a visitor will be penalized for. Know the laws and follow them. Who knows, with today's cell phones and surveillance cameras, you can never be sure who might be watching or reporting you.

Dogs are unpredictable, and you really never know when the need to go will strike them. My dog Sadie embarrassed me at a swanky hotel in Washington, DC. I stopped at a roadside rest area before we got into the city and took Sadie for a bathroom walk. She obediently fulfilled her duties and I was quite relieved to have this over with before getting to the hotel. We pulled up in front of the Mayflower Hotel and were greeted by the uniformed doormen. One of the doormen opened my door and I went around getting Sadie out. She jumped to the sidewalk, and as I was watching them get the luggage out of the trunk, Sadie stretched to the end of her leash and decided to christen the sidewalk. I couldn't believe it since she'd just completed this task. I was horrified. The doormen jumped into action with a nifty pooper scooper and a hose and all was well. I guess Sadie was just overwhelmed at the thought of staying in the historic hotel, but I was totally chagrined as I hurried into the lobby avoiding the stares of the other guests.

You can also break the law when traveling by leaving your dog alone in a vehicle. During the summer this situation gets immense media coverage, and sadly many dogs perish. However, the law doesn't cover just days with high temperatures. Only eighteen states have laws prohibiting leaving a dog unattended in a car.

- Arizona
- California
- Delaware
- Florida
- Illinois
- Maine
- Maryland
- Minnesota
- Nevada
- New Hampshire
- New Jersey
- New York
- North Dakota
- Rhode Island
- South Dakota
- Tennessee
- Vermont
- Virginia
- Washington
- West Virginia
- Wisconsin

All of the laws start with the base restriction that it's illegal to leave an animal alone and confined in a parked vehicle. The conditions at the time must be such that the animal's life would be in danger, which would include either extreme hot or cold temperatures. Additionally, some of the laws spell out what the conditions are, such as what the extreme hot or cold temperatures are, if there is adequate ventilation in the car, and if there is food or water available in the vehicle. Some of the laws are quite indefinite and you could be fined if you're not aware of the restrictions where you're traveling.

In most states leaving the car running with the heat or air-conditioning on is not permitted either. I've met people who vehemently defend this, saying their dog is comfortable, but what about if the engine quits running? An exception to this law are law enforcement or first responder vehicles, which are equipped with anti-stall devices.

While some of the statutes make this crime only a misdemeanor with a fine, some statutes provide that the dog be impounded and kept until all fines, any expenses for the care of the dog, and the impoundment fees be paid before the dog can be bailed out. This would be traumatizing for your dog and you and most definitely would ruin a trip.

Deciding what to do can be difficult if you're traveling alone and need to run in somewhere to use the restroom and have no one to leave your dog with. In my own experience, I've perhaps used less-than-good behavior when facing this dilemma. I've never seen any signs saying it's a crime or a person will be fined for taking their dog into a roadside rest area bathroom. Yes, signs saying No Pets are on the doors, but no mention of a fine, nor have I found a restriction in the law against this. I've also not seen anything in those bathrooms that a dog could damage. You guessed it, I just take her in with me. We make a quick trip in and back out, and so far, so good. I simply will not leave her alone in the car.

Conversely, many pet parents are met with the dilemma of what to do when they see a dog in a car that's in danger. Very few pet parents know if it's legal or not to use any means of force, including breaking a window, to save a dog's life that's in a hot car in danger of heatstroke. Of the eighteen states that make it a crime to leave a dog in a vehicle, all of them have provisions for rescue except West Virginia.

Rescues are limited to the use of "reasonable force" to rescue the animal, and most of the statutes only allow specific persons to do so. These generally include police officers, humane officers, fire department employees, or employees of a humane agency. People in these categories are exempt from any criminal or civil liability. However, many jurisdictions even without statutes prohibiting animals in cars have not held members of the general public liable for breaking windows to save the life of a dog in a car. Some of the statutes are ambiguous and use terms such as "volunteer," which anyone can be. In fact, you can be volunteering to rescue the dog at the time you break the window to get it out. Seriously, though, call 911 immediately, and if the dog is in obvious distress, let your conscience be your own dog—what would you want someone to do for her?

Most of us travel by car with our dogs. But what are the legal ramifications for your dog if you're in a car accident? Does your car insurance cover your dog if she's injured? What if the accident wasn't your fault; can you depend on the other driver's insurance to cover the cost for care of your dog if she's injured? The answer is generally yes, and this seems to surprise many pet parents. Think back to the prevalent view of dogs in our justice system; they are still considered property. In any accident, personal property that is harmed or lost, such as your automobile or any of the contents, is covered. You can expect no less for your personal property dog.

Dogs are covered under the Property Damage Liability provision in auto insurance policies. Most insurance policies only cover your dog's injuries if the accident wasn't your fault. Since all auto policies in the United States specify bodily injury coverage only for humans, this is again another dichotomy of the pet/property designation. It's fortunate in this situation that your dog *is* considered property. However, as we've seen in other instances, the property designation is problematic.

Some companies, such as Progressive, cover your dog's injuries even if you caused the accident. Progressive has pet injury coverage regardless of fault under its collision coverage section. This means that if you cause an accident and have coverage through a Progressive policy, a maximum of one thousand dollars is designated to cover injuries to your pet. There's no extra charge for this coverage. As of the writing of this book, no other insurance company covers pets under the collision portion of an auto policy, but keep in mind that if the other driver caused the accident your dog will be covered under the liability portion of *their* policy. Knowing this, if you are ever in an accident, get yourself and your dog checked with peace of mind about the expense.

Since May 2005, the US Department of Transportation (DOT) has required all United States airlines that operate scheduled passenger flights to file monthly reports on pets that died or were lost or injured during transport, pursuant to the requirements of Section 710 of the 2000 Wendell H. Ford Aviation Investment and Reform Act for the 21st Century (as subsequently codified at Title 49, Section 41721 of the United States Code and Title 14, Section 234.13 of the Code of Federal Regulations). This report is published on the DOT website, but it's difficult to find. Even when you do find it, not every animal incident is required to be reported. The following situations are *not* required in the report the airline submits.

- Animals that are not kept as a pet in a US family household. (Doesn't include dogs shipped by breeders.)
- Animals that are carried on all-cargo or unscheduled flights. (However, reports are required to be filed for incidents

involving animals that are carried as cargo, as opposed to checked baggage, on a scheduled passenger flight.)

- Animals that are carried on a flight operated by a foreign airline, even if the flight carries the code of a US carrier. (However, reports are required to be filed for incidents involving animals on a flight operated by a US carrier between two foreign points, as well as on a flight operated by a US carrier that carries the code of a foreign carrier.)

What does an airline owe you if your dog is injured or dies during a flight? Sadly, the answer is, very little compared to the value your dog has to your life. In 2015, seventeen pets died while traveling in the cargo hold of airlines, according to the US DOT. Considering that approximately two million animals fly in cargo holds each year, that might not seem like many, but what if it were your priceless dog?

Pet parents need to take responsibility for anything that happens to their dog when transporting her in the cargo section. Flying your dog in a cargo hold or a baggage section is inherently dangerous. Sometimes it's not the airline's fault: for example, if a dog becomes extremely stressed and dies as a result. Pet parents are often so desperate to get their dog to a different location that they ignore blatant red flags, such as the dog's age or health condition. Even though your vet must fill out a health certificate for your dog to fly, they can be filled out in haste, ignoring pertinent health issues resulting in the dog's death.

Flying in cargo is a frightening experience with vastly varying temperatures and air pressure. Unforeseen deaths occur even when the dog is out of the cargo hold. A dog on a United Airlines flight was being walked on the tarmac and got loose. It was hit by a vendor van and died. A show dog heading to the Westminster Kennel Show got free and ran away during a ground transfer. The dog was never found. Pet parents must put the welfare of their dog first, considering even the most remote occurrence before crating her up and putting her in a cargo hold. Certain breeds are not accepted by airlines, such as American, English, or French bulldogs. Pugs and shih tzus, snub-nosed or brachycephalic breeds, are prone to breathing difficulties, which is exacerbated in the cargo hold. Breed-specific legislation has also spread to airlines, with some refusing to transport pit bulls or rottweilers.

Pets travel as personal property the same as your luggage, and airlines have historically only been responsible for the market value of the dog. Unlike your luggage, though, you're required to have certain health certificates and veterinary medical records for your dog. Often these records have to be certified from your vet within a short time period before the flight. Your dog could be denied access to the flight, even though you've already paid the fee, or denied entry at your destination. Make sure you know what is required and have it in the specified time period before your flight. There are three ways your dog can travel on an airline:

- In the cabin. If she can fit in a carrier that fits under the seat in front of you. On today's airlines you're lucky if your feet fit there, let alone your dog.
- As excess baggage. This means your dog would be in a lighted, pressurized baggage hold where other fragile items are transported.
- In the cargo hold, which is the worst option.

Just as airlines have liability limits for your lost luggage, they also have liability limits for your dog. Unless you buy extra liability coverage for your dog, if something happens to her, you'd have to accept the airline's decision as to what it will pay for your loss or her damages if she survived.

International travel is covered by separate rules, and pet parents must check with the individual airline for the details. Liability limits apply to all three forms of travel: in the cabin, as excess baggage, or as cargo. On the back of every airline ticket is a "Notice of Baggage Liability Limitations" that clearly states what the airline will be responsible for. You always have the option of declaring a higher value and paying an additional fee, which I strongly recommended if you are transporting your dog on an airline.

Airlines can't deny all financial responsibility. The federal government allows them to limit their liability to two thousand eight hundred dollars, and they take advantage of this. In theory, the airline's position is that you created a "contract" with them. You agree to the liability limit in exchange for an inexpensive rate to ship your dog. This agreement, or contract, exists only in theory, as you don't have the opportunity to bargain for a price or agree to different terms other than purchasing excess liability coverage. In the hotel reservation contract example, you do have the choice to choose a different rate and other items for your stay, making it an actual contract, unlike the airline ticket.

If your dog's loss is worth more than two thousand eight hundred dollars, you can take the airline to court. These cases are decided upon a few easy factors. Did you have notice of the limit and did you have an opportunity to declare a higher limit? In most cases, the answer is yes. However, if the notice was not obvious or the circumstances of your purchase did not offer excess coverage for any reason, you have a better chance of winning your case.

Generally, if the liability notice is in print smaller than anything else on the back of the ticket, courts will consider that insufficient notice. It must also be in clear and easy-to-understand language that a reasonable person would understand. Another factor that can be considered is how sophisticated a traveler you are. If you travel a great deal, you'd be expected to know about this provision and the opportunity to purchase extra coverage. If you're not, then it's reasonable you didn't know about it and possibly won't be held to the limit. The airline's Contract of Carriage, available at the ticket counter, spells out the terms and costs of the excess coverage. This isn't a short document and reading it a few minutes before your flight is not a good idea. You can also access it on the airline's website and become familiar with it while your trip is still in the planning stages.

To get the airline to agree to a higher liability limit, you have to declare that your dog's value is over the liability limit. The airline will charge you a higher fee, and if anything happens to the dog you'll be covered for the value you declared. For example, say you are shipping a show dog worth ten thousand dollars as excess baggage and the airline limits its liability to two thousand eight hundred dollars. Before the trip, tell the airline that you want to declare a higher value on the dog. The airline will charge you an extra fee based on the seven thousand two hundred dollars of excess declared value.

Airlines can limit the extra amount you declare to a few thousand dollars. To get coverage above that amount you'll need to deal with private insurance coverage. Planning well in advance will help avoid any legal snafus should a problem occur.

Once you get to your destination, you may want to travel on public transportation such as taxis, subways, or buses. It's very common on the Tube in London to see dogs as passengers. I've shared my seat with several different breeds of dogs. Almost every metropolitan city has different rules for dogs on public transportation; again, this is a matter pet parents must check ahead of time. Many legal issues can arise when you take your dog on a train or subway. They could become frightened and bite someone or chew the seat and cause damage. It happens. A major airliner made an emergency landing when a service dog decided to "foul the aisle" twice. The owner most likely wasn't fined or penalized, as it was a service dog and by law permitted on the flight, but you can be held responsible on public transit for any damage your dog might cause.

Almost all cities in the United States allow dogs on public buses, subways, or trains. It's not like in Europe, though, where you can just climb aboard with Rover on his leash. Most urban transportation systems require the dog be in a carrier that can be held on your lap. That definitely eliminates taking all but dogs twenty pounds and under, which is the weight limit most often imposed. You'd think with approximately 65 percent of American households having at least one pet,[38] that one or two cars or rows of seats could be set aside for pet parents and their dogs.

The Metropolitan Transit Authority in New York City follows the above guidelines on all its systems for pets. The Seastreak Ferry system, which provides daily year-round ferry services from Atlantic Highlands and Highlands, New Jersey, to Pier 11/Wall Street, East 35th Street, and shuttle service to the World Financial Center, allows pets on a leash, but they must remain on the outside perimeter of the ferry. That means you have to stay out there with them no matter what the weather conditions. Pets are allowed on all the trips to and from New York City, but not to New Bedford, Massachusetts, or Martha's Vineyard.

The other option when you need to get around a city with your pet is to use a taxi. If the taxi is owned by the operator, they can make an independent decision whether or not they'll welcome your dog as a passenger. If it's a company-owned system, be sure to ask when you call them. I've never had any problems taking Sadie in a taxi in New York City, either privately owned or a company cab. They've never charged more either.

---

38. American Pet Manufacturers Association; www.americanpetproducts.org/press_industrytrends.asp.

However, we got into some interesting situations in Philadelphia and Washington, DC.

In Philadelphia, I asked the doorman at the Center City hotel we were staying at to please get us a taxi to take us to a radio station about eight miles away. He flagged one down, opened the door, and in we went. I wrote down the cab's telephone number and the taxi number so I could call them after we were finished with the radio show.

When the company answered the phone, I asked for that driver and, thinking I was doing the right thing, complimented the driver for being so nice to my dog.

"Your dog?" the woman on the phone asked, and I said yes. She rudely said, "We don't allow dogs in our taxis," and hung up on me. I had no idea what to do. There I was in four-inch heels in an area I didn't know very well. Walking back to the hotel was not an option. I knew there was a Saks Fifth Avenue down the street, but how far I couldn't remember. I'd been in other Saks stores with Sadie and they were always dog friendly, so if nothing else we could hang out there and ponder what to do about our predicament. As I was trying to remember how far it was to Saks, I saw a hotel across the street with eight traffic lanes in between. I was elated, though, because there were taxis coming and going in front of it.

Clutching my heavy travel purse and holding Sadie's leash tightly I decided to go for it in my formerly fabulous four-inch-heeled shoes. Once we reached the hotel's front area I spotted a cab sitting to the side with the driver reading the paper. I approached his front passenger door, keeping Sadie's leash very tightly to my side, hoping he wouldn't see her and maybe I could just sneak her into the backseat.

I tapped on the window and he looked my way and gestured toward the backseat, which I took as a good sign until Sadie jerked from my grip and stood up placing both paws on the partially opened window. He looked startled for a moment, and I launched into my woeful story of abandonment and how I just had to get back to Center City. He looked from me to Sadie and back to his newspaper, then he put it down and said, "Perro . . . okay."

I'm no linguist, but I knew "perro" meant dog and okay was the magic word, so I quickly opened the back door, hustled Sadie in, and collapsed on the seat. I think if he had said no, I would have gone into the hotel and asked for assistance, but other than that I had no plan. I certainly wasn't going to carry my shoes and drag Sadie back the eight miles to our hotel. Pet parents can get into pretty miserable situations if they don't check out the local ordinances concerning pets on public transportation before their trip.

Despite Sadie's transgression at the Mayflower Hotel in Washington DC, when we came out of the hotel later that night to go to the convention center and prepare for our book signing, we were warmly greeted and she was given a treat. There was a line of cabs picking guests up and the doorman escorted us to one and opened the back door. Just as I was about to let Sadie jump into the back seat the driver got out and said, "No dog."

The doorman ignored him, continued to hold the door, and gestured to me to put Sadie in, but the driver came to the back door and said, "No dog," even louder. We were at a standoff for a few seconds until the doorman pounded on the roof of the cab, slammed the back door, and told the driver to get out of the cab line. He said, "This dog is a guest of this hotel, and if you won't take her in your cab, you're not taking any other guests. Get out of here and don't come back."

The driver got in his cab and left. The doorman blew a whistle, the next cab moved forward, and we got in. We had no other problems with taxis in our nation's capital.

Ask your hotel about the city cab policy if you plan to take your dog in a taxi. If the city has an ordinance against taking dogs in taxis, you need to know ahead of time. Check the city website before you go so you can prepare for alternate transportation.

So there you are in a great city, with friendly cabs, obeying the leash laws, and picking up after your dog. You did your homework and are in no danger of any fines or problems. Evening comes and you think you'll just sit at an outdoor café with your dog and enjoy dinner. Sounds good, but make sure it's legal. Rules governing dogs at public eating establishments are governed by county health departments. Therefore, they can differ from city to city if they are in different counties. The general rule is that dogs are not allowed in areas where food is being *prepared*. If it's just being served and it's outside, it's usually fine to have Rover at the outdoor restaurant. Like everything legal, though, it gets complicated when you look at all the conditions in different jurisdictions and even within the same city.

Some counties allow dogs to be *beside your table* as long as they are on the other side of the fenced-in area of the outdoor dining area. This was the case at a popular Washington, DC, restaurant we dined at. It was interesting to learn that the tables lining the perimeter by the fence were the most sought-after seats at the restaurant.

In Los Angeles, California, it's the opposite. You *are* allowed to have dogs at outdoor dining areas providing there are *no* barriers between the patrons and the pedestrians. Their viewpoint is that it's unreasonable to ban dogs from these types of outdoor cafés if a pedestrian can walk by your table with their dog.

In 2015, a new law went into effect statewide in California that allowed dogs to dine at all outdoor restaurants. Governor Jerry Brown signed the bill into law, and the California First Dog, a seven-year-old Welsh corgi named Sutter, posted on his Twitter page: "Woof! No more doggie bags! A new law overturning a ban on pets at restaurants."

The ban on dogs in restaurants is rooted in the Food and Drug Administration food code, which is enforced by local health departments. Local authorities can follow the FDA's model rules or they can enhance them or allow more leniency. Service dogs are exempt from this ban that prohibits dogs from being in public restaurants and, in fact, makes it a crime to refuse service to anyone with a service dog.

Florida was the first to enact a law explicitly allowing dogs in outdoor areas of restaurants. Sheri McInvale, the former state representative who introduced the legislation, says the biggest opposition to the bill had to do with concerns over dog bites and fights, not health issues. The final bill signed into law contained a provision that restaurants had to carry a minimum level of liability insurance in order to participate in the program.

Around the time our first book was being released, "Yappy Hours" were popular at bars, and Sadie and I were invited to many of them. For these events, people are permitted to bring their dogs with them in the hope that their dog will be attracted to a dog and they will be attracted to the human holding the leash. It never happened for me or Sadie, but it was interesting to watch.

According to the Americans with Disabilities Act, service dogs are allowed in restaurants except for the kitchen and storage areas. Under this law business owners are not allowed to ask what service the dog provides or for any kind of documentation proving the dog is a service animal. Owners of service dogs are not required to have any form of proof or identification, and therein lies the problem. Many people "fake" that their dogs are service dogs just to get them in places. As a pet parent you should never do this. It makes it difficult for people who depend on service dogs when other dog owners try to take their dogs into places the law prohibits by pretending they are service dogs. Additionally, it's illegal and you can be fined and even face jail time if you are caught pretending your dog is a service animal when she's not.

Perhaps the worst place to break a law with your dog is in a foreign country, where everything is unfamiliar and often difficult. The last thing you need is to be in violation of one of their laws trying to bring your dog into their country. All countries have strict requirements for allowing animals from other countries to enter. The United States Department of State website (www.state.gov) is the best place to get information about bringing a dog into this country as well as taking your dog to other countries. The State Department assists hundreds of its employees all over the world as well as other government agencies' employees working abroad with the transportation of their family pets. The website's information is always up to date and accurate and is immensely helpful to those traveling or relocating outside the United States.

Another helpful website is Pet Travel (www.pettravel.com/passportnew.cfm). The site has a drop-down menu where you can choose your destination country and get an overview of what's required for your dog to enter the country.

The State Department has the following instructions for members of the general public traveling outside of the United States with a dog:

- Call the appropriate embassy in Washington, DC, to confirm the entry requirements for the country you are moving to. Some embassies will provide forms printed in English and in the host language for your veterinarian to complete. Some countries do not permit importation or have long quarantine requirements.
- Take a look at the useful list of International Animal Export Regulations compiled by the US Department of Agriculture.
- Check the requirements to see how close to departure the required veterinarian examination, shots, and tests must be scheduled.

- Arrange with your veterinarian for required shots and certificates within the specified time period. *(Even though not always required, it is recommended that you include shots for distemper and hepatitis.)*
- Pet Travel lists import information for about one hundred countries. (This is an external link for informational purposes only and does not indicate endorsement by the US government of the site, the accuracy of information it contains, or its privacy policies.)[39]

All but a few foreign countries have a period of time a dog must be quarantined when she arrives. This can range from a few days to several months. The rationale behind a quarantine period is to observe the dog and make sure she has no health issues that will be a danger to other animals in the country. Rabies is the premier disease that no country wants brought across its borders. It also gives the immigration department time to verify all records supplied by the pet parent. During the quarantine dogs might have to receive vaccinations if they're required by the country you're traveling to but are not required by the United States. Denmark doesn't have a quarantine time for dogs that meet their requirements.

All countries require that you have vet records, certain vaccinations, and a health certificate. Most of these documents will also be required to board the flight, but check with the US State Department and the country to be absolutely sure your dog doesn't end up in quarantine for a lengthy time due to your negligence by not obtaining the proper documents. It's traumatic for your dog and can be extremely expensive.

Although Hawaii is part of the United States, it has a complicated system for dogs entering the state from a one-hundred-twenty-day

---

39. United States Department of State.

quarantine period upon arrival to qualifying for direct release at the airport if certain procedures are completed on the mainland beforehand. Rabies is the primary vaccination that's universally required. In addition, the dog's home country must have a rabies-free record or a very low incidence of rabies.

One expensive international quarantine incident occurred when Elizabeth Taylor was filming a movie in England. As she was accustomed to traveling with her dogs, she planned to take them with her to England while the movie was being filmed. Taylor discovered that England had a six-month quarantine period. Her solution? Taylor rented a yacht and moored it on the Thames River. She and the dogs along with her husband Richard Burton lived on the yacht during the filming, which solved the problem since the dogs technically never entered the country because they didn't set one paw on English soil.

Germany doesn't allow any bull or Staffordshire terriers, including pit bulls, to enter the country; however they may be exported. Make sure your breed isn't banned in the country you're visiting or moving to. Almost every country requires that your dog be microchipped with a fifteen-digit International Organization for Standardization (ISO)–compliant microchip.

Dogs returning to the United States also must fulfill specific requirements. These requirements can be found on the Center for Disease Control[40] and US Department of Agriculture[41] websites. The US Customs and Border Control has a helpful booklet to assist pet parents in returning to the United States with their dog. Shipping pets back into the United States as cargo requires a registered agent, and information to assist in finding an agent can be found on the websites listed above.

---

40. www.cdc.gov/animalimportation/BringingAnimalToUs.html.
41. www.aphis.usda.gov/wps/portal/aphis/ourfocus/animalwelfare.

Travel within European Union countries is easily facilitated because they have pet passports. Initially created to protect the spread of rabies, the passports have become widely used, and many United States pet parents request them from the State Department, but the United States doesn't offer them. This doesn't stop you from making your own unofficial pet passport. Just like you have copies made of your vital records in case an original is lost, you should do the same for your dog's records, including all the necessary records needed for travel to another country. The "passport" should be a concise folder with all the necessary veterinary records, health certificates, and most prominently proof of rabies vaccination. A photo of your dog, her microchip information, your international cell

phone number, and any other important information should be included.

Taking Rover on the road doesn't have to be a stressful experience. Know the laws of the area you're going to, make sure you have your dog's medical records with you, plan ahead of time, and make it an enjoyable experience.

You've been a good if not excellent pet parent and enjoyed many years of companionship from your dog. You've protected her, taken her to the vet, and made sure she had safe food and toys that didn't harm her. You fought for her right to live in apartments and stay in hotels. You sacrificed to give her the best of everything possible, from a fenced-in yard to a soft bed. You've shared a life together, but neither you nor your dog will live forever.

It's sad and devastating when we lose our canine soul mate, but what if you die before your dog does? Have you thought about what happens to your dog if you're no longer there to care for her?

Chapter 11

DON'T DISINHERIT THE DOG
(In Dog We Trust)

Too many pet parents believe they'll outlive their dog, which is understandable, since dogs' lives go by at an approximate rate of seven years to our one. As a first-time dog mom, I had no idea of this. I realized that dogs' lives are much shorter than humans' when I was reading a local paper in the Smoky Mountains. Sadie and I were there working on our first book, and I was drawn to the editorial titled, "Good-bye, Old Friend." It was the story of the editor's dog that had died recently.

After graduating from college in Louisiana, the editor packed up everything she owned in her old car and took off for her new job in a rural North Carolina town. Fate intervened on the way out of town when a small puppy ran in front of her car. She stopped and made several inquiries to find the owner of the dog. No one admitted to owning the small, scruffy puppy so she put him in the backseat. Now, sixteen years later, she was mourning his loss.

That's when it hit me—Sadie would most likely die before me. For a year after that, I still believed that I would be the one left grief stricken in the future and never considered that the opposite might happen.

Then one evening my boyfriend Rodney and I were playing ball with Sadie in the parking lot next to my house. The ball bounced off the side of the house and rolled into the street. I ran to get it, but tripped on the curb and fell. Sadie rushed over and began whining and licking me. I was touched by her concern and asked her, "Sadie, what will you do if Mommy dies?"

To which my very wise boyfriend responded, "If you died, I'd have to show Sadie your dead body so she'd know you were gone, and then she'd grieve for a long time." At that moment I realized I needed to make sure someone would care for Sadie if I should die before her.

Leona Helmsley's provisions for her dog Trouble are perhaps the most outrageous and generous ever constructed. When Ms. Helmsley died in 2007, she left twelve million dollars to her dog. After relatives refused to care for the dog, the general manager of one of the Helmsley hotels took custody of her.

A judge eventually ruled that twelve million dollars was excessive and trimmed it down to two million dollars. Trouble lived her life out in splendor. The judge was able to make the decision to reduce the amount that dog would receive because a provision exists in more than half of the country's pet trust statutes that allows courts to decrease the amount of money left in a trust for an animal after the person who created the trust (settlor) passes away if it's excessive.

Trouble's caretaker had requested one hundred thousand dollars a year, which would pay for Trouble's needs, the caretaker's fee, a security guard, eight thousand dollars for grooming, and one thousand two hundred dollars for food. Trouble died in 2010, but the controversy raged on among the executors of the will demanding accounting for Trouble's expenses.

State legislatures and the Uniform Law Commission could easily remove the excess funds provision from state pet trust statutes and the uniform codes where it originated; however, the trend is that more states are adopting it. Pet parents need to be aware of this provision when allocating funds in a pet trust. The money left when Trouble died eventually went into a Helmsley Charitable Trust, but the amount was never revealed.

Ms. Helmsley was obviously an excellent businesswoman, but she made two big mistakes in providing for her dog after her death: she failed to choose a caretaker for Trouble before she died, and she left an outrageous amount of money in the trust for Trouble. This was perhaps to send a message to her two-legged relatives who fought over it in court for years. Designating money in a trust for your dog is a good choice, but choosing the person who will best care for your dog after your death is the most important decision you will make for her. It's also the most difficult.

Nothing is easy when thinking about your death, but making sure your dog will be cared for if you die before her is imperative.

We'll start with the easiest part, setting aside enough money to make sure your dog continues to have medical care and everything else she's used to after you die. If you've learned one thing from reading this book it's that dogs are property in our justice system. Since they are property, you can't leave money directly to them any more than you could create a bequest to your house.

Traditional trust and estate law in the United States did little to provide pet parents a way to provide for their pets after their death. Things started to change in 1990, when a provision in the Uniform Probate Code (UPC) was adopted by the National Conference of Commissioners on Uniform State Laws. This signaled a change in the law and included a provision allowing a trust to care for a pet that outlives her owner. Uniform Probate Code Section 2-907(b) included a provision that allowed enforceable trusts for the care of a designated domestic animal and the animal's offspring.

Section 408 of the Uniform Trust Code (UTC), approved in 2000, updated the provision by referring to a trust for any animal, not just a pet, and authorizing persons with an interest in the welfare of the animal to petition for appointment or removal of an enforcer (trustee) of the trust. That means if the person the deceased named to take care of the money and use it only for the benefit of the pet was mishandling funds, an interested party (someone with a relationship to the pet) could file a court action to have them removed. That's one reason why it is so important to pick the right person as trustee and caretaker for your dog.

As of December 2015, forty-seven states had adopted one of these model law provisions or their own version of animal trust legislation. A majority of these laws have only been enacted in recent years, as courts have begun to see pets as integral members of families and slowly recognize they are entitled to the same rights as other members of the family, both before and after the death of their pet parent. Mississippi is the latest state to adopt such a law. In 2014, Mississippi created their own state law based on Section 408 of the UTC, set forth below as an example of what you can expect if your state has adopted these laws:

Uniform Trust Code 59-12-0. Trust for Care of Animal

1. A trust may be created to provide for the care of an animal alive during the settlor's lifetime. The trust terminates upon the death of the animal or, if the trust was created to provide for the care of more than one animal alive during the settlor's lifetime, upon the death of the last surviving animal.

2. A trust authorized by this section may be enforced by a person appointed in the terms of the trust or, if no person is so appointed, by a person appointed by the court. A person having an interest in the welfare of the animal may request the court to appoint a person to enforce the trust or to remove a person appointed.

3. Property of a trust authorized by this section may be applied only to its intended use, except to the extent the court determines that the value of the trust property exceeds the amount required for the intended use. Except as otherwise provided in the terms of the trust, property not required for the intended use must be distributed to the settlor, if then living, otherwise to the settlor's successors in interest.

Kentucky, Louisiana, and Minnesota are the only states that do not have laws authorizing pet trusts. The other states all have statutes similar to the one above.

The trust allows a person to set aside a sum of money to care for the pet. This may occur in regular disbursements of the funds or in the manner the trust specifies. Further, an owner can make specific instructions regarding feeding, housing, and veterinary care. Such provisions are difficult to monitor or enforce. This makes it of great importance that a trustee can be removed. Generally, the trust lasts as long as the last animal named lives. Some owners specify that the remaining money left in a trust after the pet dies should be provided to a nonprofit animal welfare organization. This benefits a worthy animal charity, and it provides no incentive to the trustee to conserve spending the trust money for the dog because they personally will not be receiving the remainder of the money.

This is a complex area of law and pet parents should consult an attorney familiar with the state's pet trust law. Following are some things to consider and decide before consulting an attorney to create a pet trust:

1. Who do you want to control the money (trustee) in the trust fund for your dog?
2. Who do you want to accept responsibility for your dog and care for her (caretaker)? This can be the same person as the trustee or you can have a different person for each. Remember, the caretaker will have to get money from the trustee for your dog's needs, so these people need to be compatible.
3. You need to designate an alternate caretaker in case the first one becomes unable or unwilling to care for your pet.
4. Do you want your dog cared for in the same manner as she is accustomed to? Special food, schedules for exercise, and medical care may all be part of the caretaker's duties outlined in the trust.

5. Where will the money come from to fund the trust? Do you want your life insurance to be used for the trust or do you have money set aside for this?

6. Where do you want the remainder of the money to go after your pet dies? It could go to the caretaker or anyone else you choose. Many pet parents designate that it be donated in their name or their pet's name to a charity for animals.

After you have considered all these questions and made your decisions, make an appointment with an attorney experienced in animal law. A pet trust created by a competent animal law or estate attorney is the most enforceable means to provide care for your dog in case you die first.

However, creating a pet trust is not the only way you can provide care for your dog. Whatever you choose to do, don't neglect this important responsibility. You can put a general clause in your will leaving your pet to a person of your choice. This is simple, and if you don't put this clause in when your will is drafted, you can add it later in a codicil. A codicil is an addition to your will by a separate document that becomes part of your will. Codicils prevent having to rewrite the entire will and are as valid as if they were included in the body of the will.

Here's one example that you could tailor to your specific needs, either as a clause within your will or as a codicil at a later date.

I give my dog Rover and any other animals I may have that are living at the time of my death to my friend Sally Arthurs, presently residing at 136 Brook Street, PA, 12634. It is my express condition that she treat him as a companion animal, allow him to share her home with her, and provide for all of Rover's needs including, food, medical care, and anything else needed for his well-being. I leave the sum of $5,000.00 (five thousand dollars) *to Sally Arthurs to be used solely for the care and needs of Rover. This will include, but is not limited to, food, treats, medical care, toys, accessories such as leashes and beds, nutritional supplements, and grooming costs.*

If Sally Arthurs is unable or unwilling to accept this responsibility, I appoint Charles Edwards, currently residing at 61 Abbey Street, Charlotte, NC, 54321. It is my express condition that he treat Rover as a companion animal, allow him to share his home with him, and provide for all his needs including, food, medical care, and anything else needed for his well-being. I leave the sum of $5,000.00 (five thousand dollars) to Charles Edwards to be used solely for the care and needs of Rover. This will include, but is not limited to, food, treats, medical care, toys, accessories such as leashes and beds, nutritional supplements, and grooming costs. If he is unable or unwilling to accept this responsibility, I direct that my executor shall choose a competent and willing person to assume the care of Rover, and I hereby give Rover and any other animals that I might own at that time to that person. That person shall receive the sum of $5,000.00 (five thousand dollars) and its use shall be restricted to the above conditions.

It is vital that you specify that your dog must be alive at the time of your death if you are leaving money to the person specified as caretaker. Otherwise, even if a person cannot fulfill a condition in a will—can't take care of your dog because your dog is no longer alive—she would still get the money. This was the situation in a lawsuit with a similar clause. The clause, which ended up creating extensive litigation, stated: "I hereby give $5,000.00 (five thousand dollars) to Irene Morrison, should she survive me, for the proper care of my dog Duchess."

Duchess died before her owner did, but a Colorado court ruled that Morrison should still get the money.[42]

Other courts faced with similar situations have ruled the same way. The theory is that the obligation to care for the dog doesn't arise until after the gift of the money is made, and because it's not the beneficiary's fault that she can't carry out the condition, she's entitled to keep the gift.

It's easy for you to prevent a similar result. When writing your will, ensure that you word the clause so it states that the money is given only if your dog is still alive. Here's an example: "If my dog Casey is living at the time of my death, I leave her and $6,000 (six thousand dollars) to be used for her care to Jack Adams. If Jack is unable to care for Casey, I leave her and the $6,000 (six thousand dollars) to be used for her care to Denise Young. If Casey should not be alive at the time of my death, I direct that the $6,000.00 (six thousand dollars) be given to the Old Dogs Senior Dog Sanctuary."

Another option is to leave the money to one person and the care of the dog to another. However, this can cause hard feelings. The caretaker might feel you trusted their judgment to care for your dog, but not to handle the money for your dog's expenses. The caretaker might resent having to ask another person for money for food and vet expenses. If you choose to do this, here's an example of the clause to use as a guide:

"I leave my dog, Casey, if she is alive at my death, to Jack Adams. If my dog Casey is alive at my death, I leave $6,000 (six thousand dollars) for her care to Karen Adams. I desire that she give her brother, Jack Adams, as long as he has custody of Casey, $100 (one hundred dollars) a month for Casey's care. In addition, I also desire that she use the money to pay Casey's veterinary bills or reimburse Jack Adams for any veterinary bills he pays for Casey's care."

42. In the Matter of the Estate of Erl, 491 P.2d 108 (Colo. App. 1971).

Remember that legally, the six thousand dollars goes to Karen outright if Casey is alive when you die. The instructions about how to use it aren't legally enforceable, but they make your wishes clear, which should be enough if you choose the right people.

It's often difficult to find a person willing to take on the responsibility for your pet. Many friends and relatives are great as weekend dog sitters or helping out if you're sick. Asking them to assume full responsibility for your pet is a different story, since your pet will be going through a huge adjustment and may grieve for a long time. Realizing this, many pet groups have developed programs to work with pet parents and agree to accept custody of pets upon the death of the owner.

The San Francisco SPCA Sido Program finds loving homes for its members' pets that are left behind when their pet parent dies. The program is named after Sido, a dog that was slated to be euthanized after the owner died. Anyone who is approved and gives a good home to a pet that has lost its owner receives free veterinary care for the life of the dog at the San Francisco SPCA Veterinary Hospital.

Other organizations offer similar programs. The Washington Animal Rescue League helps by finding new caretakers for the pets of donors who are incapacitated or deceased. The organization's Guardian Angels Program provides assurance to pet parents. While membership is not required, pet parents are asked to make a five-thousand-dollar contribution for the first pet and one thousand dollars for each additional pet. A large portion of the donation/fee is tax deductible.

Similar programs can be found at universities, such as the Perpetual Pet Care Program at Kansas State University College of Veterinary Medicine and the Stevenson Companion Animal Life-Care Center at Texas A&M University. Research to see if a similar program is available in your area.

Whether you use a will, a codicil to a will, a pet trust, or an informal agreement, choosing the right person to care for your dog following your death is an important decision and should not be made quickly. Love you, love your dog is not always the feeling of relatives who find themselves with a dog they hadn't planned for. If you don't name a new owner in your will or trust, one of two consequences will result.

- If you have a will, your dog will go to the residuary beneficiary of your will (the beneficiary who inherits everything that's not taken care of by the rest of the will).
- If you don't have a will, the dog will go to your next of kin, as determined by state law.

This could be the sister who is highly allergic to dogs or another relative who lives in a small apartment and travels constantly for work. They could be someone who simply doesn't like dogs. So, unless by fate the person is suitable, they will most likely not be the person you would have chosen.

If you're lucky, you know immediately whom your dog will be best cared for and most welcomed by. Whether you know immediately or not, you must be sure to *ask* this person if they would assume this responsibility before you name them in a will. Also, you should have a list of things that would be expected of them. Hearing that they've inherited a dog and its care at the reading of your will is not the best way to find this out. You must discuss your plans and what you expect of the proposed caretaker with them. Even if they love your dog, there could be reasons that would make it difficult or impossible for them to make your dog a part of their life. Here are some guidelines to use when choosing a custodian for your dog.

1. First, this must be a person your dog knows and likes. No matter how much you like someone, if your dog doesn't, this will never be a good situation.
2. This person must like your dog as much as she likes them.
3. The person should have experience in caring for dogs and has previously cared for your dog.
4. They should have similar living conditions to what your dog is used to: for example, a fenced yard, able to come home for lunch or take your dog to day care if she's used to that, allow her to sleep with them, and other things your dog is accustomed to.
5. If this person has dogs, you should make sure your dog gets along with them.
6. They must have similar beliefs about the roles of dogs in society and not that they are merely a piece of property.
7. They must be someone who treats their own pets in a manner that you approve of and understands your plan for your dog's end-of-life care and final arrangements.
8. If they have children, see how they interact with your dog. If your dog has not been around children, this might not be a good situation for her.
9. This should be a person you are in regular contact with so that you will know if any of the conditions in their life change that would affect them being able to care for your dog.
10. Trust your gut, but not your relatives. Never assume a relative will be the best choice for your dog. Don't allow personal "family feelings" to influence your choice for the best person to care for your dog.

Ensuring that there will be a minimal amount of change in your dog's day-to-day activities after she loses you will make things easier for all involved. Dogs grieve. They may not eat for days and could become depressed. Choose the right person carefully to help your dog through this difficult time.

The story of how the dog of a newspaper heiress stayed by her bedside for weeks while the woman was dying is legendary in Charleston, West Virginia. The dog had to be led outside almost forcibly to go to the bathroom, and her meals were brought to the woman's bedroom. After the woman died the dog remained in the bedroom while the body was placed on a gurney and removed. The dog followed the gurney to the top of the stairs and lay down and watched her beloved dog mom be taken away. The dog never left that spot despite urging from everyone. She would not be moved. Three days later, she died.

Choose carefully who will make this transition for your dog the gentlest possible. Obviously, this has to be a person you trust. In addition, you need to be confident this person will use the money as directed for the care of your dog. Once the will is probated and your estate is distributed, there is no one to ensure the chosen caretaker is carrying out your wishes.

As a lawyer, I've drafted many wills. After I created a will with provisions for my dog Sadie, it became standard practice for me on my "will checklist" to ask the clients what provisions they wanted to make for their pets. Most clients were glad to know they could do that, and it gave them comfort. However, I was quite surprised when one of my clients had a completely different plan for his pets if he should die before them. He wanted them euthanized.

At first I thought I misunderstood him, but he made it quite clear that his dogs were to be humanely killed at the time of his death and cremated with him. He had no relatives or close friends he felt he could depend on to provide care for his dogs. Since he had no relatives, I suggested he ask his veterinarian to find homes for his two dogs. He disagreed. I offered to take his dogs and find them good homes, but again he refused.

It's normal for pet parents to be anxious about the care of their dogs following their death. Many of us worry and make several calls to boarding facilities if we board our dogs for a weekend. There will be no calls and no control for the well-being of our dogs once we have died, so it all must be carefully planned beforehand.

I feel people take this fear to the extreme when they decide to euthanize their pets because they have no one to care for them or believe no one will be able to care for them adequately. If a pet parent puts this request in a will, there is a chance it could be ruled invalid if challenged. This happens particularly if the dog is young or in good health and other alternatives are available.

Of course, there are cases when euthanasia could be appropriate if the dog is very ill and requires extensive treatment for a health condition that will not improve. A serious illness coupled with the stress and grief of losing a pet parent may be unbearable for an older dog. I can't make that decision for anyone, and I found that I couldn't facilitate it for my client either. I offered to get another attorney to write his will.

My own dog Sadie is now fourteen years old. I watch her closely for the slightest sign that she is slowing down or that I am expecting too much of her. As much as I dread the time when she will leave me, I will be at her side, God willing. If not, I am peaceful that arrangements have been made for her to be taken care of by a person who at least will make an attempt to love her as I have and is wise enough to know that he will never accomplish that. He knows that she will miss me terribly, but he will comfort her in every possible way.

I've made sure this person knows her routines, her food preference, her love of the beach, and her fear of storms and loud noises. He knows she gets a treat for everything from finishing her dinner to going outside for a "peester" and after every bath. He knows she must be allowed to chase seabirds and dig a hole to rest in the wet sand. He knows Sadie and I have been a pack of two and has been content to love us as a package deal.

I cherish each moment with Sadie while I hear time ticking away seven times faster for her than it does for me. I want to be the one to take her on that last trip to the ocean, sleep beside her that last night, and hear that last soft breath. However, if I'm not, I rest assured that I will be with her in her heart and that in those moments I'll be with her in spirit and it will be me waiting for her at the Rainbow Bridge instead of the other way around. Plans are never certain, but my plan is that someone who loved me and loves her will be there sending her to me. I wish the same for you and your precious canine companion.

Knowing the love of a dog is one of life's greatest blessings and one of great responsibility. Keep your dog safe, know the legal rights you have as a pet parent and your dog has in our society, and you will live a life unimagined together. I know of no other constant source of joy that life has bestowed on me than my amazing dog, Sadie. The blessings of a canine soul mate far outweigh the duties and obligations. What happens to your Rover depends completely on you.

EPILOGUE
A New Leash on the Law

It is late, and I am still writing. About an hour ago I covered Henry and sent Sadie out for the last "peester" of the day. I assume she is asleep under my desk until I feel her paw on my arm, accompanied by a very soft but urgent bark. This is not the, "I need another peester," bark, this is, "Hey, I think the raccoons are on the deck and I want to go chase them." Such is our bond that I know what she is thinking.

"*No*," I tell her. "Let's go brush your toofens—you already went out."

Sadie, ever the dutiful dog daughter, leads the way to our bathroom and thumps down into a sitting position in front of the sink, but her look is not the one that says she's waiting for her teeth to be brushed. I feel her distraction and longing to be doing something "more important" at this moment.

"I won't always be able to chase raccoons," I imagine her saying. "I'm fourteen years old now, which is pretty old in your years. I have to chase raccoons while I can."

So intent is her gaze that I can feel her desire to be out under the night sky taking a run around the yard. I start to cry realizing that fourteen years have passed in an instant. I get down on the floor with Sadie, and as I hold her closely I feel her impatience to get going.

"Sure, let's go see if they're on the deck," I say. Together we hurry down the stairs and I open the door to the deck.

While Sadie is my dog daughter and every bit a "person" too, it is her dogness that continually amazes me, and I rejoice in it. I see her take that little sideways challenge hop simultaneously with a soft bark as she alerts the raccoons that she is on her way. Her tail is high and all the beautiful hairs on her body are alive as if charged with night ions from the stars. She turns to look at me, sticks her head through the deck railing, and with a quick turn she is off and running through the yard in the cool late summer air. Her beautiful long hair flows as she runs around the yard and as she passes the solar lights she shines. I see her through the dim yard lights as she makes her rounds and then returns. She is breathing quick little breaths that signal she is satisfied. This moment of life has been seized and not wasted.

This is what I long for the courts of the future to see, to know. That Sadie, although so unique and special to me, is a sentient being like millions of other animals. These animals need a justice system that not only recognizes this, but defends and protects them.

I see a time when dogs get as sufficient justice as possible for wrongs inflicted upon them. I foresee a time when those who harm dogs receive as stringent a punishment as if they had harmed a human being. I see courts recognize dogs as beings, not property, in custody battles, and in all matters they are given the rights and dignity owed to all living creatures. Sadie is oblivious to her inferior, almost nonexistent status in the legal system because it hasn't affected her life. She is the center of my world, and in that world we have been safe and happy.

Someday court clerks will routinely place the letter "A" in court citations. It will be like "F" for felony cases and "C" for civil cases. "A" will denote an animal case, with all the rights to be heard like any other matter before the court. In this new enlightened legal system, I see a world where dogs will have legitimate standing in courts of record in all jurisdictions.

I envision courts recognizing the rights of pet parents to include the well-being of their dog in all their legal decisions and relationships. That every dog will have a designated caretaker legally recognized should something happen to her pet parent.

I see dog-friendly cities with reasonable, not overly restrictive regulations for the coexistence of people and dogs. In my vision there is public transportation that's not dangerous or inaccessible for dogs, and restaurants where they are welcome to share a meal inside with their pet parent. In this world I see in the not-too-distant future dogs will be protected from negligent veterinarians. I see them safeguarded under the law in many of the same ways as people are with malpractice, housing, neglect, abuse, public access, and all other rights they have been denied for far too long.

Am I asking too much? I don't think so. Once upon a time I was not a dog person. I didn't know the joy of being loved completely and without reservation. I didn't know I was capable of returning that kind of love. If this miracle can happen in my life, surely Lady Justice can give it a chance.

Checking the yard, making sure the raccoons are in their place and the deer aren't eating our garden, these are the things Sadie believes are her duties for me and the home we share. They are, however, just a minuscule part in the impact she has had on my life. It took a four-legged furry girl with a tail to make me into a woman worthy of being her mom. As a lawyer, she has inspired me to spread the word of the wonder of dogs and the changes needed in our justice system.

travel a great deal, you'd be expected to know about this provision and the opportunity to purchase extra coverage. If you're not, then it's reasonable you didn't know about it and possibly won't be held to the limit. The airline's Contract of Carriage, available at the ticket counter, spells out the terms and costs of the excess coverage. This isn't a short document and reading it a few minutes before your flight is not a good idea. You can also access it on the airline's website and become familiar with it while your trip is still in the planning stages.

To get the airline to agree to a higher liability limit, you have to declare that your dog's value is over the liability limit. The airline will charge you a higher fee, and if anything happens to the dog you'll be covered for the value you declared. For example, say you are shipping a show dog worth ten thousand dollars as excess baggage and the airline limits its liability to two thousand eight hundred dollars. Before the trip, tell the airline that you want to declare a higher value on the dog. The airline will charge you an extra fee based on the seven thousand two hundred dollars of excess declared value.

Airlines can limit the extra amount you declare to a few thousand dollars. To get coverage above that amount you'll need to deal with private insurance coverage. Planning well in advance will help avoid any legal snafus should a problem occur.

Once you get to your destination, you may want to travel on public transportation such as taxis, subways, or buses. It's very common on the Tube in London to see dogs as passengers. I've shared my seat with several different breeds of dogs. Almost every metropolitan city has different rules for dogs on public transportation; again, this is a matter pet parents must check ahead of time. Many legal issues can arise when you take your dog on a train or subway. They could become frightened and bite someone or chew the seat and cause damage. It happens. A major airliner made an emergency landing when a service dog decided to "foul the aisle" twice. The owner most likely wasn't fined or penalized, as it was a service dog and by law permitted on the flight, but you can be held responsible on public transit for any damage your dog might cause.

Almost all cities in the United States allow dogs on public buses, subways, or trains. It's not like in Europe, though, where you can just climb aboard with Rover on his leash. Most urban transportation systems require the dog be in a carrier that can be held on your lap. That definitely eliminates taking all but dogs twenty pounds and under, which is the weight limit most often imposed. You'd think with approximately 65 percent of American households having at least one pet,[38] that one or two cars or rows of seats could be set aside for pet parents and their dogs.

The Metropolitan Transit Authority in New York City follows the above guidelines on all its systems for pets. The Seastreak Ferry system, which provides daily year-round ferry services from Atlantic Highlands and Highlands, New Jersey, to Pier 11/Wall Street, East 35th Street, and shuttle service to the World Financial Center, allows pets on a leash, but they must remain on the outside perimeter of the ferry. That means you have to stay out there with them no matter what the weather conditions. Pets are allowed on all the trips to and from New York City, but not to New Bedford, Massachusetts, or Martha's Vineyard.

The other option when you need to get around a city with your pet is to use a taxi. If the taxi is owned by the operator, they can make an independent decision whether or not they'll welcome your dog as a passenger. If it's a company-owned system, be sure to ask when you call them. I've never had any problems taking Sadie in a taxi in New York City, either privately owned or a company cab. They've never charged more either.

---

38. American Pet Manufacturers Association; www.americanpetproducts.org/press_industrytrends.asp.

SAMPLE DOG RÉSUMÉ

AGE/BREED: Approximately fourteen years old–cocker spaniel/German shepherd mix.

TRAINING: Sadie was crate-trained, house-trained, leash-trained, and attended four weeks (eight classes) of group obedience training at Top Dog Training. Sadie has been attending Camp Critter Creek day care for eight years.

LIVING EXPERIENCE: Sadie has been an indoor dog since she was adopted at eight weeks old. She was initially left home for four hours in the morning in her crate, given a walk break for lunch, and spent four more crate hours until late afternoon. She spent all her time out of the crate and freely roaming in our house at all times when I was home. She has resided in the following types of properties:

- Single-family home with fenced yard
- Condominium unit in a one-hundred-ninety-unit complex
- Rental vacation properties, both multi-unit and single-family units
- Numerous hotels

SOCIALIZATION: Sadie has traveled extensively to numerous public venues for book signings and public events, such as the Southern Women's Shows (approximately ten thousand visitors daily), the NBC Women's Show, Book Expo America, and Broadway Barks. Additionally, Sadie has been on the *CBS This Morning* show, CNN with Daryn Kagan, numerous local network affiliates, and dozens of radio shows. All this experience has made Sadie the lovable dog she is today, and she has no issues with either people or other dogs or cats.

HEALTH: Sadie is a very healthy dog with no illnesses. She receives flea and heartworm medication monthly; is up to date on all shots, including her rabies vaccine; and receives a yearly physical at her local vet as well as at the Virginia School of Veterinary Medicine at Virginia Tech.

BEHAVIOR ISSUES: Sadie is not a barker; her only bad habit is wanting too many treats. She is also not a destructive dog, and even as a puppy she never chewed one shoe.

EXCELLENT REFERENCES UPON REQUEST

@DAVID VOISARD '16

ACKNOWLEDGMENTS

Huge thanks to my fantastic agent, Barbara Ellis of the Scribes Agency. You fought for this book and believed in it and in me. Thank you so much. We have more work ahead of us on new projects!

Rover would not exist as it is if not for my fantastic editor Nicole Frail at Skyhorse Publishing. Consistent and patient as well as enthusiastic and receptive to ideas—she is the best.

Thanks to everyone at my publisher, Skyhorse. They shared my vision and worked to get the book out to the world. The entire team is enthusiastic and did an amazing job to bring our book out in the world.

Special thanks to my publicist, Jaidree Braddix, who jumped right on board to get *Rover* out to the press. She is receptive and supportive, and tolerant of pretty crazy ideas, but most of all just fun to work with.

During the writing of this book I met some amazing people through Tinkerbelle, a mixed-breed pit bull–type dog that was unjustly ordered to death. Her story is in the book, but thanks to these dedicated people, I was fortunate to assist in her defense. Her death sentence was reversed by the West Virginia Supreme Court of Appeals and the case is cited as precedent in numerous jurisdictions.

Michael and Kim Blatt, Tinkerbelle's amazing pet parents who believed in her and fought for her.

Buck Crews, Chuck Garnes, and Cindy Kiblinger Fernald, all lawyers who worked on the case. Chuck Garnes in particular, you gave an amazing argument in the Supreme Court. It was an honor to be a small part of this life-changing case.

Richard Rosenthal, Esq., and cofounder of the Lexus Project whose advice and assistance to us during the case was much needed.

The shelter workers at the Huntington, Cabell, Wayne Animal Shelter who fell in love with Tinkerbelle and gave her excellent care while she was held there during the legal proceedings.

Capri Billings, a passionate and dedicated animal advocate and founder of River Cities Bully Rescue. Her dedication to Tinkerbelle was unwavering.

West Virginia Supreme Court of Appeals Justices Benjamin, Ketchum, and Davis who cast the deciding votes saving Tinkerbelle's life.

Lisa Wolford Moore and her husband Brent who fostered Rusty, my sweet boy dog, until I could get him and "find him a home." Thanks to the Facebook friends who brought Rusty to my attention, he went from death row in an impoverished West Virginia shelter, to being on the cover of a book, but most importantly being part of our family where he is loved and cherished.

Jessica Hill White, a one-woman wonder in Logan County, West Virginia, who rescues hundreds of dogs, gets them vet care, sends them to rescue, all while working full-time as a nurse. Jessica scoops up injured and sick dogs she finds and assists owners in re-homing pets they can't care for. Her insight and methods are the real foundation of animal rescue. ARTBAR (A Reason to Believe Animal Rescue) rescues hundreds of abandoned and sick dogs in rural southern West Virginia, relying solely on donations and an amazing vet, Dr. Koch.

Janice Mitchell, who though she suffered great tragedy in her personal life, saw the need in rural Rutherford County, North Carolina, for a humane rescue. Persistently she faced animosity and adversity to create PAWS of Rutherford County: Pets Are Worth Saving, a 501(c)(3), providing food and shelter for dogs and cats, enabling pet parents to keep them, rescuing hundreds of dogs and cats, sending them to forever homes, and becoming a voice for responsible treatment for the dogs and cats in this county.

Darlene Arden, the pet expert and successful author who listened to my whining and whose sound advice and encourage-ment were priceless.

Jimmy Thaxton and Kanawha County, West Virginia, Circuit Court Judge James Stucky who made it possible for us to shoot our amazing cover with Rusty in the historic Ceremonial Courtroom in Charleston, West Virginia. Also the Kanawha County deputy sheriffs who had to keep running into the Courtroom when Rusty hit the panic button on the bench.

Thanks to all the people who let me share their stories in this book. Some had happy endings and some were devastatingly sad, but these people are heroes for fighting for their four-legged family members.

Special thanks to Patty Stahl, owner of Camp Critter Creek, where my dogs are safe and sound when I can't take them with me. In the competent care of Brent, James, Desiree, Sandy, and numerous others over the years, Sadie and Rusty have been happy at their dog school by the beautiful creek.

Last but never least, my gratitude to my own dogs, Sadie and Rusty, is endless. It is from the lessons they teach me every day that I become a better person and was encouraged to write this book so pet parents everywhere have a better understanding of what they must do to keep their pets out of the legal system and how to make that system better for all animals.